THE
BICYCLE RUNNER

ALSO BY G. FRANCO ROMAGNOLI

Italy, the Romagnoli Way: A Culinary Journey (with Gwen Romagnoli)
Cucina di Magro: Cooking Lean the Traditional Italian Way
*A Thousand Bells at Noon: A Roman's Guide to the
Secrets and Pleasures of His Native City*
A New Kettle of Fish
La Cucina Tex-Mex
La Cucina Americana

BY MARGARET AND G. FRANCO ROMAGNOLI
Zuppa!
The Romagnolis' Italian Fish Cookbook
The New Romagnolis' Table
The New Italian Cooking
The Romagnolis' Meatless Cookbook
The Romagnolis' Table

The author on the right, at seven years old—a certified ice-cream dribbler—with his older brother, center. In just a few short years, ice cream would be a distant memory and Franco would find himself practicing with dangerous, scaled-down rifles alongside many other children.

THE
BICYCLE RUNNER

A MEMOIR OF LOVE, LOYALTY,
AND THE ITALIAN RESISTANCE

G. FRANCO ROMAGNOLI

THOMAS DUNNE BOOKS
ST. MARTIN'S PRESS ≋ NEW YORK

The names of certain persons have been changed.

THOMAS DUNNE BOOKS.
An imprint of St. Martin's Press.

THE BICYCLE RUNNER. Copyright © 2009 by G. Franco Romagnoli. All rights reserved. Printed in the United States of America. For information, address St. Martin's Press, 175 Fifth Avenue, New York, N.Y. 10010.

www.thomasdunnebooks.com
www.stmartins.com

Book design by Phil Mazzone

Frontispiece photo courtesy of the author

Library of Congress Cataloging-in-Publication Data

Romagnoli, G. Franco.
   The bicycle runner : a memoir of love, loyalty, and the Italian resistance / G. Franco Romagnoli. — 1st ed.
      p. cm.
   Includes bibliographical references and index.
   ISBN-13: 978-0-312-55454-5 (alk. paper)
   ISBN-10: 0-312-55454-0 (alk. paper)
   1. Romagnoli, G. Franco—Childhood and youth.   2. World War, 1939–1945—Underground movements—Italy—Rome.   3. World War, 1939–1945—Personal narratives, Italian.   4. World War, 1939–1945—Italy—Rome.   5. Guerrilla couriers—Italy—Rome—Biography.   6. Italy—History—1922–1945.   I. Title.
   D802.I8R66 2009
   940.53'45092—dc22
   [B]   2008046904

First Edition: August 2009

10 9 8 7 6 5 4 3 2 1

To all the Roman friends with whom I grew up:
Thank you; this is your story.

And to Gwen, who found this manuscript lost in a
bottom drawer and brought it to light:
Thank you; this is your book.

CONTENTS

CONTENTS

ACKNOWLEDGMENTS

My gratitude goes to Joy Tutela, my agent at the David Black Literary Agency, who dedicated her utmost energies to have this book published; and to Rob Kirkpatrick at Thomas Dunne Books, St. Martin's Press, who believed in her efforts and who accepted, edited, and printed my manuscript.

THE
BICYCLE RUNNER

Of Memorials and Memories

T RAVELING THROUGH THE ITAL-
ian south in the summer of 1995,
my companion and I had made a
policy to quit whatever we were doing at noon and take
shelter from the intense sun. David J. was a young American
journalist here to report on "the new Italy"; I was accompanying him as photographer, mentor, and interpreter. He took particular pride in this assignment: most of Italy had been rebuilt,
many years back, from the devastations of World War II with
the help of American funds or, as David liked to say, "with my
father's money." Moreover, his father had been a war corre-
spondent in the last two European wars. "He liked the First so
much," David joked, "that he came back for Seconds." Now he
longed to see the lands his father had written about some fifty
years ago.

The "stop at high noon" policy was essential that July: a
merciless furnace heat, carried across the Mediterranean by
African winds, had enveloped Calabria with a taste of the

Sahara, hot enough to smother my young friend's enthusiasm. And I, old enough to be his father, was not faring much better.

Even our rented car seemed to pant going up the winding road through the barren hills. At one point a smaller, unpaved road branched off, leading to a village that we might have passed by, dismissing it as another pile of sun-baked rocks, if a bell tower—actually the rusty iron cross topping it—had not given it away. The village looked very poor, a few stone houses huddled together, but it was now past high noon and we were as far from any urban center as we could be. We turned off and drove up the hill, trailing behind us a white rooster tail of dust.

The road took us to the main and only square, a rectangle defined on three sides by houses and on the fourth by the church, all whitewashed, all devoid of traits apt to soften the starkness. The sun still poured down molten lead, and its light, mirrored by all that whiteness, gave no shade. All windows and doors were firmly shuttered; not a soul was to be seen. The square was so immaculately clean that either the village was deserted or whoever lived there was too poor to afford the luxury of waste. It was then, in all that absence of color and sound, that the monument in the center of the square captured my eye.

Atop a tall, square pedestal, a soldier, World War I helmet on his head, stands stiffly facing a taller, winged figure. She, wearing a toga, represents either Victory or Glory, or perhaps simply the Angel of Death. She holds the soldier by the shoulder, putting a laurel branch in his hand. A life for a few laurel leaves. It looks as if the angel is waltzing the little soldier around, leading him in an awkward, clumsy dance. Time and weather have softened and pockmarked their features, and her open wings are frayed and chipped.

I searched the monument for an artist's signature, but I found none. Someplace, somewhere, I thought, there must be a factory spewing out war monuments of different models, in materials ranging from sumptuous marble through impressive bronze to modest plaster and concrete. Perhaps even the epitaphs came off the shelf in a range of affordability, so much per letter: "Whoever dies for his Country will live in Glory forever!" "The City, in Perennial Gratitude." "Gratefully, the Town."

The memorial I was facing must have been the bottom of the line, all that this poor village could afford. Even the most customary element, the Motherland's flag, was missing, giving the soldier a generic nationality. A poor soldier, from any poor village, remains poor even in his monumental heroism. But he is not anonymous: on the pedestal's front panel seven names are chiseled in, with the dates and places where they fell.

At that moment it came naturally, for me, to make ourselves metaphorically embody our countries.

"This," I told David, "was World War I, and from the rout of Caporetto to the victory of Vittorio Veneto, it was our very own war. Then in 1917 you joined the Allies and made it your own as well."

With befitting utilitarian sense, the gratitude of the village toward two fallen soldiers of the Ethiopian war was offered on the back panel. "And this, 1936," I told him, "is when you were against us. Not really shooting at us, only trying to starve us with economic sanctions."

A side panel was inscribed with further names and dates: World War II. I counted five names, and the chiseling looked more recent.

"Here things get confusing," I continued. "In 1942, two

died in Russia. In 1943, one in North Africa. You and I, we were enemies then. In 1944, one year later, two died near Florence—same war, but we had had a change of heart then, and we fought on your side, friends again."

Just then a young man appeared in the square. He was as surprised to see us as we were glad to see him. We explained that we were in search of shade and food. Was there any to be found around here?

"Americani?" he asked, more as a confirmation to his judgment than as a question. At David's nodding, he told us, smiling, that if our expectations weren't too high, both shade and food could be had at a small place, *qui vicino.* A hole-in-the-wall really, and not too far. It was no trouble for him to lead us there. He was barely past adolescence, neatly dressed in military fatigues, and told us he was home on a short furlough. No, he said, the village was not totally dead. At this time of day people took shelter inside, enjoying the coolness of the night stored up by the thick stone walls of the houses. After a brief walk we were in a cool, grottolike trattoria with four or five tables. There the young soldier announced that we were his friends and deserving of the owner's total attention. We asked him to join us, and he did, but just for a cold, refreshing glass of wine.

The coolness of the place—and a simple lunch—did much to restore us. I asked the soldier if he was a *"volontario."*

"No," he said, *"Sono stato chiamato alle armi."* He had answered the call to arms, the Italian obligatory twenty-four-months military service, war or no war. He wanted to know about America: did they have obligatory military service there? He told us that many men of his village had emigrated to America, never to come back.

Reaffirming his friendliness, he walked us back to our car. At the monument on the square, he snapped a salute, clicked his heels, and introduced himself in proper military fashion.

"Soldato Semplice Corsi Primo," he said, *"ai vostri ordini!"*

Behind the curtain of hot air rising from the pavement's stones, the angel's wings seemed to quiver. I circled the monument once more and looked again at the panels on the pedestal. The fourth was pristine, unmarred. A blank slate.

I felt the urge to remove this last panel, to obliterate it. Make it impossible for the Country, any country, to be Grateful, forever, to another single Private Corsi.

As I watched the young soldier walk away, he reminded me of myself at his age, of another hot day, on a dusty road in Tuscany.

A platoon of American GIs marched in two single files, one at each side of the road. They were heading away from the front line; young, beardless, tired, they were smeared with sweat and dust. Like adolescents after a rowdy game.

"Over there! Over there!" one file sang in cadence with their steps, following it with a few bars of raunchy lyrics. The other file picked up the song: "Over here! Over here!" answering with another string of barracks verses. They sang loosely of this fucking Italy, of the fucking Italian boot, of what they were fucking going to do with it. From the side of the road, resting on makeshift crutches, I watched them go by. One of them acknowledged me with a lift of his chin and a wink, and I winked back. I remember wondering, on that long-ago day, how many of these boys were going to be as lucky as I was.

I was going home.

"Over there! Over here!" they kept singing. I remember that it struck me as ironic, then, that the place where I was born and brought up, the only place I had ever seen, for these young soldiers was a vaguely remote, temporary "Over there." For them, it could have been any other country.

Over here, I thought, and I am it.

I am grateful now to have these memories. They remind me of a life, of a compelling era the world lived through. Amusing or tragic, they are all vivid, all real to me. I feel as if, from the height of my age, as from a tall observation tower, I can look back and make some sense of these events.

I

A Birthday

IN THE SUMMER OF 1939, VICTOR Emmanuel III, of the House of Savoy, Sovereign of Italy, King of Albania, Emperor of Ethiopia, was sixty-nine years old and five feet tall. In that same summer, I was almost five feet tall myself and in a few months, fourteen. I do not know what Victor's aspirations were then, but for me the most cherished one was that I would soon stop wearing short pants. After our family returned to Rome, the family tailor would turn my older brother's knickerbockers inside out and refit them for me. I could stand the wait until then because even if I had received the almost new pair of almost long pants right away, I would not have worn them. These were the last few days of summer vacation at Cattolica, and the only thing I was going to wear, I had promised myself, was *il mio slip,* my scant triangular bathing suit.

Cattolica was a small fishing village on the Adriatic coast, a quiet family place, with a few hotels and guesthouses open only for the summer. A few miles to the north was Riccione, and a few miles again was Rimini; both bigger, fancier, and more expensive places than Cattolica. They were also the favorite summer resorts of the Mussolini family, and as such they attracted big shots and fashionable, moneyed people. Each mile south toward Cattolica marked a descent in status and affluence. We came to Cattolica simply because in his boyhood my father had summered here, long before vacationing on the Adriatic had become fashionable.

My mother, younger sister, older brother, and I—escorted by my father—had arrived in the middle of June to take possession of the fisherman's house we always rented for the season. During our vacation, my father would shuttle back and forth every weekend between us and Rome, sometimes staying with us for a full week. He described the four-hour train trips as the price he had to pay for the joy of being a temporary bachelor "on the loose" in the sweltering city. My mother did not seem to appreciate the whispered jokes about summer bachelors and summer widows that provoked such hilarity within their circle of friends, and I certainly didn't make much sense out of them.

Someone might say that at almost fourteen I should have known better, but I didn't. Nobody had felt it necessary—or perhaps, considering my childlike appearance, appropriate—to explain to me the facts of life. My knowledge of these arcane facts was patched together from secretive confabulations with kids my age or gleaned from hearsay and imagination. Actually I am grateful, now, that my parents did not diagram for me the exact workings of the nuts and bolts of the construction of life. The way we figured it out, my friends and I, lying in the shade of an overturned boat during the day or on the cooling sands of a summer night, it was much more complex and fantastic than reality. Even though I was close to adolescence, the hormonal awakening had not corrupted my feelings for the opposite sex. I had been in absolutely platonic love many times already, making up adventurous fantasies in which I played all the heroic parts. Rescue and unrewarded sacrifice were essential elements of these dramas, with the real heroines of the day—teachers, schoolmates, comely maids, sisters of friends—absolutely unaware of the amazing ordeals I dreamt up for them.

My major preoccupation that summer was being almost fourteen and looking more like ten. It weighed heavily on me. How could anyone, friend or foe, let alone a girl, take me seriously? And yet in a year I had grown half an inch: there was hope. For my propensity to swing from everything swingable I had earned the nickname *Scimmietta,* Little Monkey. Now I had graduated to a new one: *Selvaggetto,* Little Savage. It wasn't much better, nonetheless I had been promoted from the animal kingdom to the human race. "Savage" I could take, but that "Little" hurt.

Probably it was an appropriate nickname. Amid the clean-cut, scrubbed, and well-behaved middle-class group of vacationers, I must have stood out as a miniature, scrawny Tarzan.

In the Italy of 1939, conforming to fads and fashions was of primary political importance, and striving for status was an essential task. Consequently, lower civil servants, small merchants, and minor professional people simply had to do the right thing and send their families on a vacation, whether they could afford it or not. Vacations provided a big stage on which to show off, compare ranks, act out hopeless aspirations.

Costuming for the play was all-important. The wardrobe was incomplete without pre- and after-swim outfits, morning and afternoon clothes, and appropriate dress for the *passeggiata,* that crowning event of a vacation day. Before or after dinner, people would stroll up and down the main street in their best garb, or sit at a café to sip a coffee or have an ice cream, watching and being watched, estimating and judging each other's deceptions. At any time, but especially for the ritual of the *passeggiata,* the children were meant to be the family's show-pieces. Walking fashion plates, they had to embody the family's affluence and good taste, its status, education, and manners, and they had better meet this responsibility. The *passeggiata* was the downfall of many a child's nervous system.

It was of mine.

Perfect demeanor was rewarded by an ice cream, or soft drink or pastry—your choice but same price—but let there be any melting, dribbling, or other soiling of the immaculate wardrobe, and the rewards would be withdrawn for days. In my childhood years, I was a virtuoso ice cream dribbler, a master white-sailor-suit spoiler. More than once, when denied my own ice cream, I managed to run head-on into another white-sailor-suited, ice-cream-licking innocent and make a mess of both of us.

But this summer was going to be different. When we first arrived, I made my *pronunciamento.* I would wear only, and always, my bathing suit. Not surprisingly, I found an ally in my father. "Let him," he told my objecting mother. "It's his last chance. He will grow up—"

"To be a savage," she cut him short. "You are going back to Rome and I'll be left here to deal with a savage. What a figure I'll cut!"

An otherwise intelligent, pragmatic person, my mother

was a fanatic follower of fashion's dogmas, of the accepted
dos and don'ts of the moment. My looks upset her even more
than my behavior. A few days of total exposure to the sun had
turned me into a brown pygmy, and seawater and sand, along
with the inexplicable loss of my comb, had transformed my
hair into a veritable fright wig. I was decidedly skinny or, as
Mamma despairingly defined me, undernourished. What she
meant was unfashionable. Proper children from proper families had to be plump, rosy, and constantly combed.

On this last item, to tell the truth, Mamma had given up on
me. That spring I had begun my fight against wearing hats, or
plastering my hair with brilliantine, or molding it under a hairnet at night, the common practice of the day for unruly hair.
Mamma had retained the upper hand, however, in our battle
by reproving me constantly for my unsightly coiffure. So I
came up with a solution worthy of a Solomon: I simply took
a pair of scissors, cut my brilliantined hair, wrapped it neatly
in the hairnet, and presented it to her.

"There!" I declared. "Now it will keep combed forever."
Victory! I had, however, wildly underestimated my parents' reaction. To win one freedom, I lost another. I was confined at
home and kept out of sight—the family idiot!—until my hair
grew to a reasonable length and its shortness could no longer
suggest that lice (oh, how low-class!) had attacked. For the duration of my house arrest, my mother, following her principle
of immediate justice, had added a few physical bruises to the
moral ones. My father did not speak to me or even acknowledge my presence, the most hurting punishment.

I do not mean to suggest that my parents did not love me.
They loved me very much, and I them. The pity of it all was
that my attempts to rise to their level of beauty, intelligence,
and self-assurance so often ended in disaster. Many times in

the darkness of a despairing night, once the emotional hot flame had cooled, I reached the conclusion that I was not part of the family at all, that they had just found me abandoned in some garbage heap and, out of the generosity of their hearts, taken me in and brought me up as one of their own. When I tried to compare myself with them, it was a disaster, great enough to uphold my theory.

There was my mother. A tall, Junoesque beauty, always fired by unmasked feelings, attractive with the knowledge of being so . . .

There was my father. Tall, handsome, athletic, elegant in thought and manners . . .

There was Marco. Two and a half years my senior, six feet tall, with the looks of a Greek god (Adonis, I had heard him called by the whispering girls on the beach—and I hoped it was a dirty word), an A-plus student, a champion at sports . . .

There was Anna. Three years my junior and almost as tall as I, as graceful as a reed, Nilotic in her beauty, a charmer, constantly charming, the doll of the beach . . .

And there was me.

I had been generously allowed to be part of the group but had been unable to show my gratitude and love with some practical action that would please them, like getting plump, keeping combed, or just simply growing up.

These morose attacks of self-pity did not last long, nor did they, fortunately, depress me seriously. The world would soon see my worth. In a few months I would be fourteen, things would change.

For the moment there wasn't much to do but let the days go by, enjoy the childish games on the beach, and wait.

Waiting was the trademark of that summer. Waiting was

in the air. Everybody seemed to be waiting for something to happen, or not to happen. There was a lot of uneasy talk among the grown-ups about England and Munich, Germany and Poland. These names had been popping up throughout the summer in the one o'clock radio newscasts, and the official announcer mentioned them with the same excitement and high spirits as if he had been talking of an upcoming World Cup soccer game. Except that the official voice seemed to know already which one was the winning team. There had been more and more martial songs on the radio, along with words and phrases such as "Vindication," and "Third Invincible Reich," "Marching Ahead Toward Ineluctable Destinies," and "Inalienable Rights."

Even the carefree atmosphere under the beach umbrellas had been marred. Sooner or later the ladies' conversations would switch from fashions, needlepoint, and general gossip to international affairs. My mother, not a political person, had more trouble than most adjusting to the new situation. Even with Signora Paoli, her most simpatico of summer friends, my mother's peal of laughter sounded forced and hollow when politics came up. Signora Paoli was the wife of the Fascist prefect of the city of Piacenza and its province. Signor Paoli was a balding, round man, a family man. The mid-1920s had found him a jovial wine merchant of reasonable wealth, and circumstances had brought him slowly into the Fascist political arena and then to prominence. Since his last weekend visit, Signora Paoli apparently understood it to be her duty to fire sarcastic broadsides at the Polish, French, and English military. In accordance with the propaganda party line, she made bold—especially for a lady—allusions to these soldiers' sexual inadequacies, and my mother felt it her duty to laugh. She knew very well that my father did not approve of party lines, especially the boastful, blustering kind, but she was afraid that sooner or later he would say something out of order in the Paolis' presence and get into trouble. To balance this possibility, she went along with the jokes. After all, simpatico is one thing, political foolhardiness another. Then too Signora Paoli had been most cordial, kind, and friendly, and all without the least condescension, quite unusual for a person of her status. Even if the Paolis were not huge stars in the Italian political firmament, here in Cattolica they glittered.

I had become friendly with the Paolis' son, Vincenzo. A few months older than I, for his age he was a giant, but not terribly imaginative or bright. I soon found out that the relationship had definite advantages. In Vincenzo's company, minor mischief was overlooked. When we bought snacks from an obsequious beach vendor, for ten cents we got twenty-five cents' worth of goodies. Caught drilling peepholes in the girls' dressing cabanas, we got only a bland reprimand from the cabanas' attendant, instead of the standard beating. Besides, my holes were too low for a rewarding view, Vincenzo's too high to do me any good.

Signora Paoli looked benevolently on our association. She was pleased, she confided to my mother, to see Vincenzo act like a boy his age and not like a *polentone*—a dull, big blob of polenta. To conform to the official mold, a Fascist boy had to be strong, courageous, a smart aleck and a bully. And a winner. Slow, oversize, dumb *polentoni*—or undersize, losing ones, *mezzecartucce* (half-loaded cartridges)—were scorned as anti-Fascist and un-Italian. For boys, the official template was Balilla, a Genoese street urchin who in 1746 threw a stone at an occupying Austrian soldier, yelling "Enough is enough!" His defiant, accurate pitch was the example that fired up a popular revolt, and freed Genoa from Austrian domination. The Opera Nazionale Balilla (the Fascist youth organization) was named after him, and every young member belonging to it was called a Balilla.

Vincenzo and I, together, made one Balilla. I had the daring and speed, he the muscle. With that kind of teamwork, we could pick and choose our membership in any of the gangs on the beach and could commit, unpunished, all sorts of minor sins. We stayed away from the major ones, the premier of these being "bad language," a sin not tolerated and, as we had been warned, punishable by death, it being vulgar and inappropriate to our age and station in life; it was much preferable to be caught committing murder than to be heard saying dirty words.

Soon the temptation to commit major sin arose. Vincenzo had been informed—by an expert on the Orient, he assured me—that we could use the most foul language under our parents' noses and get away with it. There was, the informant said, a most revolting, brutally dirty, blasting Chinese curse so terrible that not even Chinese people would dare to verbalize it; they could only express it in sign language. Make a **V** with the index and middle fingers of your left hand and stick your nose through it: the Chinese curse to end all curses. Yes, it deserved to be put to the test.

Among the peddlers who plied the beach was a diminutive, nattily attired, most gentle middle-aged Chinese man. How he got to Cattolica—or even more amazing, how he made a living out of his trade—was a mystery. He carried strapped around his neck a mahogany box with brass fixtures and an incredible number of small drawers, all full of costume jewelry for the ladies and wooden puzzles for the children; festooned around

the box were ties for the gentlemen. Sometimes he trailed behind him, high in the sky, Chinese kites in the forms of eagles
or dragons, and sometimes he would let us, just for a moment,
hold the string. He sold very little but, constantly smiling, did
not seem to mind spending hours showing off his merchandise
and describing it in a most broken Italian. We liked him and he
us. He just happened to be the perfect foil for testing our re-
bellious, dirty-language, antiparents scheme.

Vincenzo convinced me I should try it first. He could not;
considering his father's position and the Chinese's nationality,
he could have started an international incident.

And so I did. First from quite a distance and then, since
the peddler had not even flinched, closer and closer. It must
have dawned on him, after a while, that a gesture repeatedly
performed only in his presence meant something—and from
our leering attitude, that this something was bad and offensive. Either his restraint was remarkable, we thought, or the
curse nonexistent. A waste of time. But one afternoon, when
I was making a last attempt with my V-nose gesture—I had
even developed a confident flourish to it—he sprang like a jack
from his box and went for my throat. I ran for my life. He pur-
sued me relentlessly. My diversionary tactics, zigzagging and
doubling back among the beach umbrellas, proved useless. Finally he caught me. With lightning expertise, he thoroughly
pummeled me into immobility and stripped me of my mi-
nuscule bathing suit.

He then walked away with calm and dignity—and with
my suit—as if nothing had ever happened. I, naked as a worm
and feeling like one, was left to crawl into the sea to hide my
shame.

Even worse was the impossibility, later, of revealing to our mothers the cause of the incident. The peddler, honorably, declined to explain—let bygones be bygones—and, to show his magnanimity, he gifted me with one of his Chinese wooden puzzles. Nevertheless, for three days I was relegated to the immediate surroundings of the family beach umbrella. An unnecessary restriction. Even if I had wanted to, I could barely move.

Vincenzo and I spent interminable hours trying to put together a defective Chinese puzzle. We secretly nicknamed the gentle Chinese 'Phan-Koo. It could pass for Chinese, we thought, but actually sounded like and meant "up your ass" in foul Italian dialect. It was something that our mothers should never, never hear.

What we heard a lot in those three days were my sister Anna's renditions of many popular songs, cutely and teasingly performed for us, a most captive audience. A favorite of hers was a leftover from the Ethiopian War, a song of encouragement to a "black-faced, pretty Abyssinian girl to wait and hope; the hour is getting close when our strong, handsome Fascist legionnaires will arrive, unshackle you, and give you our Duce and our King . . ." She poured into it all the feeling she could muster.

Anna's singing delighted Signora Paoli. "Isn't she adorable?" she would croon. "She is the most beautiful thing on the beach!"

She was wrong. The most beautiful was Luisella Paoli, Vincenzo's sister. Almost seventeen, Signora Paoli's only daughter, she was indeed the recognized beauty of the beach. A photo of Luisella, in bathing suit, had appeared full-page in the local paper with the caption "Our Italian Youth! (Luisella Paoli)." She had also appeared in the regional paper—I had seen it framed in Vincenzo's room—wearing the uniform of a Young Fascist Girl, giving the Roman salute. The photo had been taken waist up from ground level, emphasizing the Fascist insignia on her prominent breast. She wore a brilliant smile, and her dark eyes were focused on the future. A real beauty. The caption read, *"Primavera di Bellezza,"* Springtime of Beauty, which playing on the words of the Fascist anthem, cleverly suggested the physical rewards of political involvement.

Her character was as beautiful as her body. Generous and happy, she never laughed at me but with me, and when she called me Little Savage, she made it sound like a compliment. If I wrestled with her in an attempt to capture a beach ball during the splashy games we all played in the sea, she did not, like certain other girls, scream bloody murder for all the parental authorities to hear that I, filthy little pig, had attempted to paw her. I loved her. But she had a definite predilection for Marco. They were always and boringly inseparable.

All during the summer the open-air movie theater ran, before the feature, a double dose of obligatory newsreels, through which we were exposed to interminable parades of German troops and tanks. Either *Il Duce* or an Italian delegate in full uniform appeared in the reviewing stands "shoulder to shoulder with our German comrades." Their Roman salute, right arm outstretched to the sky, was getting more and more horizontal and Nazi-like. The soldiers were "iron-willed," the machines of "tempered steel," the goose-stepping formations of "granite strength, a thousand men with the beat of one heart." This anatomical puzzle was, without fail, the signal for some Fascist zealot, appointed to stir up the audience, to cheer and encourage the rest of us to cheer. It was interpreted by most of the immature public (us) as a license for vocal mayhem. The newsreels also showed the British navy on maneuvers in the North Sea; the sight of Chamberlain (close-up of his rolled umbrella) and his admirals sipping tea (the sissies!) on the bridge of a battleship provoked the same instigator to give vent to a riot of boos and rude noises. But the sequences we waited for most were the comic relief ones: the lines of the commentary were straight, but the commentator's voice turned sardonic, with a poorly hidden chuckle here and there, and that's how we knew it was comic. These sequences usually involved news items from America (the term *americanata* had become common usage to describe something outlandish, or slightly deranged): an airplane built like a tube with (chuckle) a propeller inside (chuckle); a mailman making his rounds on (chuckle) roller skates; a collegiate (chuckle) contest of (pause for effect) goldfish swallowing!

The newsreels were a rich source of inspiration for the next day's games on the beach. It was fun to have Vincenzo try to stuff a fish down someone's throat, or to play mock battles from the trenches of sandy Maginot and Siegfried lines. Forever fascinated by anything that soared in the air—bird, stone, or plane—I originated a game called Stukas. These were the German dive-bombers, which according to the newspapers, magazines, newsreels, and radio, constituted the definitive weapon. The deadly planes would swoop down from the sky, each dropping a single bomb; in their headlong descent toward the target, they produced a noise so piercing and terrifying that, even if not directly hit, people in the vicinity went nuts forever. The pictures of the young Aryan pilots in their Stukas gave me ambivalent feelings. They were all blond and blue-eyed, and their countenances showed a powerful determination. They looked at you from the photos with an air of superiority. On the one hand, it was rewarding to know that they allowed us to be their "comrades," to share their power with us; on the other, their cold attitude, along with their incredibly powerful war machines of the air, land, and sea, gave me the creeps. They made me, and my country, feel like a pretentious weak bumpkin.

Not fourteen yet, but capable of distinguishing between reality and games, I settled the issue with my new game. The players *were* the dive-bombers: armed with sand pails full of water, we bombarded the unwary. Oiled ladies on beach towels, men buried up to their necks in the hot sands of noon, all were in danger. It was a great game, and soon Vincenzo and I had a full squadron in operation. In all innocence, we proudly called ourselves *Los Novios de la Muerte,* the Betrothed of Death, after the air squadron that had bombed Guernica in Spain. We ran like the wind, holding our loaded pails with arms outstretched like wings; having spotted our targets, we would swoop down and—with the most bloodcurdling screams we could produce—drench them. Unfortunately, the victims' screams turned out to be louder than ours, and our glory was short-lived. A bunch of unpatriotic mothers confiscated our pails and grounded us.

But most of the fun had already been blown out of what remained of summer. Some of our best companions—and/or adversaries—had packed up and left with halfhearted promises to meet, to resume playing or square the accounts, next year.

I was even admitted, instead of barely tolerated, into the fringe of my brother's small group. But there was an abyss between me and the seventeen-year-old boys and girls. They talked interminably of the university studies to come, and of philosophy and books, and used big words and kept going at a single subject for hours. Most of them were of military draft age, and that subject took long hours of discussion.

It made me wonder if, once grown up, I too would turn so distressingly boring.

By the end of August, Luisella had become my brother, Marco's fiancée. It's true that, at that time and place, if a boy and a girl showed a fancy for each other and were seen alone together more than twice, they were considered engaged. But Luisella loved Marco, and Marco loved to be loved. Even if I felt that Marco did not deserve her, I had to agree with everybody else, with some pride and a lot of envy, that they indeed made a beautiful couple.

Finally my father arrived to spend the last few days of vacation with us and then take us up to Frontale, our maternal grandfather's village in the country. After a few weeks at Nonno Nicola's farm, we would return to Rome. It was high time. Summer, the spirit of summer, was over. Killed not only by the first winds of fall, and by the ever-present martial music and slogans, but especially by the building tension in the grown-ups, who showed a confusing mixture of bravado and apprehension. They repeated the official line of elated assurance, but amid all the boldness, like lonely whistlers in the night, here and there transpired a tremolo of fear. Some said we would be at war in a few days, but then quickly added that the war would be over a few weeks after that. Many families had already left for the cities, and the few that remained closed ranks, as it were, with the camaraderie of survivors.

Signor Paoli also came to take charge of his family and take them back to Piacenza. He had arrived in a black, official Alfa Romeo limousine, driven by a Fascist militiaman, who wore, like Signor Paoli himself, the Saharian, the summer colonial-style white uniform. Signora Paoli and Mamma packed a lunch for us children, and Signor Paoli had us driven to the hills in his car—official flags flying on the fenders—for a last picnic.

The colors and fragrance of the orchards and the vineyards laden with grapes were intense, and the hills had never been more beautiful, round and soft like the body of a reclining woman. The sea breeze had cleansed the air of the haze of summer, and Bruno, the militiaman-chauffeur, said he could see—it was that clear—the Dalmatian coast, all the way across the Adriatic. Anna agreed with him. Vincenzo and I, from the vantage point of the highest branch of a tall chestnut tree, could see better and farther. It wasn't Dalmatia, only threatening gray clouds at the horizon.

We also saw Marco kiss Luisella, and we were elated; now we could part more than friends, almost brothers-in-law. On the way back, Bruno sang and taught us parodies of opera arias with raunchy lyrics, making us swear not to tell a soul where we had learned them. We laughed, but under the laughter there was a streak of sadness. We were wondering how long it would be before we saw each other again.

Luisella started crying, and she cried all the way back to Cattolica.

The Paolis left quite suddenly early the next morning, September 1. I felt cheated of the many plans Vincenzo and I had made for the rest of our vacation. Nobody paid much attention to me that day. The grown-ups were glued to the radio all day. I went fishing for crabs, alone.

On the beach, in the afterglow of sunset, September the first, Anno Domini 1939, the seventeenth year of the Fascist Era, the third of the Italian Empire, there I was by myself, and not a fraction of an inch taller or more grown-up than I had been yesterday. Goddamn! Goddammit!

Suddenly it dawned on me. To be almost an adult was to be able to speak your mind aloud, forcefully. A grown-up might yell the most horrible words, words that a child should not even think of, let alone whisper. What might happen if I went for it? What if I gave vent to an escalation of dirty words?

Making sure I was alone, I walked to the edge of the beach and faced the sea.

"Damn pig!" I yelled at nobody in particular, to the world in general. And then louder, with no references at all:

"Damn bastard, fucking pig!"

What a glory! And now for something bigger, stronger, more mouth-filling:

"Shitty cuckold, fucking asshole bastard pig!"

Ah, what a satisfying burning of the lungs, ache of the jaws!

"Goddamn the shitty cuckold soul of your most bastard pig-fucking ancestors!"

Elation, the soul swelling with the pride of daring and, having dared, flying away like a balloon, chasing the echo of the horrible curses. How easy to grow up! Come out of the sea, Neptune, I can tear you apart! Good-bye, laughable little savage child, cup your hands around your mouth and destroy childhood with one final blow:

"Bastard prick pig! Prickhead! Cuckold shit and fucking bitch son of a bitch!"

I saw my father only as he passed me by, almost brushing my shoulder. Without looking at me, without turning, silently he walked into the sea and swam.

I stood still, galvanized. A flame shot through the soles of my feet and up and up, incinerating my hair. That's it, when you die: one long, burning flame, the burning lungs and the burning heart stop, everything in the burning eyes turns red and you are dead.

Though a powerful swimmer, my father took only a few strokes, then swam back and walked out of the sea. He was bigger, much bigger than Neptune. He stood somberly over me and looked for a long moment into my eyes. Then, weighing his words carefully, he said slowly: "You are right, *Selvaggetto.* It is war. . . . The goddamn son of a cuckold German bitch is murdering Poland."

Then he put a huge, strong hand on my shoulder, and together, we men walked home.

2

The Best of Enemies

ON HOT SUMMER NIGHTS I SPENT forbidden hours camping under the stars. My camp was the little marble-floored balcony that looked down on the big courtyard of our building from five floors up. With considerable aggrandizement, the building was referred to as a *palazzo*. It was actually a bastion of middle-class living in a middle-class section of Rome, a square, six-story structure built like a fortress around a soccer field–size courtyard. The building, in fact the whole quarter, had been built between 1910 and 1930 to accommodate the explosion of civil servants after Rome was made the capital of Italy. The establishment in the twenties of the Fascist party swelled the ranks of bureaucrats even more, but with the right recommendations or some palm greasing, some nongovernment people also resided in the *palazzo*.

The architect's Renaissance aspirations were satisfied by a fascia of colorful murals, painted just under the eaves and here and there around the many windows, representing classical acanthus leaves draped around nymphs and satyrs; the colors were somewhat faded but good enough to relieve the functionality of the construction. The courtyard, in a similar attempt at aristocratic grace, was divided into geometrically shaped flower beds, some adding up to circles, some to squares, hedged by myrtle shrubs and planted with all sorts of carefree flora. Dwarf trees and palmettos made a perfect jungle gym for the many resident cats; a fountain at one end of the garden splashed gently all the time, to the happiness of the fat red carp swimming in its pool.

Like a fortress, the *palazzo* had only one entrance, a large arched entryway—a truck could easily pass through it—defended by a humorless, stern *portiere,* doorman-janitor, and by glass-and-wrought-iron gates that he banged shut each night at exactly 11:00 P.M. Once one was through the gates and into the courtyard, one's first impression was of entering a green oasis, away from the congestion and noise of the city. But in a minute it was easy to realize that some sixty families, most of them blessed with numerous offspring, lived here. From the open windows seeped the familiar noises of mothers calling children, the clanging of kitchen pots and pans, a voice singing to the rhythm of a slapping mop, an unrelenting piano lesson in progress. Many terraces and balconies, guarded by wrought-iron railings whose floral design echoed the acanthus of the murals, also faced the courtyard and frequently served as pulpits for the exchange of news and the broadcasting of gossip. Not much stayed secret in our *palazzo.*

Access to the apartments was through eight independent entries-staircases, evenly distributed inside the periphery and wide enough to accommodate elevators at a later time. For now, though, the residents had to climb the many broad marble steps leading to the various landings. There, on opposite sides of each landing, were the doors of two apartments. Each stairway, identified by a Roman numeral, had massive oak doors that opened onto the courtyard to reinforce the feeling of fortress. These doors too were closed and locked at night. This was the hour when everything went quiet, only the burbling fountain and a few subdued cat fights gave life to the warm night.

My little balcony was kitty-corner from the balcony of my friend Piero Mazzetti, only his was one floor lower. Piero and I had connected the two balconies with what we called a *teleferica,* a cable car. It was a big name for a small piece of engineering: a string tied to the wrought-iron railings, across which, riding on a pulley, we passed back and forth a basket no bigger than a shoe box. Because of the incline produced by the one-floor difference, I had to spool the basket up to me with a second string or, by free-reeling this out, let it slide back to Piero. The forty or so feet that separated us were then covered with swooshing speed, ending with the hollow thump of the basket hitting Piero's railing. The muffled swooshes and thumps underlined the silence of our adventurously inno-cent nights.

We had started this operation in third grade, inspired by a much ballyhooed event. Mussolini himself, with a small group of uniformed and bemedaled Fascist VIPs, had cut the ribbon and taken the inaugural ride on a new *teleferica.* The little car, suspended on a cable over the abyss, went from the bottom of the Gran Sasso Mountain—the tallest of central Italy, in the Abruzzi region—up to the modern hotel at its very tip, Campo Imperatore, a skiers' paradise. It was one of Mussolini's many public works, some flashier than others, meant to bring Italy up to speed with the leading nations of the world. Mussolini himself would never have guessed, then, that he had built his own jail. Years later, when he was forcibly ousted from office in 1943, Italian *carabinieri* took him manacled to that impregnable peak, a prisoner in that same hotel.

Piero and I used our *teleferica* to pass to each other pieces of candy, or a new toy to touch, admire, and send back. Once we thought of having a real living thing take the trip; Piero tried to stuff one of the many Mazzetti cats in the suspended basket, but the animal, with admirable perception, scratchily refused. Above all, we used the *teleferica* to exchange secret messages. Written in our newly acquired and barely tested handwriting, the messages, scribbled in the glow of a dying flashlight, turned out to be so secret that most of the time we ourselves could not decipher them. We had to complement the secret communications by loud balcony-to-balcony whispers, in a long and finally boring guessing game.

Our nocturnal activities were all the more fun because they were forbidden. At least in theory. After going through the motions of lying down in our beds, as soon as our households had quieted down, we sneaked out onto our balconies, with an apple or a cookie as survival rations. Our parents usually closed their ears to these supposedly furtive goings-on, but if our shenanigans threatened their sleep, they would shoo us back into our beds and put a quick end to our adventures.

Our *teleferica* lasted a few years, through fourth and fifth grades and up to our first secret smoking experiments, when our lungs lost their virginity to chamomile leaves rolled in tissue paper. One night, Piero's aunt Ada took us by surprise and discovered the smoldering thing going back and forth in the basket. Then and there, with a swift snip of scissors, she cut the connection.

We had outgrown the game anyway, so the broken string of the *teleferica* was left dangling to rot.

But despite all that followed, and throughout our lives, much stronger strings of friendship and affection kept Piero and me connected and bound together.

The Mazzetti family was deeply religious and just as deeply devoted to the Fascist cause. They professed both creeds with the same unquestioning diligence and considered them inseparable parts of the same faith.

It was very confusing for me to see all over the place, side by side, the portraits of Jesus and of Benito, as Mussolini was familiarly addressed. I had been going for a while to catechism classes, and all I got was that Jesus was some abstract figure who told me to obey him unquestioningly. If you don't, when you die, you'll burn in hell. Benito's philosophy sounded almost the same to me. *"Credere, obbedire, combattere!"* Trust me, obey me, fight for me, and shut up. If you don't, I'll have my goons beat you up right now, no waiting. That was his constant aggressive slogan. The differences between the two were their accoutrements and postures: one in a flowing white toga, seraphic expression, a golden aureole floating over his head; the other in black military uniform with lots of decorations and tassels, fierce determination expressed by his chin jutted out to touch his nose, and piercing black eyes. Sometimes he was pictured sitting on a white charger; but then Jesus was portrayed floating on white clouds. Uncannily, the eyes of both portraits seemed always focused on you, following you. The best thing I could do was to sneak silently by without looking at them, hoping they didn't notice me.

My father was anticlerical (a.k.a., in Italy, a *mangia-preti,* a "priest-eater"), an agnostic and a freethinker. His generic classification, then, was "communist," a synonym for anybody with thoughts not conforming with the official Fascist line. As for my mother, her religious belief was closer to superstition than faith, and her political one ranged from noninterested to neutral.

The Mazzettis had moved into their apartment about the same time that my parents had moved into theirs; this fact helps to explain their maintaining a polite, long-lasting, and extremely peculiar "good neighbor" relationship.

When they moved into their new apartments in the *palazzo,* the two young couples were open-minded enough to discuss their opposite opinions in a civilized manner; somehow each hoped, I think, to make the other see the light. It was the very beginning of the self-proclaimed "Fascist Era," imbued with a general and revitalizing optimism—considering the messy situation of the immediate post–World War I period, any change could only be for the better—and not many people, especially among the young, were capable of foreseeing the harsh times in store for the opposition, any opposition. This became increasingly clear in five or six years, but even so, they—now with growing families—remained polite to each other. When they met in the courtyard, they just smiled and limited their conversation to the weather and the health and the bringing up of children. As we children grew—parallel in ages and numbers—they did not discourage our being friends and perhaps secretly hoped that we would become the catalysts for spiritual and political conversion.

In the battle of philosophies, our side, by the sheer number of the opponents (our five versus their eight), was doomed.

And of course there was something beyond the different political inclinations, something different in personal attitudes and lifestyles.

To begin with, my father was a *settentrionale*—born in northern Italy—hence a sort of expatriate in Rome and considered by the *meridionali* (Rome in this scheme could be seen as the beginning of southern Italy) as a snobbish intellectual, dedicated to rationalization and cautious long-range planning of everything, therefore more interested in a positive future outcome than in an alluring, chancy present. It is true that a certain prudence made him stretch his engagement to my mother for eight years. In other words, my father was not given to the sudden impulses, extroverted and noisy emotions, loud-mouthed and hot-blooded behavior associated with the South. Tall and light-skinned, slender and athletic—versus dark, short, and roundish—he dressed with quiet elegance—versus colorful flash. He had an artistic bent that led him to appreciate beauty in whichever expression of life he could find it. From certain rumors jokingly circulated—and from my mother's clenched-teeth smiles in reaction to them—I gathered that these included feminine pulchritude. Which, the same rumors suggested, was a reciprocated interest.

My father studied at the Accademia delle Belle Arti, which gained him the honorary title of Professor; then he furthered his studies and became an architect. With a growing family, and lacking the taste or the aggressiveness for a freelancing career, he joined the ranks of government employees working for the Ministry of Transportation and State Railroads, developing and designing railroad stations. The job gave him and his family great lifelong benefits plus the opportunity to travel, which he loved to do, enough spare time to dedicate to his pen-and-ink drawings, and generous vacation time, which we all treasured. He was well-liked and had a witty sense of humor that kept the whole family in a good mood. My mother adored him, and willingly played second banana to his jesting.

She was a Roman, and her character was almost the opposite of my father's. Dark-haired, with flashing black eyes, visceral in her feelings, she always preceded her reasoning with action. She would do things—generally involving money matters—on the sly, convinced she had fooled my father, and he generously would let her believe it. She met my father when posing as a nude model in one of his art classes. Not taking too warmly to his comment that she could have modeled for Rubens, she grabbed the object closest to hand, and a small clay bust of Leonardo met with my father's head. It was the spark that provoked, besides a trip to the emergency room, a relationship that lasted a lifetime. She was a loyal general and soldier, his army of one, and indeed she would have jumped in the fire for him, although, naturally, not during those short intermezzos when she wanted to kill him. She supported him blindly and absolutely. She was very conscious of fashion, and I always suspected that her Sunday appearances at church were mostly opportunities to show off her latest attire and check out the other ladies' style. This attitude, among other reasons, influenced her political conduct. She simply refused to wear the Fascist Women's uniform: it was absolutely crude and unfashionable.

She became a dedicated mother—without much changing her worldly outlook—with the appearance on the family scene of my older brother, Marco. After my parents' eight years of bohemian engagement and a city hall wedding, Marco was born legal and perfect—to the day and hour—nine months later.

This gift for perfection was the trademark that stuck to Marco all his life. The anecdotes that testify to this quality are too many and too painful for me to recount, since they were offered to me—and how frequently!—as examples to imitate in whatever circumstance I was not up to snuff. One of the earliest involves one of my father's artist friends. He used Marco as a model for a putto angel on a mural for a church altar, and it turned out to be so lifelike, my parents asserted, that they were tempted to change Marco's name to Angelo. It was enough to make me puke.

I followed Marco into the world by almost two and a half years, and follow I did for all our growing years. There was not much I could do to match that paragon of excellence. I was left with the options of crawling under the nearest stone or doing something stupidly outlandish, anything to call attention to myself. And on the rare occasion I did something that outshone him, it was generally judged an aberration, that chancy exception that confirms the rule. This all gained me the reputation of an eccentric, with a strong negative implication. I must admit that my feelings toward Marco were mixed, and remained so for a long time. I couldn't help feeling both envy at his seemingly effortless achievements and pride in sharing space and family name with him, basking in reflected glory. Being fingered as Marco's brother had its pros and cons.

My personal battle for equality within the family took a turn for the worse with the birth of my sister, Anna. Three years my junior, she turned out to be a feminine version of Marco, with the added attraction that, while he was aloof and self-centered, she was absolutely outgoing and sociable. She had taken the best genes from our mother and father; her character and beauty were a mix of earthiness and elegance, cunning and intelligence. A homespun, smiling Nefertiti, by the time she was a teenager, Anna had assembled a large circle of friends and admirers, many from social strata higher than ours, a circle that kept expanding throughout her life and to which I was admitted without condescension. I liked her. When she was a baby, I made games and handcrafted toys for her, and I took much pride in her joy. In return, she was the only one convinced that I was a genius.

While the makeup of our family was heterogeneous, the Mazzettis presented a monolithic front. In fact, this geologic adjective was later adopted and widely used by Fascist image makers to signify the massive unity of the ideal state: no cracks in the granite. One single will, no wavering; hard, straight, erect, and macho as an obelisk; strong as a single piece of stone and, subliminally, no moss gathering here.

The Mazzettis' extended family was perhaps more monolithic in spirit than in fact. The family cast of characters, in chronological order, began with the nonagenarian grandfather, Nonno Salviotti—a skinny five-footer affectionately called Nonnetto (Little Grandpa) for his diminutive size—father of two daughters, Ada and Teresa (Mrs. Mazzetti), and once a civil engineer on the project team of the Simplon Tunnel, which ran under the Alps. Tended with loving care by his daughters, he spent all day in his room checking over and over again the figures of his past projects. He was considered harmless but somewhat balmy. He came out of his room-hermitage for sorties to the toilet, with uncanny precision in timing, only when the facilities were already occupied; then he would stand there, knocking petulantly at the door until he was let in. In meeting the exiting customer, Nonnetto would whip up his little arm in a Fascist salute and squeal *"Viva Il Duce!"* The official answer to that, accompanied by the same gesture, was a perfunctory and loud *"A noi!"*—To us!—after which everybody could go about their business. His real political weight in the family lineup was light, but after all, he was still the honorary head of the tribe.

Then came Nana. She was of considerable vintage, undetermined but close to Nonnetto's. She had been Ada and Teresa's nanny and then, as they grew up, their maid-housekeeper. Now she was kept in the family, out to pasture as it were, by the affection of the two women. Having decided that more than one bath per season was a modern-age extravagance, she usually smelled quite ripe. She was of elephantine proportions: if you met her in the long and narrow corridor of the apartment, advancing deliberately, shuffling her slipper-clad, massive flat feet, you had better retreat or get squashed against the corridor wall and be imbued with what, once we grew up, we remembered as Essence de Nanà. Elephantine also was her devotion: she would have defended with her life the Mazzettis' children and, if they met with her approval, their friends. As tangible proof of her gruff affection, she prepared for us all sorts of delicious afternoon snacks and goodies, the messier the better. She made the creamiest, fluffiest, sweetest of pastry creams, even tastier when she let us use our fingers instead of spoons.

Signor Ulisse Mazzetti, husband of Teresa Salviotti, was the official head of the household, giver of the family name, father of my friends, entrepreneur, adventurer, conquering hero, soldier of fortune. He was, for me, of mythical proportions. I don't remember meeting him in person more than four, perhaps five times in my life, but I felt as if I knew him just as well as all the other members of the family. Photographs of him were all over—on walls, on mantels, on mirrors, on desks; there was hardly a corner of the house where you did not feel his presence. Together with Jesus and Benito, he made up, for me, the holy Trinity. He was squat and muscular, with a full head of curly hair, a Roman nose, and a square, uplifted chin, mouth always in a confident smile. His most striking features were his eyes, dark, piercing, shining, searching, and like those of the two other members of the trio, always focused directly on yours.

The gallery of pictures pretty well covered his curriculum vitae: seated in a skeletal World War I airplane, goggles on forehead, white scarf flowing; on the stairs of a church, a protective hand around Teresa Salviotti's shoulder, in a wedding photo; in the uniform of a *squadrista,* a member of the elite squad of Fascist commandos who started it all with the march on Rome; near a delivery truck, its side emblazoned with "U. Mazzetti Co., Ltd./ Industrial Bleach and Soap"; in a white Saharan jacket, the official colonial attire for the Libyan campaign; in the uniform of the East Africa Corps, with pith helmet and sand goggles, and a pretty little Ethiopian girl at his side; with a tasseled cap at a rakish angle on his head, near an army truck loaded with Spanish Falangists.

He was rarely at home, but he frequently wrote separate letters to his wife and his children. These Piero read to me, or sometimes he narrated their contents to me, which I preferred. I could close my eyes and follow the adventures of Signor Ulisse as in a movie. The letters invariably had the same openings ("I hear from your mother of your behavior. I'm so proud of you") and closings ("I am confident that you will continue to be good Fascist children; do your duty and protect and defend your mother, your family, and your Country").

Sandwiched in between opening and closing, told in a matter-of-fact way, were brief but colorful tales of his life, things that were meant to impress us, springboards for our imaginations. "With my truck broken in the middle of the desert, I had to take a long ride on a camel." (Was he rescued by a caravan? Taken by desert marauders?) "Not to offend a touchy chieftain, I had to partake of the host's meal of roasted grasshoppers and snake meat." (Did he swallow? Did he like it?)

I shared vicariously with Piero his pride in his father but also felt a tinge of jealousy. My father was likewise frequently away from home, working on location for various periods of time. Sometimes he sent us postcards from ho-hum places, such as Florence or Venice or Milan—"Thinking of you. Many kisses, Papa"—and generally he came back home even before we received them.

Big deal.

The really big deal, delivered by acquaintances or carried by Signor Ulisse himself on the rare occasions when he came home, was a series of incredibly exotic presents to his children: a barely domesticated capuchin monkey, a scary chameleon, a large, red-bellied turtle, a squawky, multicolored parrot. The gifts were intended not only to entertain but also to teach responsibility for the training, maintenance, and love of living things. The Mazzettis' living bestiary, which included a large family of cats, was a thing of wonder and admiration for me—and of considerable aggravation for the neighbors. The animals—even if in theory well cared for and kept clean by the designated custodians—emanated a very distinctive, zoo-like aroma. It permeated the apartment's walls and its inhabitants' clothes.

All told, Ulisse Mazzetti was, in my eyes, the template of

the Fascist he-man: dashing, dynamic, not bound by boring conventions, a free spirit. He was my potential role model, if I ever grew up. Too bad that my parents, as I gleaned from their whispered conversations, thought of him as a charming braggart, an irresponsible buffoon, a ne'er-do-well, a fortune seeker, not much of a family man. I may have sensed a remote shadow of truth in their judgment, but it saddened me. Deeply.

It took me a long time to distinguish between Signora Teresa and Zia Ada, so similar were they in appearance, character, and as it appeared to me as a child, their roles in the family. They both had the fine-chiseled and delicate features of mother-of-pearl cameos, and a refined composure that totally masked their toughness and determination. Eventually I came to think of Signora Teresa, in her role of mother, as more important— hence older—than Ada, who was merely an aunt. Later I came to see how really immature was my judgment.

Teresa Salviotti had obviously married below her status, a fact given away by her, and her sister's, aristocratic countenance and manner of speech. Signor Salviotti—Nonnetto— had been a distinguished professional, as attested by the many diplomas on the walls of his room. In addition, it was said that the Salviotti family had been "connected with the Vatican," and Nonnetto had done important work for the Vatican state. What had provoked the social downslide and brought the two sisters, accustomed to reasonable wealth and status, to share with their aging father the decorous but definitely middle-class quarters of our *palazzo,* I was never able to find out.

While Signora Teresa, as an understanding, nurturing

mother and accomplished housekeeper, fulfilled one Italian idea of womanhood, Aunt Ada, a dedicated spinster, represented another. Men considered her sexually attractive, probably due to her holy purity attitude. My first memory of her, by my accounting, goes back to my infancy. She must have been in her mid-thirties then, and already accomplished in her spinsterhood. She was soft-spoken and kind, like her sister, albeit three times more of a perfectionist concerning order, obedience, and discipline—the old iron fist in a velvet glove—and with Teresa she shared the duty of educating and raising the Mazzetti children in the Roman Catholic and Fascist doctrines. Together they sculpted the family into a particular form of pure Fascism, as in "pure mathematics," in which the working of numbers is a mix of theory and philosophy, an end and a reward in itself. Their Fascism was totally removed from personal gain; it shunned the elbowing for power or for preferential status. It was as pure as a dogma, a Faith, something you believed in absolutely, without doubt or scrutiny. Yes, a reward in itself.

This communion of politics and religion reached a climax in Ada: while the celibacy of nuns is explained by their being spiritually wedded to Jesus Christ, Ada's was justified by her being spiritually wedded to Benito. Side by side over her headboard she kept an oil portrait of Jesus, with a dried-out bough of Palm Sunday frond inserted between the frame and the wall, and a portrait of Benito riding the white charger, always a fresh flower below its silver frame. She had a doctorate in social sciences and held a position of relative importance in the National Institute of Workmen's Social Insurance. After so many years of competent, loyal employment, she should have held a position in the directorate of the institute, but she had two strikes against her. First, she was a woman, and second, she was too pure to debase her political creed with office politics. She had little chance against the sharp-clawed, scheming male party climbers. These were the ones who formed the hierarchical garlands, the descending spirals of saints, angels, and cherubim around Il Duce's high throne.

Federico Mazzetti, eldest of the three children, and two months younger than my older brother, was the first of the next generation. Tall and slim, he was gifted with a swinging, double-jointed elegance of movement; always smiling and easygoing, he had a subtle and gentle sense of humor that prodded him to invent hilarious schemes, planned at length but seldom executed. He possessed a quick-to-learn intelligence and would manage to save each freewheeling, less-than-satisfactory school year by last-minute cramming. I identified with him because I was not much of a student either, and because we had in common a sense of amused curiosity about the world around us.

The family lineup continued with Piero. Almost exactly my age, Piero had his father's stocky and muscular build and thick, curly hair. He had a well-organized, purposeful mind and did things the way they were supposed to be done; if others did not, he would police them and see that they mended their ways, and his quick temper and strong physique ensured that his suggestions were most often followed. Piero was an A student and had an uncanny sense of coordination that made him excel in gymnastics and sports. With stones, javelins, archery arrows, or blowguns (and later with real guns), his aim was lethal. With his slingshot, he could stop cold a lizard on the run or a swallow in flight. We were natural friends by reason of our age and had been close since birth. We took our first steps together at the same local park; we sat at the same double desk throughout nursery and elementary school. I always learned something from him, and afterward, occasionally, I resented it. Sometimes I wanted to punch him in the nose, and the few times I did, or attempted to, even then he taught me a lesson: get stronger or smarter, or avoid confrontation. And he was too much of a by-the-rules gentleman (I being weaker and dumber) to beat me up. Not too harshly, anyway. A real friend.

And finally came Tina, the youngest. Three years younger than Piero, she was a pretty, leggy girl with thin lips, the same age as my sister and, like Anna, one minute full of coquetry and the next of spite. I ignored her, or at least I tried to, until we grew up. Then it became impossible.

Any sketch of our lives in the *palazzo* would be incomplete if the Mazzettis' revolving menagerie of pets was left out. One that lasted a long time was the multicolored parrot, Pippo, Federico's favorite; the only squawking words that he ever said were *"O! Che bello!"* The old bird never specified what was "Oh, so beautiful"; perhaps he was easily satisfied by whatever he had or saw, and perhaps it was this sunny attitude that rewarded him with an incredible longevity. On the other hand, Noah the turtle, Tina's ward, was so unhappy about its condition that it tried several times to commit suicide; now and then it sneaked through the balcony railings and hit the pavement four floors below. The only injury was to Tina's ego, which I tried to soothe by telling her that I too would go for hara-kiri if left in her care.

Permanent members of the set were a family of cats who had grown up with their own fascist tendencies: they operated as a group and in union strength, they made their own laws and ruled their own turf. Pride of them all, especially to the Mazzetti boys, was Ponzo. With a velvety, lead-colored pelt, he was a large, powerful beauty and the terror of the neighborhood's legged and winged fauna; even several of the large red carp swimming in the courtyard fountain showed marks of his claws. More than a cat, Ponzo was, for me, like a midget puma; he moved and stalked silently, in slow motion, head low between bulging shoulder muscles, belly to the ground, yellow and malevolent eyes fixed upon his prey. He held that pose at length, like a sculpture, until his target got accustomed to his presence. Then he would spring and strike in a blur of teeth and claws. Whenever I had to share a room with Ponzo, I found myself keeping my back to the wall and my eyes on the vicious beast—the same tactic used by Negus, the Mazzettis' playful, mischievous little monkey. A master at spitting seeds or throwing fruit pits at the other cats, when Ponzo was in the vicinity, Negus retreated to his high perch in the corner of the room and sat quietly there, trying to be invisible, his long leash hauled up from the floor and gathered tightly under his arm, out of Ponzo's reach.

Piero was the only one who had some control over the feline, and had trained him to attack any fingered target. Ponzo had made the courtyard his special domain and needed no solicitation to provoke mayhem; the jagged edges of his ears were the badges of a fighter, a gladiator. With Ponzo around, even the other Mazzetti cats respected the law of the watering hole: they kept a respectful distance from the common food bowl and approached it only when Ponzo had finished

his meal and moved away. While the other cats had a preference for fish, tidbits set aside by the local fishmonger, Ponzo
was mostly a carnivore. He gulped down with equal relish
beef hearts, livers, and lungs (butcher's special), and he had an
inordinate liking for tripe. Ponzo savored it slowly as a connoisseur, deliberately, with lip-licking gusto. His mean features
seemed to soften, his eyes semiclosed in beatitude, an elemen-
tal, four-footed gourmet tasting a piece of heaven. I frequently
wonder if my lifelong fondness for *trippa* began then, inspired
by Ponzo.

Once, and only once, I asked my mother to let me have
my own pet. With enormous benevolence, she agreed that pets,
and animals in general, are loving and lovable creatures of
God and as such have a rightful place in this world. But that
place was not—firmly and definitely not—in her house.

Looking at this gallery of portraits and the events of those
childhood times as they appear to me now, I find it hard to
read in them any prophecy of the tragedies to come. The
Greek theater masks we were all wearing pointed, if anything, more toward comedy. As a matter of fact, the whole
country—after a promising start in rebuilding itself morally
and physically from the upheaval of World War I—seemed
to have embraced a form of public display of postures, gestures, and uniforms that, seen with after-the-fact wisdom,
were ridiculously histrionic, mock-heroic, amateurish. How
could sedate, well-thinking, middle-aged men get dressed
up in military uniforms from an operetta stage, and mothers
and grandmothers, wearing Colombina-like dresses, hold the
hands of toddlers in quasi-military getup, calling them "Sons

of the Wolf"? How could they (we) all have fallen for the huge masquerade? It soothes my love-of-country feelings to know that the whole world fell for it too, and it took quite a while to discern between comedy and reality. It is unfortunate that Mussolini's proud announcement that "our trains are running on time again" provoked hilarity around the world. The trains did run on time again, and they reached towns and villages once isolated. The running on schedule symbolized the return to order after the political and economic chaos. Temporarily a new sense of purpose and of pride returned to the country.

But then megalomania set in, and appearances became more important than substance. Actually, nationally and internationally, the appearances *were* the substance. The "Fascist Nation," by my wild estimate, was composed of (A) 1 percent intellectual philosophers; (B) 2 percent self-made politicians honestly believing in the new order; (C) 10 percent privileged party members, who hoarded all they could get—and more; (D) 15 percent sycophants and bullies-enforcers; and (E) 72 percent conformists who, for their safety and that of their families, went along with the charade, ostriches with their heads buried in the sand, not wanting to see or know what really was going on. Mixed in with the (E) there was the vast layer of silent anti-Fascists, officially nonexistent. But if they became too active or too outspoken and were found out by the frightful OVRA (Organizzazione per la Vigilanza e Repressione Antifascismo), the Fascist secret police, they were persecuted and dealt with. But by and large, self-preservation was stronger than anti-Fascist beliefs.

3

Book and Rifle

T AGE NINE OR TEN, MY schoolmates and I knew more geographical details about Ethiopia than about our Motherland. In 1935, for the cleansing of a "shame" that had occurred in 1896 and for the honorable purpose of "civilizing" it, Italy invaded Ethiopia. Every morning, before the beginning of classes, we heard the war's developments blow by blow. Standing at attention beside our desks, we listened to our teacher reading the official war bulletin: "Advancing in a pincer formation from Makale and Abur-Aich, against massive hordes of foreign-trained and highly armed natives, our invincible legionnaires, under the heroic command of Generale Badoglio, have annihilated and routed all resistance. In a swift advance, our victorious army has conquered and freed the village of Tass'aran. The village was burned to the ground by the enemy before its retreat."

Then the most deserving pupil moved a little Italian flag on a map of Ethiopia stretched on the classroom wall. Most of the locations mentioned by the war bulletins were not on the map, but that did not matter; the important thing was to move the pins in the right direction. This duty often fell to Piero Mazzetti, on his own merit as a good student and also because his father was a legionnaire—"legionnaire" not as in Beau Geste but as in "Roman legions." The term was meant to give our soldiers the aura of conquerors and colonizers, and make the whole exercise a repeat performance of the empire building of ancient Rome. Signor Ulisse Mazzetti wasn't really a full-fledged legionnaire, but close. He dressed like one, pith helmet and all, but without military insignia. As the troops advanced, the Corps of Engineers followed, building roads, bridges, airfields, and a system of transportation where none had existed before. Most of the intensive work was carried out on contract by big and small civilian companies, militarized for the occasion so that they were directly under the army's orders. Out of patriotism or opportunism—or both—Signor Mazzetti had joined the fray, supplying four trucks to move whatever was necessary to be moved. His fleet's size kept growing with the expansion of the theater of war operations.

Because of his father's exalted status, and because he reported brief essays from his father's letters home, Piero had become the Ethiopian expert in residence. Ulisse Mazzetti sent tidbits such as these: "Dear children: 'Yes' in Ethiopian is *eeshee;* it also means 'perhaps,' 'no,' or whatever they think you want it to mean! Their bread is a spongy, thin, and acid pancake. They call it *enjira,* and they use it with their fingers to scoop up food instead of a fork! The natives live in huts called *tucul* [it sounded like "your ass" in dialectal Italian; some kids chuckled and blushed, others grabbed at the chance to say dirty words with impunity] and most of their children run around naked. The first thing the legionnaires do, after entering a village, is cut the slaves' chains (!!) and free them."

The Ethiopian campaign intensely touched our lives not only for its duration but for years to come, and in more ways than one. My feelings were constantly teetering from patriotism and national pride, out of loyalty to the Mazzettis and the official stance, to shame and doubts. These latter were due indirectly to my father—indirectly because his own feelings and conversations were not meant for me to listen to or to understand. I know now that it saddened him not to be able to express openly to his children his feelings about certain things; he deemed, rightly or wrongly, that we were at that stage where life is confusing enough without any outside help.

Sporadically, his architectural work took him just across the border to France and Switzerland, and on his return he would confide to my mother what uncensored news he had gathered there and what people abroad thought of us. I concluded, from these discussions not meant for my ears, that our African war was a sham, a naked act of aggression against a practically defenseless, poor, backward country; and that we had behaved cruelly by bombing and strafing civilian populations; that our General Graziani—a national hero, the "Conquering Lion of Ethiopia"—had a reputation abroad as particularly ruthless and cruel, responsible for mass executions and gassings.

So there went the image of the conquering heroes. Where was the truth?

It was unsettling. As a good and true Italian youth, I had to be loyal to the official line, but my conflicting loyalty to my father and his opinions, no matter how outlandish, was natural and incorruptible. And then there were the Mazzettis. They lived one of Mussolini's mottoes, "Who is not with me is against me!" and I was ashamed that my father had to be different, had to be on the "against" side.

This situation of mine was aggravated because it was impossible to forget Ethiopia. Our public lives were inundated by things with an Ethiopian slant, from songs and music to games and food. Anything fun and good with a chocolate or other dark color was called "Abyssinian" (it even became the Italian name for what Americans called an Eskimo Pie). Negus and Ras, Tafari and Menelick became the most common names for pets and puppet show characters. Once the war was over, the "Kingdom of Italy" was declared "Empire," and our diminutive King Victor Emmanuel III was promoted to Emperor. Mussolini took for himself the title Founder of the Empire. As in the old Roman Empire times, spoils of war were brought back home for all to see: the huge, monolithic obelisk of Aksum was carted away from its place in the African sun and again erected back in Rome, near the Circus Maximus.

And so I found myself, and I wasn't alone, marching to the sounds of several different drummers, and frequently the marching was painfully real. Every Saturday afternoon—sometimes also on weekdays—we wore our blackshirt uniforms and reported to a local headquarters to practice formation marching, or to learn the care and use of army rifles, scaled down to our size, perfectly working, folding bayonets included. Federico and Piero Mazzetti were the shining paragons of our group; I tried to emulate them, and sometimes I felt a surge of pride in being a Balilla myself. Various groups formed a legion, and then groups competed with groups and legions with legions to outshine the others on the parade grounds. Thousands of children and young adolescents—male and female—convened in stadiums to perform hours-long, exhausting, synchronized exercises for "Authorities" watching from the reviewing stand. After the practices and the performances, with the final "At ease!" great baskets of freshly baked buns together with baskets of chocolate bars were set at the edge of the field. We were to file by and take one of each treat; if there were any left over, the most deserving got a chance at another round. The Mazzettis always got double rations, and being generous friends, they shared them with me.

I did not mind these weekly musters. Besides spending a few hours playacting the soldier with kids my own age and testing my wits on how to squeak by under the rules, I appreciated being treated as a worthy member of a group. And I liked the free bread and chocolate. I was hooked on them.

Sometimes at night, after a particularly tiring mock-military day, I had a recurrent dream. In a perfectly pressed and starched Balilla uniform (in the dream I even added a few nonordinance frills), I marched at the head of a parade, beating a drum, just in front of Il Duce. I was the much admired personal drummer of Mussolini. It was a dream I wanted to wake up from but also one I wanted to replicate on subsequent nights.

Unconsciously I had developed, when at dinner with the family, the habit of playing on the table—baraba-mbamba, baraba-mbamba, barram, barram—a marching tattoo with fork and knife for drumsticks.

"Stoppit!" my parents would yell. "You are driving us crazy!"

And perhaps I really was.

My parents' attitude toward these Balilla matters was suffering compliance. My being kept out of these exercises, or not showing up regularly, was not advisable. Each absence, even if justified, was a demerit point in my schooling, and several absences meant a suspension from classes. Then my parents had to accompany me to headquarters to explain our aberrant family behavior and be subjected to scolding and long lectures. So they saw to it that I complied with the rules and had my own uniform. I never had a new one. Complying was one thing, but spending good money for it was something else. I made do with a uniform that originated somewhere among my older cousins, passed down to my brother and finally, with a few tucks here and there, fitted for me.

From top to bottom, the uniform began with a black fez hat with the brass emblem of the Fascist eagle and the markings of one's legion sewn onto it. The fez, topped by a long string ending in a black tassel, was held on the head by a black elastic chin strap. With trained, circular motions of the head, one could make the tassel spin like a slingshot and hit someone in the face; but that someone could grab the swinging tassel, pull it until the elastic chin strap was fully extended, and then let go. With luck, the brass eagle would hit the owner's head with a rewarding thunk. Part of the uniform was a black shirt, and on this rested a blue bandanna, folded on the diagonal to form a triangle, two of its corners tied in front with a sailor's knot, the third reaching exactly the middle of one's back. Assorted ceremonial braids, anchored to the left epaulet, swung under one's armpit. The uniform's olive green short pants, of military cloth as smooth as sandpaper, were held up by a five-inch-by-six-foot black cummerbund wrapped several times around the waist. The torso accoutrements were completed by gun belt and bandolier. Leggings of the same cloth as the pants wrapped the legs, spiraling down from the knee into black army boots. These were heavily hobnailed and could make you glide over marble floors like an ice skater and, with the right twist of the foot, screech like fingernails on a blackboard.

That was the uniform of the Balilla, a corps of warriors aged eight to fourteen, and whoever designed it could not have invented a more dangerous and entertaining suit of clothes. Besides the previously mentioned possibilities of the fez, the cummerbund and leggings added to the general merriment. Or torture. They had a poor hold on slender waists and skinny legs, and frequently became unbound, easy inspiration for an alert comrade to pull hard on the loose end of the cummerbund and make you spin like a top, or to step on dragging leggings and make you trip. Belt, bandolier, braids, and bandanna were all handles easily grabbed to stop you cold in your progress. Or flight.

It was almost impossible to obtain sartorial perfection, and under inspection any one item could be found not up to snuff. This gave a Balilla pause and taught him to be smart and cultivate a good relationship with the inspecting platoon commander. Which wasn't always easy. Whoever occupied a top position felt finally able to revile and humiliate the underdog, and enjoy it.

I developed the habit of stopping at the Mazzettis' apartment on duty days, so we could all proceed together to the local headquarters. Invariably I joined the Mazzetti children's lineup in the corridor. Zia Ada, wearing the uniform of a Fascist Women officer, gave us a final inspection before we left, pulling here, smoothing a crease there on the Mazzettis' tailor-made uniforms. When she got to me, she just shook her head and gave me a little tap on the cheek. I understood from this most eloquent gesture that I was beyond improvement but that she held me blameless; whatever fault I displayed, it rested with my uncaring parents. Then we marched down the street and to the reunion point, Zia Ada, Tina Mazzetti, and my sister, Anna, at the head of the troop.

"*Giovinezza, giovinezza,*" we sang, keeping in step. "*Primavera di belle-e-e-ezza . . .* "

Young we were indeed, and it could have been called a springtime of beauty. I was ready for duty, whatever it was. And for bread and chocolate.

If my father was somewhat uneasy about my spending too much time with the Mazzettis, my mother was not. She felt that if I was in the proximity of Piero, by natural osmosis, some of his sense of order and purpose would rub off on me. I did my homework with Piero, so at least she did not have to worry about that. She was also reassured of my safety, if not of my behavior, when once homework was done, we moved to the local park. Once in a while she made surprise visits to the park to observe us playing soccer or tag, or king of the hill with a myriad of other kids. All this among a mob of nannies, maids, aunts, and *pensionati* who knew us all by name and, in a pinch, would administer first aid to a skinned knee or a bleeding nose. To this my father could not object. What he felt uneasy about were the sessions we had at the Mazzettis' when, at dusk, we returned from playing.

It was then that the complete Mazzetti household convened in their large dining room, moved the big table to one side, and knelt in a circle to recite the evening prayers, the litanies, and the novenas. Once these were over, Aunt Ada asked everybody to say a special prayer for whoever needed it most that day ("God Omnipotent, Lord of Heaven and Earth, protect our brave soldiers in Spain . . .") and then sat us children around the big table, now back again in the middle of the room, for a "discussion of daily events." I do not remember when that routine began, but once I was part of it, I found it fascinating. Sitting informally in discussion with a grown-up—sometimes two, when Signora Teresa joined the group—was pretty novel to me. At that time communications with my parents were limited to the most mundane and superficial things, mostly at mealtime. Accomplishments at school, fun events at play, and simple jokes were accepted subjects, but my parents considered me too young and immature to discuss substantial, important things. Doing so would have given me, as my mother used to say, "Too Much Importance," or wrong ideas about my position in the family hierarchy.

Zia Ada's "discussions" were nothing less than political lectures. Besides caring sincerely about our knowledgeable devotion to the cause, she was using these "discussions" as rehearsals for the weekly lectures she gave at the local *sezione,* the political office–meeting place. Each city section, every so many blocks, had one. All the small *sezioni* answered to the larger one of the city district, and all the district ones to the main headquarters, the pinnacle. A pebble dropped from there made ripples that reached down to the smallest neighborhood. Zia Ada volunteered her services at our *sezione,* but given her knowledgeable dedication, education, and administrative abilities, she held a position of influence that reached way up. Once in a while, elegantly and unobtrusively, she dropped a polished pebble in the main pond, and sooner or later its effects would lap at our shore.

In the discussions, Ada dedicated a lot of time to explaining in a progression of steps the ideology of Fascism—sometimes having to stop and explain the meanings of words like "ideology." Then we were asked to repeat and explain in our own words whatever we had learned. Fascism, she told us, was the total submission of the individual to the State and absolute dedication to its glorification. The many had to be absorbed by the One, to their reciprocal benefit, just like so many twigs tied together form a strong bundle—a *fascio*! There, that was the meaning of the word.

Ada progressed to the theory of the survival of the fittest. Not only among all living things but also among nations. At this stage, her voice grew louder and her oratory more demagogic and bombastic, the politically de rigueur style. Fat, sleepy, complacent old nations were "Doomed to Perish" to make room for young, aggressive, hungry ones. The confused, wandering, namby-pamby, selfish, bourgeois capitalistic nations were condemned to disappear when challenged by one led by a strong, single-minded, authoritarian leader representing the "Will and the Highest Ideals of the Whole Country." Plutocrats, Jews, dirty bourgeois, and other fat-cat individualists, no matter how intellectual and well-meaning, could do nothing against the Imagination, Stamina, Creativity, Vision, and above all, the Willpower of . . . well . . . Come on, *say* it!

"*IL DUCE!*" we screamed together, at full voice. The mandatory answer was a release, and we tumbled down four flights of stairs for a last run around the courtyard before dinner. We chased each other playing tag, and whoever was It we called a dirty bourgeois.

"*Giovinezza, giovinezza . . . ,*" we sang, out of breath, running, and our voices reverberated in the courtyard like the trills of Roman swallows.

. . .

On Sundays I often took long walks with my father. While my brother was busy with his brainy companions, we left my mother and sister to visit relatives and went out into the city. My father loved to walk, and I loved to walk with him. He took me to museums. He showed me every single Roman fountain and building and church and old stone. He seemed to know the history of each one of them, and he could tell it in such an interesting way, so unlike our art and history books, that I was sure he was making it up as he went along. He was not, I found out later.

Not a great talker, on these occasions he became practically loquacious, and this encouraged me to talk. The switch from the Roman Empire of Then to the Roman Empire of Now came naturally, and that brought up the Mazzettis, and that brought up my incredible knowledge, big words and all, of the "corporative state and the Fascist ideology." And I passed it on to him freely, in exchange for his on-the-spot history of the art of Rome.

"It is good that you know all those things," he told me seriously one afternoon, "but don't give up on thinking for yourself. The *fascio*/bundle idea, it's not bad. But think of this: a single, healthy little twig can be straighter and stronger than a whole bunch of rotten ones all put together."

I visualized a bunch of rotten sticks, and it made a great impression on me. If I recall correctly, it was the first time I understood the workings of a metaphor.

"One of these days," he said, "I shall have a talk with that nice Signorina Ada."

On our way to pick up "our women," we took the long

way around so that we could look at the Bernini fountains in Piazza Navona, not just to admire the sparkle of gold the setting sun cast on their waters but also so he could buy me an ice cream cone at a special place in the piazza.

Then he used his linen handkerchief to clean the ice cream off my face and my hands so Mamma wouldn't get upset with us.

On rainy days we played inside. For these occasions, as a protection to her sanity, Mamma had invested in a box of *Monopoli* and some more traditional table games, like Parcheesi and Lotto. We huddled around the dining table and played at length, until some obvious cheater was discovered and we had to switch games to stop the ensuing squabble. A parlor game we all enjoyed was *Libro e Moschetto,* Book and Rifle. We liked it because we had invented it ourselves. We sat on the floor in a circle, and then a starter opened the game by reciting the beginning of one of the thousand mottoes found on schoolbook covers, on posters, stenciled on the walls of railroad stations and farmhouses, on every water tank, on any available vertical surface (they were all signed with a big cursive "*m*" for you know who), and the next player had to complete it, fast. If unable to, or too slow and hesitating, the loser would get "the Book and Rifle": a bump on the head with a telephone book (*il libro,* the book) and a strike with a ruler (*il moschetto,* the Rifle) from each of the other players. And so on around, quickly.

Libro e moschetto . . .	*Balilla perfetto!*
(Book and Rifle . . .	a perfect Balilla!)
È l'aratro che traccia il solco . . .	*ma è la spada che lo difende!*

(The plow cuts the furrow . . .	but the sword defends it!)
Credere, obbedire . . .	*combattere!*
(Believe, obey . . .	fight!)
Meglio un giorno da leone . . .	*che cento da pecora!*
(Better a day as a lion . . .	than a hundred as a sheep!)
Se avanzo, seguitemi . . .	*se indietreggio, uccidetemi!*
(If I advance, follow me . . .	if I retreat, kill me!)
Rosso di sera . . .	*bel tempo si spera!*
(Red sky at night . . .	sailors' delight!)

This last one, and other traditional sayings, such as "When it rains, it pours" was a trick, and whoever fell for it and completed it got the Book and Rifle.

Generally, and it was part of the fun, the Puzzetta twins were the ones who reaped the penance. The twins frequently joined us in (supposedly) more sedate indoor games, their chancy physical condition not permitting them the rough-and-tumble play more suited to our age. My mother felt sorry for them and insisted that we invite them when we played at home; she also tried to protect them as much as she could from being the butts of our jokes, which were really gross and intended, with that tinge of innate cruelty children have, as comeuppances or revenge toward their father, Commander Puzi. The sins of their father visited on the sons.

If there was a single most disliked, even hated, person in the whole neighborhood, Commander Puzi was the one. He was a short, round, uneducated, irate, loud, and venomous little man. He had produced nine children, spanning from ten to twenty-six years in age. A widower, he had recently married his not too smart maid-housekeeper, younger than his eldest son, and it was common knowledge that his purpose was to have her continue to perform, permanently and without pay, the same work as before. He had also married, with a vengeance, the Fascist cause and was the self-appointed political soul, guardian, enforcer, and spy of the immediate neighborhood. He spent most of his time at the *sezione* headquarters, where with his infiltrating, oily personality, he had weaseled himself into the position of moral censor of everything. Rumor had it that he had a little dirt on all the other local authorities, so they humored him and let him have, up to a point, his way.

Even though he was often ridiculed behind his back as a character from a comic operetta, Comandante Puzi could do real damage. He strutted around in full regalia at all times, all shiny brass and silky sash, medals and tassels, a bantam rooster, yelling orders and threats to anybody he considered his inferior but especially to young people: "Stand erect! Do not lean on that wall! You are disgracing the uniform! Stand at attention when I speak to you! Oh, the only way of teaching you is with *il Santo Manganello!*" This last, of the "Holy Bludgeon," was one of his favorite phrases, referring to the weapon that Fascist bullies used to crack the heads of "subversives," "communists," and any opposition in general, and that had allowed the movement to gain supremacy over the despised milquetoast, nonviolent bourgeoisie.

We named the twins Puzzetta I and Puzzetta II. Twisting a little the diminutive for Puzi, *Puzzetta* meant "little fart," and referred both to their size and to their propensity, because they were fed mostly beans and cabbage, for breaking wind. The twins were more or less my age but practically half my size, and I was small enough. It took the two of them together to reach normal brain speed. What made them really peculiar—the main reason for our taunting and teasing—were their squeaky, highly nasal voices, always full of braggadocio, underlined by bossy gesturing learned from their father, who in turn, aped Il Duce. But the little farts that roared seemed not to mind our behavior toward them, and on rainy days they always came back for more. They were accustomed to it, we explained to Mamma when she told us to stop our cruelty. That was the way they had been treated by their father and by their mob of older brothers. This reality brought moisture to my mother's eyes and larger pieces of cake to them. We thought it was real generosity on her part, but perhaps she too was buttering up the kids as an antidote against the venom of their father.

It was the twins' suspected snooping around our house that made my father, following my mother's advice, thumbtack a portrait of Il Duce in a corner of his studio. It was a somewhat crumpled and finger-marked cover of one of my notebooks (most textbooks, school diaries, and homework books had pictures of Il Duce on them), and he considered the gesture of posting it a talisman against the ill will of tattlers or squealers. A picture of Benito on the wall was not obligatory, but its absence could be interpreted as noncaring at best or if added to other elements, downright anti-Fascist.

It was the Mazzetti boys who, in the days when the larger outdoors was off-limits to us, came up with ingenious ways of letting off steam. The games had a strong Fascist undertone, showing daring and courage, reinforced by Piero's loud prodding with *"Giovani Fascisti, avanti!"* Young Fascists, chaaaarrrge! One that involved nerve and coordination was the game we called Monte Bianco, after the Italian mountain in the Alps, tallest of Europe. It involved starting at the bottom of the stairwell and climbing four floors to the Mazzettis' apartment on the outside of the banister, holding on to it and using as footholds, on the stairwell side, the spaces between the iron railing and the steps: mountaineers going up Monte Bianco. So far so good, I could do that. If I forced myself, I could even look down into the abyss below my feet. On reaching the Mazzettis' landing, before vaulting onto it, spitting down into the stairwell substituted for the ritual planting of the flag on the mountaintop. The tear-shaped spittle fell, revolving slowly on itself, taking amoeba shapes, sometimes dividing and then re-uniting, catching the light of the landings' windows, and finally splatting at the bottom. Piero could do it beautifully; Tina and my little sister, Anna, could do it too. At that stage, my mouth was too dry and my spittle inconsequential.

Another, much more dynamic rainy-day game was Bagno Pulci (Flea Bath), which required one to enter, in her absence, Nana's room, crawl on top of the chest of drawers, from there to the top of the armoire, and from there jump down on Nana's bed. This was the supposed pool of fleas; once landed, you had to trampoline out as fast as possible, faster than a flea could jump on you. We allowed Tina and Anna to participate because of the graceful, balletlike fluttering of their skirts when they were arching between armoire and bed, and because between jumps they could be on the lookout for Nana. Quickness was essential, given her erratic comings and goings. If someone hesitated to jump, he or she was pushed down, paratrooper fashion, by the next in line. We had learned this from movie newsreels portraying hundreds of Germans in full battle gear jumping off planes. Excessive zeal from the pusher could provoke a poorly calculated jump. It happened to Anna, resulting in a broken arm and a big lump on her head. But worst of all was her telling my mother not only about my pushing her off the armoire but also about all the other dangerous and forbidden games I had been involved in.

"Since you're not capable of breaking your head by yourself," my mother yelled at me, "I'll do it for you!"

It is said that a moral punishment is more painful than a corporal one. Not true, in my mother's case. She administered both equally, with trained efficiency.

To make sure I had learned my lesson, I was grounded and forbidden to engage in any sort of commerce with my friends for an undetermined length of time—"until you grow wings" was the way she put it—and for the duration, as a bonus moral punishment, I had to eat in the kitchen with the maid. It was humiliating to be the pariah; being banned from the dinner table was like being banned from the family. But then, eating in the kitchen with the maid offered certain rewards. Like picking the ripest fruit out of the bowl before it was brought to their table. Or, with impunity, sticking my finger into my sister's dessert. My mother's theory and practice of pedagogy were simple and direct. While the Montessori system, much in vogue at the time, advised careful explanations of whys and what-fors, and allowed the child to "develop his own sense of decision making," my mother's system had only two basic tenets. One, you do what you are told; two, if you don't, I'll make you do it anyway. It was a lean and unencumbered system and, by eliminating a lot of explanation, discussion, and arguing, left her with more time to dedicate to our day-to-day care, such as feeding us excellent food, teaching us good manners (or else!), and keeping us in clean, proper, and fashionable clothes.

Her law changed with the circumstances, the character

and size of the transgressor, and above all, the mood of the lawgiver; it was so full of variables that one had to be on one's toes at all times. Moreover, her administration of justice was swift and immediate, and with no right of appeal. Before engaging in any action, she believed, one will be confronted by two choices—one right, lawful, honest; one wrong, unlawful, dishonest. One should never expect a reward for doing the right thing, and if one chose to do wrong, one should accept the final bill without bellyaching. The price tag had been there and posted all along for everybody to see.

For her, it all came down to the simple operation of adding and subtracting the rewards of good against evil. The bottom line would help you make a decision. No room for self-congratulations or rewards, or for regrets, self-pity, or guilt. This simple theory was generally taught during one of her law-and-order performances. "Even if you are as innocent as you profess," she would say, "what you're getting now is for the times you went scot-free." In response to my assurance that such a thing had never, never happened, not even once before, she would just tell me to put the retribution in progress on account toward some future unrecorded misdeed.

My mother's belief in my facility for creative misdeeds stimulated my curiosity to see how far I could go down the forbidden path, which in turn, honed her power of intuitive detection. It became a cycle that we were able to break only years afterward, when we discovered that we were—indeed we had been all along—the best of friends.

I was too young and self-centered to understand all the pressures and extra requirements my mother was subjected to in those not-so-simple times. She was the buffer and the shield that protected our family from the wolves (and hyenas) at the door. My father's political thoughts—and his determination to stick to them—cost him advancements in his career and put his actions, and those of his whole family, under constant scrutiny and tests. He had been forced out of the opening ceremony of one of his own projects, a public building, for not wearing the required Fascist uniform; many times he had been ordered to report to the local *sezione* and asked of his whereabouts on a particular day, or why he was associating with certain persons. Much as he tried not to bring them home, these harassments were reflected in moody mutterings and sometimes, contrary as they were to his nature, by loud and elaborate strings of invectives accompanied by fist pounding on his drawing table.

That was when my mother sang.

No matter what time of day or night it was, she went into most energetic and clear renditions of operatic arias, loud enough to make the windowpanes vibrate and drown out my father's outbursts. It was not healthy to have his opinions about this or that party member stray out of the apartment walls and seep into the ears of even the best of neighbors. It was better to listen, afterward, to their complaints about the loud singing than to hear the secret police's knock on the door.

As time went by, my mother became so skilled a singer that she could have performed with the best at the National Opera House.

Nonetheless, my father kept receiving the despised and feared *cartoline rosse,* red postcards. The red cards were summonses printed with a standard formula: "It is obligatory for

Comrade [handwritten name] to present himself on [day and hour, scribbled in] for important communications. Disregard of this notice will not be tolerated, or justifications accepted." The appointed day was generally a Saturday, and just to add a little dread, the hour was eight in the evening, the sacred hour when the family is reunited for dinner and the absence of a member is most felt.

The "communications" also followed a standard formula. Most of the time there was no specific reason given for the summons. The main one was to harass the "Comrade" and make him feel powerless and under the party's thumb. Commander Puzi, with the local Fascist Militia bully at his side, would produce a sizable dossier. "So here you are, my friend!" he would say, chuckling, leafing through the pages. "This is all of you, Comrade . . ." This performance was meant to reinforce the fact, in case you had missed it, that the authorities were watching and keeping score. Then he would begin a fishing expedition with a series of questions: "Why did you not show up for last Saturday's rally? Is it true you expressed defeatist, unfavorable political opinions? You were seen associating with undesirable elements—why? There are rumors that you are fond of telling anti-Fascist jokes, wouldn't you like to make us laugh too?" And so on.

Frequently the bully, with his shirtsleeves rolled up to show he meant business, displeased not only by the answers but by his victim's very presence, would engage in a barrage of foul-mouthed, vituperative accusations, underscored by threats of violence. Commander Puzi would then make the motions of restraining him, as if barely capable of holding back a growling rabid dog, and summon to the meeting the political officer in residence. This person went into a little sermon, finally explaining that all this was done for the country's and one's own good, and all would be forgiven and go unrecorded if one signed a promise to mend one's ways.

If the reasons for the meeting were more serious, or aggravated by unrepentant behavior, then the person summoned would be asked to purge himself of political sin. The act of moral purging was reinforced with a physical one. The sinner would be asked—or forced, with the help of a funnel—to drink one or two glasses of castor oil. Just enough to let one see his unpatriotic, uncooperative, anti-Fascist tendencies shoot down the toilet. Castor oil and the Holy Bludgeon were the trademarks of the Fascist power of persuasion.

My father had been spared these indignities and other humiliations more than once, thanks to the timely intercession of Signorina Ada. She disapproved of the use of violence and considered the castor oil–bludgeon treatment as an evil medicine for stubborn, stupid minds. She knew my father and respected his intellect, and she was convinced that an intelligent, civilized discussion would go much further than the idiotic, vulgar, offensive machinations of Commander Puzi and Co.

She also knew that my father's navigating in hot waters had officially begun with his criticism of the architectural merits, both artistic and technical, of a colleague's drawings. Unfortunately, this colleague happened to be high up in the Fascist party. The matter deteriorated from professional to political, it was brought to the attention of the department's head, and my father's long-overdue promotion was put on ice again. Ada knew that my father was a recent party member; he had not enrolled until he had to, in 1935, when membership became a requirement for keeping a government job. Thus, he was in a vulnerable position. She knew that he was trading a lot of abuse and humiliation for the basic right to work at his chosen profession, the right to support a family. A harsh compromise with one's conscience. But he wasn't the only one, he wasn't alone.

Like my father, many were under the thumb of a few. The few unscrupulous, violent men who were in power, who wore the robes of the righteous and declared themselves the Law. Their purpose, more than to convert, was to intimidate and humiliate. And they succeeded. Once even I was exposed, with my father, to a mortifying, indelible event. During one of our walks, we ran into a Young Fascists parade, two platoons marching, their synchronous steps making the cobblestoned street reverberate. We had to wait on the sidewalk for it to go by. Suddenly, from behind, a Young Fascist—perhaps a sixteen- or seventeen-year-old boy—in full uniform, his shirtsleeves rolled up, swiped my father on the head with an open-handed blow, making his hat fly away. "When a Fascist flag goes by," the boy yelled, "people uncover their heads!" The humiliation, the feeling of impotence against such arrogance, the impossibility to retaliate, froze my father, his hand almost crunching mine. His eyes, focused on the infinite, were wet with tears. I shared all his feelings ten times over, and my immediate reaction was to spit on all the black Fascist pennants. Perhaps it was the decisive turning point in my political beliefs, seeing personally and most brutally for the first time what was behind the phony facade.

Those who attempted to oppose these bullies were beaten up and jailed, outspoken dissenters sent into exile, all civil rights lost, their families left on the dole or dependent on the surreptitious handouts of friends, their children shunned and denied access to schools.

Some activists, the ones who could, fled abroad, but most

turned into opportunists, or cowards, or just people stringing along, day by day. And when told to, they, we, sang, without much blushing, the Fascist anthem:

> *Hail, Italy, mother of heroes!*
> *Hail, immortal motherland!*
> *Your children are reborn*
> *With a new faith and a new ideal . . .*
> *We are the new soaring eaglets.*
> > *"Giovinezza, giovinezza*
> > *Primavera di bellezza . . ."*

And people had to stand up and salute, right arm stretched straight to the sky.

I kept on wearing my makeshift uniform and going to the rallies with Piero Mazzetti and a million other kids. On orders, when Il Duce gave speeches, we crowded city squares, like extras in a cast of thousands, so that papers could publish photographs of public sites full to the brim with exulting people. The captions said: "Oceanic Masses of Citizens Spontaneously Convene to Applaud Our Duce." We were the masses, mostly, happy to skip classes and having a great time yelling the slogans we were told to yell. We learned to goose-step on parade—little rifles resting on our shoulders—until the hobnails of our boots became hot, and afterward we kept getting our bread and chocolate.

Commander Puzi kept finding reasons to send red postcards, my father kept going to the requested "meetings," and Aunt Ada kept discreetly—sometimes apologetically—bailing him out. My mother kept singing.

Once in a while my father, an accomplished gardener, gave me a simple bouquet of homegrown flowers to take to Ada. There were no accompanying cards, and she took the flowers with demure, whispered thanks. The flowers always ended up at the foot of Benito's portrait, the one of him riding the white charger.

I never had the heart to tell my father.

4

Zia Elena

FORTUNATELY, THE UNPLEASANT-
ness of these days was mitigated by
strong and affectionate family ties,
and ours was a large family. My father's roots were in the
north of Italy, in the Emilia-Romagna region. He had one
brother and two sisters, one of them with five daughters and
a son. My paternal grandparents were also up in the north,
near their daughters. My mother had two brothers living in
Rome. All came with several children, my cousins. One other
sister lived in a small village in central Italy. I liked them all,
and was fortunate to be with them often. We visited the out-
of-towners frequently, sometimes spending a few days or longer
vacations with them. Thanks to my father's managerial position in the Ministry of Transportation, our family had free
first-class passes on the Italian railroads, which allowed us to
travel at will. The kinfolk would always be there, waiting for
us at the station.

Among all the uncles and aunts, if I ever had a preference, it was for my zia Elena. There were many reasons for my special affection, and she had a particular influence on my life from the start, and especially in the years to come.

My maternal grandfather, Nicola, with the cooperation of Nonna Assunta, produced four children, two boys and two girls.

My mother was the younger of the girls, and my aunt Elena the oldest, though the difference in age among all of them was very little. Nonno Nicola had inherited a small farm in Le Madonnine, near the village of Frontale, in Le Marche region in central Italy. It was a family farm with a corn patch, a nice vineyard, a vegetable and fruit orchard, and a few ancient walnut trees; it produced barely enough to feed a family. After his obligatory military service, Nicola left the farm for the urban attractions of Rome, delegating the agricultural worries of caretaker and sharecropper to a friend, Domenico Bertoldi. Keeping the farmhouse for himself, Nicola returned every year with his growing family to spend part of the summer, to go hunting, to supervise the harvest and the making of the wine. His four children, all having been born in Rome and continued their studies past the third grade, were considered cosmopolitan by their country friends. Privileges came with this status, such as the girls being allowed to wear makeup, but also certain restraints, such as the boys having to wear shoes.

In 1916, with World War I still going great guns, a group of Austrian prisoners of war were billeted in the schoolhouse of Frontale, a spot remote enough to need limited security. Following the still respected rules of the Geneva Conventions, they were allowed to work in the fields, free but under guard; they were well-fed, well-housed, and generally treated humanely. The only inhumane element in their detention, as I have heard it, was supplied by my mother and my aunt Elena: the two girls, then in their late teens, would tease the sex-starved Austrians by promenading without chaperones under the schoolhouse windows, singing provocative arias from *La Traviata, La Bohème,* or *Rigoletto.* It seems that they had quite a command of the material, underlining the lyrics with operatic, suggestive gestures. Rumor had it that a Viennese count was among the prisoners, and the girls were determined to smoke him out—as a first step toward conquest—by following the romantic canons of the times. The young prisoners crowded at the windows, cheering and whistling and joining the girls in loud chorus, throwing them pieces of paper with scribbled notes. The count never made himself known, if he ever existed, but the girls did succeed in provoking the ire of one of the guards, who grew tired of having to restore the peace and calm down the excited Austrians. The guard, a tall, sturdy, and handsome military policeman, was Carabiniere Berto Dorico; he took it upon himself to scold the flirtatious girls and inform them that he had orders to shoot his gun at them—or at least spank them—if they did not cease and desist.

Elena and Berto were married shortly after the end of the war. The choice fell on Elena because, as the older of the two sisters, she had to marry first. For this unromantic reason, then, Berto became my uncle and not my father.

Berto and Elena were quite an odd couple. He was tall,

massive, silent, and generously good-natured; she was short, sprightly, loquacious, and acquisitive. She had brilliant, smiling green eyes that made her appear constantly playful—or, if she did not like somebody—spiteful.

They settled in Frontale, and under her tutoring, Berto passed the state exams (she did too) of the Ministry of Post and Telegraphs and was employed by—and in time ran—the newly established Frontale post office.

The village of Frontale was laid out on terraces at the foot of Mount San Vicino, the tallest mountain between the Adriatic Sea and the Tuscan Apennine mountains. The thirty-foot cross that stood at its very top identified the mountain from miles away and looked over Frontale's jurisdiction. This included most of the deep woods on the mountain's slopes and several farms in the valley below; all in all, the whole citizenry amounted to about one thousand souls. Besides the post office, they were served by a flour mill, a blacksmith and all-around mechanic, a shoemaker, a church, the elementary school, a midwife, and a general store cum wineshop. A mile or so down in the valley, a line of cypress trees, like a fence of exclamation marks, screened Frontale's cemetery. A doctor and a pharmacy were available in the nearest town, about twelve miles away. Frontale also had a mayor, a political appointee for life, or until he fell from grace. Having married money, he owned one of the few cars in the area (or as some wag said, owning his wife's money and having married a car) and scooted around all day long, rarely seen.

The heart of the village was the main square, a space about 250 by 50 feet, big enough for children to chase each other and, being the only horizontal, flat space around, good enough for playing bocce on Sundays and summer evenings. The square was really a huge rectangular terrace. One of the long sides—the one facing east—ended just at the edge of a 35-foot cliff, and was guarded by a waist-high wrought-iron railing. From there one could enjoy a most beautiful panorama of the valley below and of green hills as far as the eye could see. My zia Elena's house was on the other long side of the square, parallel with the railing. It was three stories high, with most of its windows looking out onto the square and the view. The rear of the house was built into the slope, and from the back of the third floor, one could walk out into the orchard and the vineyard behind. The post office occupied most of the first floor.

The economy of the village was largely based on agriculture—viticulture, really—and the making of charcoal. Few of the farms and vineyards were family-owned; most were held by sharecroppers for absentee owners. Some money was brought in by a scattering of artisans who made and shipped out pottery, and by others who were lathe masters, turning the hard boxwood of the local forest into all sorts of household things, from mortars and pestles to spoons and forks, from bowls to bocce balls. There was also, up on San Vicino's slope, a limestone quarry, but it produced only enough lime for local building needs.

All told, the area was not rich, but the people were hard-working and gifted with a serene disposition and a witty sense of humor that saw them through the rough spots of life. Many were illiterate, or practically so, so the postal activity wasn't excessive, not many letters being written or received. Most of the post office work had to do with pensions and the filling out of bureaucratic forms, the dispensing of government subsidies, and the processing of money orders; a few came in, hardly any went out. The telegraph would clackety-clack once in a while and was mostly used for post office affairs and internal memos. The general public was terrified by the telegraph machine: a telegram, if it was not for internal office news, generally meant bad family news. The post office was also the recipient of government directives, rules, bans, and the list of the young men due to report for the draft, which had to be posted in full view outside the office doors. It was generally read and interpreted for the public by Berto or Elena.

Having generous personalities, Berto and Elena fulfilled their duties graciously—without supercilious official behavior—treating young and old as friends. And having read and written their letters for them, frequently they became their advisers. The grateful villagers returned the favor with cheese, poultry, sausages, and all sorts of goodies. One of Zio Berto's responsibilities was to deliver the mail. He made the rounds accompanied by his two faithful hunting dogs, and along the way, he indulged in hunting. Even so, he had time for tending his vineyard and orchard.

Zia Elena organized and ran the local Fascist Women's chapter. The official propaganda image of the *donna fascista* had been devised so that many could identify with it: housewifely, motherly, and substantial enough to nourish large and strong Fascist families. Sometimes, waving a big Italian flag with one hand and holding a baby to her breast with the other, she represented "Motherland." She had to appeal to the Mamma syndrome of the Italian men, hence devoid of any erotic attributes. Rachele Mussolini, Il Duce's wife, fit the bill, and so did Zia Elena. Elena was petite, if somewhat chubby, but her dynamism and bounce made her seem larger.

For some of Frontale's ladies, the group's activities were a hardship, what with having to wear socks and shoes, a black skirt with a white shirt and a black masculine tie. All these accoutrements, made in city-girl sizes, were way too small and restrictive for their muscular, bosomy country figures. The women also found the political lectures and the marching up and down the square following Zia Elena waving a Fascist black pennant not their idea of entertainment after hard work on the farms. But Zia would not accept their bellyaching, and pointed out to them the many rewards: a reason to meet and gossip openly with other women once a week, away from their men, and above all the privilege of belonging to the Dopolavoro fascista, the After-Work Fascist Club. This was the organization that took care of leisure time. It offered a clubroom loaded with political magazines, a few inspirational books, and pamphlets about health, nutrition, and physical fitness. The *donne* also had the possibility of borrowing patterns for the latest Milan fashions; the Dopolavoro organized ski trips in winter and vacations at the beach in summer, with stays at inexpensive government hostels. All these things that the Frontale women's contingent needed as much as the famous hole in the head.

The men had daily meetings of their own. Their Dopolavoro was a large, practically bare room, with five tables and chairs, and a makeshift bar at one end. After their work, the men got together to play cards, drink one or two—frequently more—glasses of wine, and have a boisterous time. Politics were part of the exercise only about once a month, when a Fascist political officer came to give a lecture and check things out. But then, on those days most of the vineyards, sheep, or cattle developed some sort of difficulty that required the attention of the men, and the *dopolavoro* was practically deserted.

The person who really benefited from all her political zeal was Elena herself. She had become very visible in the Fascist circles of the region by proselytizing and promoting activities in nearby villages and hamlets, and by being present at "reunions" and meetings as far away as Ancona, the capital city of Le Marche region. By means of her political savvy and connections, she obtained special scholarships for her only son, who went to study in Rome's best schools and stay, free bed and board, at special hostels for Fascist Youth. He was actually a deserving student in his own right and graduated magna cum laude from the University of Rome. As a representative of the local Fascist Women's organization, Elena also took frequent paid trips to Rome to attend the many parades, assemblies, and demonstrations—and to visit her student son, whom she adored.

Yet Zia Elena was not selfish in the garnering of favors. With her ability to navigate bureaucratic waters and knowing at which port to call, she did many things for her comrades in uniform, such as obtaining medical care or expediting reimbursements for medicines, or having their eighteen-year-old boys excused from the obligatory twenty-four months of military service because (she vouched for them personally) they were needed at home to work in the fields and help support their families. It was now 1935; nobody wanted to see their sons shipped out to fight Ethiopians, a people who, in Frontale's common wisdom, were just one step up from cannibals.

Through her contacts in Rome, Elena was able to push along all sorts of applications and demands that would otherwise be lost in the bureaucratic labyrinths of the many ministries and departments of the government.

It was only natural that all this exposure gained Elena the enmity of the female intelligentsia of Frontale and its environs. The schoolteacher, the midwife, the wife of the mayor, the curate's housekeeper, and some of the wealthy landowners' wives assuaged their resentment toward her by spreading vile rumors. "She is a terrible miser," the rumors went, "and would prefer to lose a pint of blood than part with a penny." There was some truth in that. But then they insisted that "her sticking her nose in everybody's affairs was done only for personal advantage and that she exacted compensations in monies or goods for all of her deeds." That was a definite calumny. The most hurtful gossip was "that her inordinate attachment to material things, and her boundless dedication to her son, had excluded Berto from her life and made him only another of her prized possessions." They joked, blushing and chuckling sotto voce, that Berto (and some of them could personally testify to it, they said) "was delivering more than the mail and that his hunting was done with quite a pistol indeed."

Baseless slanders produced by the fire of envy. Mostly.

At that time many countries, as a punishment for her invasion of Ethiopia, had unleashed against Italy "economic sanctions"—trade embargos—cutting her off from any commercial exchange. It was quite a blow, since Italy was dependent on all foreign goods of primary importance. The attitude of the Italian government, for the benefit of the national population and the international press, was a nose-thumbing, boastful *"Ce ne freghiamo!"*—We don't give a damn!—but it shortly launched the Gold for the Motherland campaign.

Zia Elena, because of her influence in Frontale and neighboring villages, was sought out to sell the idea and organize the campaign. The Oro per la Patria campaign had a dual purpose: a symbolic one, to unite the populace in patriotic enthusiasm; and an economic one, to put some gold into the depleted national coffers. Zia Elena did her best, suggesting to the villagers that they'd better follow the routine or else. She had never threatened anyone before, not even in jest, so it was clear that something was bothering her. On the appointed day, a bucket was put on a table in the village square, and people marched up to it, took off their golden wedding bands, and dropped them in. The ceremony varied depending on the affluence of village, town, or city; in some places the buckets were replaced by coffers, with the local bishops blessing and surveying the operation. On a table nearby, the names of the donors were written down on an "honor roll," and if they wished, the gold bands could be replaced by steel rings. A very high percentage of Italians complied with the Gold for the Motherland campaign. My mother and father did so. Not contributing was interpreted as obstructionism, a severely condemned attitude, especially for government employees.

The inside of Zia Elena's ring was inscribed with Elena's and Berto's names and their wedding date. It had cost most of Berto's savings. Zia did not volunteer her ring: if they wanted it, they would have to chop her finger off.

I loved Frontale. My family spent at least a month there every year, generally as a close to the round of summer vacations, before returning to Rome in the fall. Exactly when depended on the weather, on the timing of the harvest and pressing of the grapes, a ritual that my parents, especially my mother, would not pass up for all the gold in the world. And neither would I.

It was the accepted routine for middle-class families to go to the high mountains after vacationing at the beach, then to finish in the country. The pediatricians (or was it old wives?) recommended the sea stay because the sea air's iodine along with intensive tanning would dry out all the bad humors collected over nine months of city life; then the mountains' pure air would cleanse the lungs of the iodine and further purify the blood; the country, with its bucolic calm and good, unadulterated food, was supposed to restore the frayed nerves produced by sea and mountains, and prepare vacationers for the coming urban onslaught. The logic of the three-part vacation routine escaped me. It was hard to have to abandon each set of friends and games—just when both were getting good— to start all over at another place.

But I always looked forward to Frontale, and often my pleas to let me skip the mountains and stay with Zia Elena were granted. My argument was that perhaps Mount San Vicino could not compare with the Alps (the family vacation destination) but it was tall enough, the tallest of the region.

Frontale was like home. Actually, I had been baptized there by Don Girolamo, the village curate, in a religious interlude during the rites of the harvest and related bacchanalia. The *vendemmia* was a yearly movable feast on which the Frontalese went from vineyard to vineyard to pick and then stomp on the grapes. The celebrations lasted well into the night; the hosts outdid themselves in providing food and music in exchange for the guests' help. Gratitude was expressed all around by eating, drinking, ribald singing, and dancing to exhaustion. Tales of the feast were made to last until the next harvest, although when something really exceptional happened—as when a visiting missionary priest eloped with the very pregnant wife of the blacksmith on the blacksmith's motorcycle—they lasted much longer. And, just like good vintages, they got better with the passing of time.

For me, one of the special attractions of Frontale was Zio Berto. He would let me follow him everywhere, and with him life was a constant discovery. At seven, I learned from him the great adventure of getting up before dawn to inhale the mixed fragrances of dewy grass and woods and the scent of fresh-baked bread wafting up from the valley, and to listen to the echoing, muffled sounds when the world is quiet and the sun is rising. When I was eight, he taught me how to use a hunting knife, how to make a corncob pipe, and how to carve a recorder out of a bamboo cane, and play a tune on it. By the time I was ten, he had shown me all the shortcuts of the valley and the hills. He took me to the mountain charcoal makers and let me eat at their bivouac and accept their wine; and then he taught me how to light and cook on a fire in the forest. He showed me how he walked in the woods without making a sound and how he stalked a wild rabbit or a wild pigeon; he let me carry his prized shotgun and once made me fire it and made such a fuss about it that I felt as if I had fired a cannon. From Zio Berto I learned how to go through the impassable parts of the forest's underbrush by following the bed of the brook, inside the green tunnel made by the thorny blackberry bushes growing on its sides.

Zio Berto was a big man and a gentle man, and he could do things I thought only Indians could do, as we saw them in American movies. He was the best hunter in the region, the paragon of all hunters. He prepared his own shells and showed me how much gunpowder to weigh for what size buckshot, how hard to pack the powder and how hard the wad. His two hunting dogs were the envy of the region and, the envious said, the only reason for his hunting success. They forgot to say that he had trained them himself and that they would obey his commands a mile away. At his whistle (it was actually a thin, almost inaudible hiss that he produced with clenched teeth), the two dogs performed like an army at the orders of a general, searching, surrounding, stalling, or rushing the prey to bring it into his gun's range. He chose just the right size shot for each animal. When he fired, he never missed, and he felled his victim instantly, with minimum damage.

Berto showed me how to find my bearings in the forest by checking the moss on tree trunks' sides and how to tell, by the smell of the wood and the angle of the leaves, when rain was close and it was time to head home, but also that this was the best time, their scent being at its highest, to find wild mushrooms. He let me collect them unsupervised and then checked them to see if I had learned his teachings. Mushroom gathering, he told me, was a great life lesson in how not to trust appearances; some of the most beautiful and colorful mushrooms were the most poisonous and some of the ugliest the best—but then sometimes the opposite was true.

I have remembered his lessons all my life, and for many years after I could travel the region alone and always find my way. I knew all the farmers and, being Berto's nephew, was always welcomed at their farms and their tables. Thank God, I was a dedicated learner. Probably his teachings saved my life when, a few years later, I found myself roaming and hiding in these same fields, woods, and mountains.

What Berto brought home from the hunt, or from the farms he visited, Elena turned into unforgettable creations. Her reputation for stinginess was perhaps supported by the parsimony of her cooking techniques. To feed Berto, she had to use ample measures, but while her portions were generous, the way she could squeeze the best out of every single ingredient was masterful. Whatever was not used when fresh she would cure, can, or preserve. Her root cellar competed in space with Berto's wine cellar—and that was quite large—and was replete with the sorts of goodies that gluttons' dreams are made of. *Prosciutti* and sausages, rabbit and goose confits, at least five different kinds of wild mushrooms steeped in olive oil, fruits in spices and syrups, marmalades and jellies and preserves of tiny wild strawberries and cherries.

The door to the cellars was semihidden in the back of the post office, and it opened onto a steep flight of stairs carved into the rock, which descended to a set of cold, cavelike rooms. The stone walls were impregnated with the musty smell of wine casks and the aroma of all the good things that Zia had squirreled away. If I could have bottled and sold only that fragrance, I could have made my fortune. But then, I am fortunate enough that I can still, vividly, remember it today. More than once I attempted a furtive visit to that treasure cave, but Zia Elena kept the doors of her gastronomic vault under double lock and key.

Zia enjoyed my appreciation of her skills and often managed to add something special for me to her daily repertoire.

My idea of heaven was a day in the fields with Berto, with a lunch packed by Elena.

My obvious partiality for her food aside, my aunt's cooking was renowned throughout the area just as much as my uncle's wines. In the course of their periodic inspections, the regional Fascist big wheels made it a point to reach Frontale at lunchtime. Elena dined them, and Berto—even if he had no taste for politics—wined them until lunch stretched into dinner. The dignitaries would finally leave at some hour well into the night, with gifts from Elena's cellar, somewhat unstable on their feet but totally reassured of her—and the whole area's—dedicated loyalty to the party. At least until the next month or so, when they would come to check again. Throughout the years, never once did they leave less than entirely satisfied.

For the celebrations of October 28, 1938, the sixteenth anniversary of the Fascist Era, a golden ribbon was pinned to the Frontale black pennant and a silver medal on Elena's pride-swollen bosom. It was the Silver Medal for Exceptional Merit, Exemplary Conduct, and Selfless Dedication to the Cause.

The Silver Medal was one of the highest recognitions given by the party for political conduct. In her case, also for culinary prowess.

In January 1940, a great lightning storm hit Mount San Vicino, and some of its woods were lost to the ensuing fire. The massive oak tree in Zia Elena's orchard was also struck and felled, a dark omen.

Two days later Berto suddenly died, with his hat and shoes on, as he had always wished to go.

At his funeral, for the first time in the fifteen years of my life, tears welled up in my eyes that were not in response to a physical hurt. It was his last lesson: there can be a much deeper pain than that inflicted by wounds of the flesh.

Once widowed, Zia Elena elected to remain in Frontale. She kept the post office going as postmistress. She also developed a galloping deafness that neither the doctors in Ancona nor those in Rome could cure or explain. But somehow she did not feel terribly handicapped by it. As a matter of fact, we thought that her deafness was not as bad as advertised: sometimes she could hear a whispered conversation from the floor above or the rustle of a field mouse in the pantry. We were all convinced that it was her way to keep everybody on their toes, never knowing when or what she had heard. She just chose when to listen or not to listen; it was her way to turn off the world.

On June 10 of that year, Mussolini gave a blustery speech from his balcony in Piazza Venezia to the usual "oceanic, spontaneous" crowd of believers. He declared war on England and France, joining forces with our German Comrades. He promised to break our enemies' bones and those of whoever crossed our path to victory. I was there with all the other schoolchildren of Rome, and applauded and yelled *"Vittoria! Vittoria!"*

Immediately the big drum-up of patriotic feelings—the speeches, pep talks, and martial music that had been going on for months—multiplied a hundred times.

Elena was tapped to help out with the propaganda, but her heart was not in it anymore. More and more she used her deafness as a shield, and people agreed, her professed zeal was just pro forma.

At first, the war did not change Frontale's life much. The place remained, in the general mayhem, an inconsequential speck on the map of the world, and if the world did not know of Frontale, Frontale did not know much about the rest of the world either. Whatever the news, whether carried by the airwaves or by outdated newspapers, it was couched in the sibylline official language that made the world seem even more incomprehensible and remote.

As the war progressed, life in Frontale began to take new and unexpected turns. Food rationing was put into effect nationwide. At the beginning, the limitations on some goods did not bother anybody much, but then shortages of basic staples became severe, especially in the cities. Either because they were hoarded by individuals or were being bought illegally at their source by black-market speculators, scarce items became even more scarce, hence ever more expensive. Many people started looking for supplies in the countryside, and Frontale began to see more outsiders in an ordinary day than it used to during a *fiera,* the monthly market day, when city merchants filled the square with stalls and farmers came from miles around to buy anything they needed, from shawls to shovels.

Now the process was reversed. People came from the cities to buy olive oil and cheese and eggs and chickens and sausages and milk and butter. And also fresh greens and fruits. Demand began to outstrip supply, and buyers strove to outbid each other. Greed took hold of the locals, and chickens in their coops and lambs in their folds were no longer safe at night. Zia Elena added more locks to her cellar and kept Zio Berto's shotgun well-oiled and handy. Some of the more enterprising left Frontale with their bags of edible goods and delivered them to the cities for big profits. But it was not easy money. The journey was chancy and dangerous. Railroad lines, stations, and bridges became prime bombing targets, and Allied planes returning from bombing missions, to avoid landing with bombs in their bellies, took to dropping whatever bombs they had left on country roads and minor railways, at random. Their fighter escorts completed the job by strafing anything that moved. Travel was not healthy.

The disruption of rail and road traffic put a virtual end to the postal service, and the telephone and telegraph were not in much better shape. In Rome the only news we had of Frontale was gleaned from tales told us by those black marketeers who made it as far as us, and from the rare notes from Zia Elena they hand-delivered. By the messengers' scary tales, the situation in Frontale and neighboring villages was appalling. They said that greed had taken over, lifelong friendships were lost to suspicion and fear, neighbor distrusted neighbor. We dismissed the tales as overinflated, so the black marketeers could justify their high prices for the risks they were taking.

Zia's notes, neatly written in administration calligraphy and bureaucratic jargon, did not tell us much more than "I am in good health. The situation here is under control. I hope the same is with you. Respectfully yours, Dorico Elena." Knowing Zia for her energy, ingenuity, and strong sense of self-preservation, we did not worry about her.

We much preferred to think of Frontale as the quiet, forgotten haven we knew, an unalterable fixture of Mount San

Vicino, and of Zia Elena and all the quirky Frontale *paesani* as being as indestructible as that mountain.

"I am sure," said my father, attempting to lift my mother's spirits, "that everybody is fine and behaving. Or that old crust Don Girò will excommunicate everybody. Either that, or shoot them on sight."

5

Don Girò

AT FIRST LIGHT OF DAY, DON Girolamo approaches the wrought-iron railing at the east end of the square, takes a deep breath, lifts his cassock, and pisses, paying careful attention not to hit the curlicues of the railing, so that the steaming stream can arch and tinkle on the stone pathway thirty feet below. Then he pats his belly a few times and, in an unhurried and sonorous sequence, first burps and then breaks wind.

Now a new day can officially begin: a donkey yawns, joining a rooster in greeting the pink edge of dawn. The red point of the sun appears at the end of the valley, and the vineyards reluctantly let go of the morning mist, which rises to mix with the first plumes of chimney smoke. Reassured that what he sees of his world this day isn't much different from the day before, Don Girolamo goes back to his church and tolls the Matins.

Summer or winter, rain or shine, Don Girolamo did not

miss this ritual once. It was his unabashed way of showing gratitude to his Maker for giving him a functioning, serviceable body. It was like an engineer's checking of the gauges, a check that he repeated, in reverse order, every single night before turning in.

That, more or less, was all the attention he paid to the well-being of his body. The rest of his time he dedicated to the care of the souls of his flock, a care that he gave in very personal, creative ways. He had done this for so long that nobody in Frontale could remember a time without Don Girolamo. Even the oldest of the villagers could not remember who had preceded him, or if ever there had been a predecessor. If asked, they would put his age at a vague "way above eighty," but whatever it was, he was still going strong. Compared with years past, he was a little more cantankerous, perhaps, a little more forgetful, a little more eccentric, but his mountain boots still trod with an assured step. His tall, lean frame was still erect under the weight of his cassock, of his cartridge belt, and of his ancient, ever-present shotgun. His biretta rested, cocked, on an unkempt mane of white hair; his eyes were still dark and piercing, and together with a strong aquiline nose and sucked-in cheeks, gave him an irrefutable air of messianic power. He had a deep, gravelly voice, and his diction was slow, determined, and loud. Before every sentence he made a sort of rumble low in his throat, as if he had to rummage around in his larynx for words.

An authoritative shepherd commanding obedience and respect from his flock, he did not stand for any arguments. If anyone laughed at his idiosyncrasies, it was out of affection and without malice; he was as much a part of the village as the bell tower, the post office, or the tavern, and the villagers would have defended him to the death from ridicule by outsiders.

My contacts with Don Girolamo began very early in my life and religious career. He baptized me, a fact that resulted in some administrative discomfort throughout my life.

Not even a month after my birth in Rome, my parents swaddled me up like a cocoon and took me to Frontale to be baptized. Baptism was against my father's beliefs, but to humor my mother and to show his open-mindedness, he allowed her to indulge in her superstitions. They had chosen for me, because of its aristocratic, romantic lilt (my mother's idea), the name Gianfranco. But that name turned out to be absolutely unacceptable to Don Girò. No such name appeared on the long list of Holy Saints. Not yet, anyway, and the idea that I could ever become one was obviously precluded. A compromise was reached by splitting the name into its two component saints: Giovanni Francesco. This double name was joined by hyphenation with Saverio. Don Girolamo's anti-Fascism was expressed by his admiration for Francesco Saverio Nitti, the last Italian liberal premier before Mussolini. My father concurred. My mother had to balance this political gesture by adding her father's name to the list, and my grandfather, in turn, being particularly devoted to this old parish church of San Paolo e Maria, wanted these names to be added, as good omen and protection.

I emerged, then, from the baptismal font as Giovanni Francesco-Saverio Nicola Paolo e Maria. This name was sent by Don Girolamo, as was his duty, to be recorded in the General Register Office. But my father had already registered my birth at the city hall in Rome, the day I was born, giving the agreed upon name of Gianfranco. There some amanuensis, in beautiful handwriting, put it down as Gian Franco. So I ended up appearing under many names in the national registers. Eighteen years later, under different first names, thanks to clerical creativity, I made twice the wanted list of the military police for dodging the draft. If caught, I probably would have had to be shot more than once. The irony of it all is that, with all that bounty of names available, I became known simply as Franco.

Even so, I still feel I was luckier than the other two infants baptized that day in the multiple ceremony. Don Girò must have been scraping the bottom of the barrel for saints' names: he named the Bertoldis' boy Ubaldo and his twin sister Erminia. It was reported that all three infants cried disconsolately throughout the ceremony.

From then on, even if our paths met every year for only a few short summer weeks, or at best months, Don Girolamo had a great influence on my way of looking at life, and not necessarily from a religious point of view. I always admired and tried to emulate his directness of thought and speech, so devoid of hypocrisy and metaphors, and his behavior, so totally ungoverned by the judgment of others. Immune to the "what will the people think?" test, he embodied the saying "to call a spade a spade," or in the Italian version, "to call bread, bread; and wine, wine."

For the latter he had a particular predilection, which he shared with his old friend, my nonno Nicola. The church of San Paolo e Maria came with a little orchard and a small vineyard, and Nonno, as a commitment to his church, supervised the growing of the grapes and their pressing. Under his care, and with the help of Domenico Bertoldi's expertise, the little vineyard produced two first-quality wines in a quantity disproportionate to its size. This was because every year, by tradition, all the vineyards in the area donated to the parish a few bushels of their best grapes. When rightly pressed and governed, this best of the best produced, even in poor vintage years, superior wine. The white was crisp and clear, a golden-green Verdicchio; and the red the robust, round, and nutritious Rosso Piceno. Connoisseurs recognized Don Girolamo's special wines by their label: the top left corner was cut off. On the market, bottles with the mutilated label were known as *vino del curato,* the curate's wine. They brought in top prices, and the proceeds were put to good use.

Naturally, to produce that sort of wine, diligence and careful strategy in all the phases of production were required.

Even in their advanced years, Don Girò and my grandfather Nicola had long and frequent wine strategy sessions before, during, and after the harvest. Also before, during, and after the aging of the wine in the oak barrels, and then again when it was finally bottled. These sessions were held at Nonno's place at Le Madonnine, in the kitchen just above the cellar with its six huge casks. After Vespers, Don Girò would trek down the five kilometers from Frontale, coming by the open fields, hoping to encounter some game to shoot at. Upon arrival, he would lean the shotgun and bandolier in a corner of the room and sit at the kitchen table, a lit candle in its center, with Nicola and Domenico Bertoldi. Frequently my uncle Berto was also there to offer his expertise. The strategy sessions consisted of tasting a glass of the old wine, comparing it with a glass of the new, rechecking with another to determine if the aging was proceeding as desired, and then again with a glass for judging the color by the light of the candle, and yet another glass to bounce its taste against bites of Domenico's fresh-baked bread and Nonno's salami and Don Girò's cheese. And then, as a diversion from this exacting work, they would produce a deck of cards and play. By that time they'd be lost to the world and having a noisy, gloriously marvelous time. A herd of pachyderms could have marched through that kitchen and gone unnoticed. But then, at that stage, even if they had seen such a thing, it wouldn't have fazed them at all.

We children were sometimes present at these sessions, supposedly incognito, generally when rain forced us to seek refuge inside or if we had no other mischief to attend to. The "we" was the generally inseparable pack composed of myself, the co-baptized Ubaldo and Erminia—Domenico's children—and sometimes Gigio Lanzoni, son of one of the other three farmers of Le Madonnine.

The major attraction of the strategy sessions was that, naturally, we were not supposed to be there. Whoever was in charge of us at the moment—parents, aunts, or older siblings—considered not so much that children had no business at the wine tastings but that the men had a right to be left in peace.

We had no interest in their activities per se, we only liked to play Indians, moving as stealthily as they did in our comic books. We sneaked like snakes (repressed giggles not counting) and hid now behind this man, now behind the other, with the final objective to end up, unseen, under their table. We thought it was the greatest game in the world. It took all of our innocence to believe the old people were not aware of us. But they played along with our game so well that, emboldened, we graduated to more daring things. Once under the table, we might tie their shoelaces together, for instance, or roll up their pant cuffs. When they discovered what had befallen them, they would go into gales of fake despair and shoo the Indians out of the room with great ado.

We spent hours planning camping expeditions to the North Pole, and once, following Erminia's disquisition on oil-cloth and waterproofing, Gigio suggested we put her theory to the test. If true, Don Girò's cassock was so greasy that it should hold water. At our next snakelike attack, we volunteered Baldo to pour half a canteen of water into Don Girò's gaping cassock pocket. Ever so slowly, Baldo executed the maneuver. Not a drop filtered out. We retreated outside and waited for the inevitable bellowing reaction. It never came.

It was tradition that, upon taking leave of Don Girò, Nonno would ask him to bless us kids. He always complied by waving an approximate cross gesture in front of our faces—for a long time I thought he was shooing away demons, or flies—and then by giving each of us, with a touch of Latin rumbling deep in his throat, a gentle rap on the head, a fatherly, loving tap. A blessing.

On the night of the water test, the benediction from those long, hard, bony fingers hurt like hell. And the next day was Confession.

As long as I remained under my mother's jurisdiction, my religious career had to follow her dictates. I had to go to cate-chism classes, obey all the precepts of Mother Church, go to Mass on Sunday and on all the other Holy Days, go to Con-fession, take Communion. Everybody was doing it, it was the right thing to do. No questions, no explanations, no excuses. Just do it. And I did.

So in my growing years, going to Confession was an accepted fact of life. Going to Confession in Frontale was an accepted fact of death, with a side trip to purgatory and a short stay in hell. Don Girolamo, the only priest around to whom we could confess our sins, was inflexible and without one ounce of compassion. He enjoyed, I am convinced, looking at us, kneeling on the hard boards of the confessional, squirming and sweating. He carried out his role with the precision and all the warmth of a tax accountant. Moreover, being slightly deaf, in a booming basso profundo voice he urged the sinner to be just as loud, so the transactions escaped the confessional for all to hear.

"Bless-me-Father-because-I-a-sinner."

Deep growl, clearing of the throat:

"*Who* are you?"

"A sinner, Father."

"Speak up, child!"

"A SINNER, Father!"

"Mmm . . . *That's* better."

But from there on, in fact, it was all downhill. He took long pauses between questions to make the misery last longer. Then he signaled that I should start enumerating my sins, beginning with commandment number 1. A growl meant I could proceed to number 2 and so on. No growl meant that he was not satisfied with the accounting, and I'd better search my soul and remember how many times I had coveted my neighbor's wife. Or committed murder since last Sunday's confession.

From the corner of my eye, I could see the whole congregation in the pews: a single, huge ear. Those beastly, gossipy womenfolk—why didn't they go outside? They could sit on the church steps or stand in the churchyard, like the men, and hear the whole confession anyway.

But finally, the most terrifying, the worst of all, the killer question:

"Mmm . . . Have *you* committed *impure* acts?"

Impure acts were sins that the catechism teacher—a young nun—had always whispered about and never explained clearly to us. We imagined these "acts," possibly involving our privates, or even sex, to be serious sins, serious enough to get you a one-way ticket to hell.

" . . ."

"SPEAK UP!"

At this point I knew that my life was over.

" . . . ? . . . ?"

"How *many* times? Alone or in company?"

Now I was asked to betray myself. And my friends.

"Alone!"

That was it. I had lied in Confession. I had committed my soul to burn to a crisp. And if I got out of this alive, I swore to myself, no more scrutinizing with Baldo, Erminia, and the other kids the reproductive commotions in the sheep's barn or in the rabbits' hutch.

Finally Don Girolamo let me go with a reluctant blessing and the penance: ten Pater Nosters, ten Hail Marys, ten Acts of Contrition . . .

Later, the comparison of my penance with those of my friends would tell how really bad—or good—I had been.

Don Girolamo was impartial in his terrorizing. With Fire and Brimstone, his two snapping shepherd dogs, he kept the flock in the fold. He chose a simple theme for his sermons and made them as straight and direct as arrows. The pulpit was a little balcony on the wall at the left of the altar, at the height of a second floor. It could be reached either through a spiral stairway from the sacristy or directly from the parsonage, where Gianna, Don Girolamo's housekeeper, had absolute dominion. After the Gospel, Don Girolamo would stomp from the altar and disappear into the sacristy. In a moment (sometimes longer if he made a pit stop in the parsonage) he would reappear in the pulpit and, like Moses from on high, begin his sermon inspired by current parish events in the very general context of the ten commandments. Pointing his finger as if lightning should issue from it, he would address by name the targeted sinners.

It was a very effective, personalized style of preaching. And nobody was safe. For one reason or another—fornication, stealing, adultery, or greed—someone in the congregation was bound to be called on the carpet.

Don Girolamo, having performed another successful Mass, was now ready for his well-deserved Sunday lunch. And if, overtaken by fervor, he dragged the sermon on too long, Gianna would appear behind him in the pulpit and tell him to wrap it up. Food was on the table and getting cold. Gianna was a strong, cunning peasant woman, the only person with any control over Don Girò. She was his *perpetua,* his maid, nurse, cook, housekeeper, and secretary—in perpetuity. Gianna gave orders and Don Girolamo obeyed.

Perhaps it was an unorthodox way to conduct a parish.

The gratitude of the faithful to their church is expressed by *pro-voto* (small silver or golden hearts affixed on the church's walls) thanking God or the appropriate saints for "grace received" in answer to prayers. The walls of the church of Paolo e Maria were covered with little hearts, most affixed during Don Girolamo's tenure.

Of course, his tenure had spanned more than half a century. Just out of the seminary, he was given Frontale's parish—considered by the bishop one step removed from darkest Africa—to prove to the higher-ups that he did, indeed, have what it took for a successful career in the church. As a seminarian, he had shown vigor, stamina, ingenuity, and a charisma that promised a fast climbing of the ladder.

What he had not shown in seminary, or perhaps had acquired by contagion after a short residence in Frontale, was an appetite for all the pleasures a country parish had to offer. Good food, good wine, good hunting, and a gregarious life spent more in the company of parishioners than in the solitary reading of the missal. Moreover, of all the vows that he had taken when he was ordained, the one he could not seem to endure was chastity. With his spirit always willing—and his flesh strong until very late in his years—he had impregnated so many wombs that the internationally accepted sobriquet "son of a bitch" had become, in Frontale, "son of a priest."

Legend had it that, during the decades of his prime, Don Girolamo had fathered quite a number of boys, generally a desired gift in an agricultural society. For the ones not welcomed in their mothers' families, he arranged admission to seminary schools. He gave generous scholarships to these, out of his own funds or the church's vineyard proceeds.

It might appear ironic that, of all of the Fascists' activities and campaigns Don Girò blasted from the pulpit, the one he attacked with particular relish was the *Campagna Demografica*.

The purpose of this effort, begun in the late twenties after the bloodletting of the Great Emigrations and of World War I, was to increase the Italian population to restore strength to the anemic nation. The core of the campaign was the "Beautiful Italian Family"; families that produced more than four children were given prizes and subsidies. These rewards would grow with the number of children, so that people who had been blessed with eight would try for nine, and then go for ten. It was not unusual to see families with a dozen or more children, with the firstborn fifteen or twenty years older than the last. The picture of the lined-up whole family, the oldest children cradling the youngest, appeared in national and local papers with the caption *"Un' altra bella famiglia italiana!"*

Don Girolamo thought the whole campaign ridiculous and a sign of governmental mismanagement. Paying people for doing what they were doing for free anyway! Moreover, how irrational! One of the official reasons given for the Ethiopian war was that, as a Fascist popular song went, "Our Italian boot is getting tight . . . but we shall stretch it down to East Africa and make it comfortable for all!" This song was one of the many darts Don Girolamo threw back at the politics—and singing—of my aunt Elena. She retaliated by going to church in her Fascist uniform. Their love-hate relationship was as legendary as his reproductive prowess. Or her frugality.

An added irony to the Demographic Campaign was that, thanks to some particular quality of the air, food, wine, water, or soil, sexual activity in Frontale was abnormally healthy. Don Girolamo's contributions were just a bonus.

. . .

The Bertoldis could have qualified as one of the Beautiful Italian Families. Domenico, with his knack for producing twins, was doing his biblical best in populating the earth. He had twelve children, all baptized by Don Girò following the uncompromising wish of Anna, Domenico's wife.

Politically, however, Domenico was at the other end of the spectrum, being an anarchist and a *mangia-preti,* a priest-eater. His friendship with Don Girò and his alliance with Zia Elena were some of the many surprising but accepted paradoxes of Le Madonnine. Even the name of the tiny burg—"Little Madonnas"—derived from an unexplained excess of devotion; where the provincial road forked into the oxcart path that led to the farms, there were two small shrines to the Madonna, one on each side of the road. They were similar little brick temples, each sheltering a doll-size terra-cotta Madonna holding the Baby, a votive candle going at all times, and a bunch of fresh field flowers. Obviously, each Lady had her own set of admirers, who in active competition, preferred her above the other.

I had grown up with the Bertoldis' children. Each one of them had something interesting or amusing to bring to the friendship, but the closest were my contemporaries, Baldo and Erminia.

Our turf was the pastures, the vineyards, and the orchards, and the ancient walnut trees, so glorious to climb and to hide in. But above all we loved the brook. It ran in its own hollow down from the mountain along the whole length of the valley; for long stretches, wild blackberry and evergreen bushes formed a canopy over the brook, hiding it, and only the muffled gurgling of water inside the green tunnel gave away its presence. The brook went by just at the end of Nonno's farm, between the cornfield and the pasture, where it was lined with poplar trees. There, in the shallow pond formed by a gentle bend of the brook, is where we spent many hot, late-summer hours.

We had played there since we were babies, under the surveillance of a grown-up or two. We played naked for the good of our skin and the protection of our clothes from elaborate mud pie making. The game generally ended in mud fights and then in washing off in the frigid waters. The little pond grew with us. Over the years we dammed it off with field-stones and made it bigger, and we continued to swim there naked until almost in our teens. It was a simple Eden, and we were not ashamed. We took our nakedness as natural; perhaps the blessings of Don Girolamo protected us from sinful thoughts. From the brook I brought back to the city the taste of grapes chilled in the rushing water and the memory of the indescribable pleasure of getting dressed after the ice-cold ablutions. Our clothes, left splayed on the grass, were saturated with the fragrance and warmth of sunshine.

Of the twins, Baldo was the funny one. He was not too smart, and he liked to act more dumb than he actually was. He had a large, frogish mouth; buttonlike eyes; and a small nose set in a round head with jug-handle ears. Because he was prone to lice, his head was always shaven, and this, together with his preference for communicating with gestures, pirouettes, and jumps instead of words, gave him a definite moronic appearance. The last in a long line of strong and capable brothers, he established his identity by entertaining, pleasing, and doing idiotic things. On command, or just on his own initiative, he might put chicken shit on his tongue and fake eating it, or make lighted cigarette butts disappear in his cavernous mouth, or walk upside down on his hands, chasing the geese around the threshing floor. He was chunky and yet incredibly agile. He ran awkwardly, his limbs going every which way, but he was the fastest and could jump from one tree limb to another like a monkey. He was also a most loyal friend and would do, without questioning, whatever we asked of him.

Erminia was the smart one, and inquisitive. She loved to play the teacher, always knowing something we did not; she was also the most responsible, and this had gained her the duties of taking the sheep to pasture, tending to the pigs, and caring for the chickens and geese. I liked to help her, which mostly meant I followed along and did what she told me to do. Even if we were the same age, Erminia's attitude made me think of her as older, more grown-up. Our parents loved to compare our growth, year to year. They put us side by side against a barn door and with a knife carved our heights, and the date. She was always taller; but then I was taller than Baldo; then again, he could eat chicken shit . . .

In June 1940 I had finished junior high and, come October, would begin my first year of the Scientific Lyceum.

The war had spread over the continent like unchecked wildfire. The import of the situation for my family was that we skipped the vacations in the mountains, despite the great sorrow of Lia, our maid. We were supposed to go for a few weeks to her village in the Alps as in the past years. Instead we went directly to Cattolica for part of July and August, then proceeded to Frontale for the grape harvest.

At the beginning of September, on our way from the coast to Frontale, my mother suggested a stopover in Assisi to pray at

Saint Francis's sanctuary for protection from the evils of war. The five of us boarded one of the superfast trains that ran on time—the Littorine—pride of the Fascist organization. But this one, coming out of a tunnel at full speed, managed, in a very fast sequence, to hit a landslide, derail, flip over, and hang upside down over a precipice. My whole family came out of it muddied but unscathed, with only a few bruises. Proof, my mother declared, that Saint Francis had performed another miracle. My father argued that if Saint Francis was so nice, thank you very much, he should have stopped the landslide from screwing up the Fascist train's punctuality. Too bad we were on it. They were spontaneous comments made in a tense moment, but they underlined for me once more the separation of Church and State in my family.

But we made it to Frontale. It had been a very good year for the grapes. The right amount of sun and rain, and now a last burst of summer were the recipe for a great harvest. Preparations were under way, but it wouldn't be like the years before; a lot of the young men were in the army. That is what Erminia told me by the pond, and we had a lot of other things to tell each other. We had put our grapes to chill in the stream, anchored to the bank like boats at a marina. We laughed about a group of religious nuts who had predicted the end of the world on New Year's Eve 1939, waiting for it on top of Mount San Vicino. There was a terrible snow and ice storm; the world survived, but those fanatics almost did not. We remembered all the fun things we had done with Uncle Berto and regretted his passing; we spoke of war with excitement and made heroic predictions without the remotest idea of what we were talking about. She congratulated me on my scholastic achievements. Surely I was to become a great man of science; I would come around with instruments, looking like the land surveyors, nose in the air, a big-city big shot, and not even notice poor peasant her . . .

As for Erminia, life had brought on new responsibilities. Four of her brothers were already in the army, one had died of frostbite in the mountains of Greece; there were more infants to help her sisters with, and she had to do more work around the farm, things that once only the men did. And, I noticed, she also had found time to grow. She still wore her hair cut short like a boy's, but her tomboyish appearance had been softened. Was it because she wore a smock instead of trousers? Were her lips redder? Perhaps it was just the red light of sunset . . .

We heard Don Girolamo's bell strike Vespers.

I noticed—how could I not have before?—that Erminia's eyes had green sparkles in them and that the light of the setting sun was accentuating the line of her breasts.

She was telling me of Baldo's great experience. He had helped Domenico take the cow to the Monta Taurina, the official insemination station, a rite of passage for a country boy. She laughed at Baldo's excitement and at his tales of cows and bulls. He had reported to her the earthshaking event, blow by blow. Laughing, she imitated Baldo's way of telling the story, with jumps and pirouettes and thrusts and big mooing. I could not resist. I caught her off balance, in midpirouette, and pushed her into the pond; she kept laughing louder, uncontrollably, spraying water and mooing and jumping. I stripped to my shorts and joined her. It was the first time we were in that pond not naked.

Eden was over.

I do not know what overcame me, but I pulled my shorts

down and, showing off my fuzzy nakedness, roared: "I am the bull!" And blushed at my own boldness.

She froze for a second and then, estimating what was offered for inspection, she developed a Mona Lisa smile.

Then, in a low, considerate tone, as if explaining things to a child: "A bull? Have you seen Don Girò's? That's a bull!" And she ran away, laughing again.

What ensued was a chase, a wrestling match, a mock fight, a mixture of shame and fury, a pounding of the blood, each beginning where the other ended. I recall it as a puppies' game: attacks are rejected and then encouraged, only to be rejected again; staring and growling and showing of teeth and then lunging and grappling and rejecting and teasing again. But then there are no more rejections, only the grappling and the pounding of the blood, the gasping for air, the aching of the loins, the stiffening of the spine.

And then all is very quiet and peaceful.

The bell pealed Benediction. It had been, for years, the signal for us to go home.

In my euphoria, I walked all the way to Frontale kicking at stones, barking back at dogs, and chasing squawking chickens out of my path. I kept thinking, and wondering, and trying to figure out if I, if we, were still virgins or not.

At Sunday Confession, I went through the public laundering of my soul with Don Girolamo. It was pretty smooth sailing, the waters unruffled by the usual growls and pauses, until we reached the rocks of his last query.

"Mmm . . . Have you committed IMPURE acts?"

". . ."

"*Speak* up, son! How *many* times?"

"*Once* . . ."

"Alone or in company?"

"ncompany."

"*Boys?*"

"*No!* No, Father!"

A silence, followed by the shuffling of vestments that indicated the end of Confession. Here comes the penance.

"*Bonum tuum! Ego te absolvo, omnia peccata tua* . . . "

With my poor Latin, I translated: "Good for you! I absolve you of all your sins."

Or that is what I thought, or I hoped, he said.

And that was my last confession with Don Girolamo. Actually, it was my very last confession ever.

It would be almost four long, eventful years before I returned to Frontale.

6

The Crazy *Maionese* Maker

TIME PASSED WITH THE PACE OF a crazed metronome, sometimes too fast, sometimes seemingly standing still. Leaders yelled Victory! but it was really defeat. All sides declared that they had the secret final weapon to put an end to war. Wait till tomorrow, or perhaps a week. But war kept engulfing Europe, Russia, and North Africa, with enormous losses on all fronts. Civilian casualties kept pace with the military's.

Food shortages were getting worse by the day. The Annona, the Fascist central agency for the supply, control, and distribution of food, had issued a set of ration coupons for most everything that was edible, except fresh vegetables and orchard produce. The coupons were metaphors for disappointment. A family of four was assigned, say, three ounces of butter a month; after long waits at the store, people were told there was no butter to be had. Or sugar. Or flour. If people arrived at dawn to be first in line when the dairy store opened, they had a chance at the family daily ration of two cups of milk, or perhaps a few eggs supplied by the store owner himself. The Annona turned out to be a most corrupt organization, in the hands of people with little knowledge of the task but with a lot of friends. There were strong suspicions that most of the black market originated there, but whoever complained was labeled a defeatist and dealt with by the law-and-order bullies. An active bartering developed among families who juggled what was essential against what was not. A ration of five cigarettes a week could be traded for one bar of laundry soap. It was common for burglars to break into a house and steal whatever food was available, ignoring the jewelry.

Food, the thought of food, was of primary importance.

Some once-common dishes now took on a mystical value, things to hold on to as reminders of a past good life and promises that good, simple things were still there to be had. Just wait a little while longer, do not lose faith. A few grains of "real coffee" would mysteriously appear, be religiously ground into powder, and made into a tiny cup of espresso. The grown-ups would take small sips in turn, the children vicariously rejoice in breathing in the old, familiar aroma. Little bits of this and that were put aside until there was enough to make one decent dish, enough to go around, modestly, for the whole family. Our family had one such special dish, a celebration. Every fourth Friday, third when we were lucky, a silvery freshwater fish would come to us. How it managed to do so was not too clear to me. I suspected that it was part of a chain of IOUs that began with a Tiber fisherman and then, like salmon rushing the rapids, passed through various hands to land finally in our kitchen. Or, following a simple barter, a bunch of cigarettes could be traded for a nicotine-addicted fisherman's fish. Neither my mother nor my father smoked, so their cumulative ten cigarettes a week, times three or four weeks, could easily fetch a whale of a fish.

These fish Fridays were ceremonial days. The preparations followed a well-rehearsed and safe procedure. Our kitchen assumed the character and mood of a hospital operating room. The fish—generally a pound and a half—was carefully scrubbed of its scales, then cut open like a book and slipped into a pan of barely simmering water flavored with an onion, a carrot, a stalk of celery, a lemon slice, and a bay leaf. After three minutes, the fish was taken out and put on a fish dish, the cooking water saved in its pan. The fish was then carefully boned, the central spine lifted easily away, more stubborn bones picked out with tweezers. Then the fish was put aside, covered with a moist dish towel.

What was essential to the celebration was mayonnaise. A fish without it was quasi worthless. What was needed was *maionese*. Real *maionese*.

And I was entrusted with its making.

On a Friday afternoon in early winter, the sky dark much too early, the apartment empty (Papa at work, Mamma shopping, my older brother at the gym, my younger sister at ballet practice), its windows streaked by rain and my soul by dampness, there I was feeling lonely and dejected.

But Lia's voice was beckoning me into the light and warmth of the kitchen. Ah, that was heaven, and making *maionese* a reward. Lia was our maid, and she remained with us until the final cataclysm of the war, when she had to return to her Alpine village in the Veneto region. She was in her midtwenties and a marvelous cook. The fact that she was so hopelessly old did not blind me to her great beauty.

Having Lia in our family was one of my mother's many wisdoms. If my father and brother—I have never been sure if I was included—had to be exposed to temptation, then let it be under her watchful eye, where temptation would never be allowed to blossom into sin. A handsome woman herself, Mamma never felt seriously threatened by competition. Lia was the last of a succession of beautiful maids who made our household very popular with uncles, cousins, and friends, for it was another of my mother's wisdoms to think that we men—but was I included?—would grow accustomed to feminine charm and beauty, so that if, when, and where these graces were used against us, we, like Mithridates against poison, would be adequately immunized. I cannot honestly prove her right, but I must say that at least she set a standard.

Lia was now getting ready to make fresh pasta, and she called me. Time for me to make *maionese.*

I approached the making of *maionese* with trepidation. I had to follow a strict, unquestioned ritual, or there were penalties to be paid. I never knew or asked what they might be, in the same way that I never cared to ask what the consequences would be if I dipped a dirty hand into the Holy Water font.

The preparation steps for *maionese* making had to be done in perfect sequence. (1) The Bowl. It had to be the bowl for *maionese,* a white china one, a half sphere with a flat base. Nothing else would do. (2) The Spoon, a short-handled, hardwood spoon, its curvature made by use to conform perfectly to the inside of the Bowl and, like it, reserved for that use only. (3) The Eggs. They had to be fresh that day and at room temperature, neither warm nor cold to the touch. (4): The Lemon, squeezed as thoroughly as possible and its juice filtered through a sieve into a small glass beaker. (4A) The rubbing of hands with the squeezed-out lemon. This was not a mandatory step in the ceremony, only an aping on my part, for I had seen my mother and Lia do that before they discarded the rinds. "It keeps the skin clean," Mamma would say.

Finally there was the Olive Oil. We had three different qualities in the kitchen: frying oil, cooking oil, and the "extra virgin." The first two were of anonymous origins and kept in nondescript vessels. The third was hand-carried to us by a farmer who insisted that he picked the olives himself and swore to the impeccability of the oil's pedigree. This oil was kept in a special crock and used only for salads, fish, and naturally, *maionese*. I treated this oil religiously, associating its name directly with that of the Virgin Mary.

It had to be poured and measured into a copper contraption with a beaky spout. A spilled drop was a sin, even if, I reassured myself, only a venial one, a small one, with minor retribution. Mortal sin was when words or deeds provoked the sky to crack open and a lightning bolt to frizzle you to nothingness on the spot. But now, in a very short time, this classification of sin relative to the wasting of olive oil had shifted. With the rationing of many foodstuffs, the farmer's status had changed to that of black marketeer, and the price of olive oil, especially extra virgin, had become astronomical. The simple *thought* of wasting it would definitely be a mortal sin.

Once I had assembled all the ingredients, including salt and pepper, I had to line them up on the kitchen table and pull a chair close to it. The positioning of the chair was all-important; it had to permit me, once seated, to reach the ingredients with my left hand and simultaneously leave me with an unobstructed view of the whole kitchen—and of Lia.

The separating of the eggs followed. Ever so carefully, I would plop the yolk back and forth from one half shell to the other, letting all the white slink into a glass. All the white. With a very fresh egg, that takes some doing. Just when you think that the white's all gone, you spy some slyly clinging to the yolk. You have to make a gambler's choice: either ignore the remaining white or go for a pristine yolk at the risk of losing some of the precious gold along with the hideous white. At this point Lia must have shared my agony, for she always stopped her activity and, holding her breath, observed me closely.

With the yolks separated, the real business was at hand. The bowl had to be nestled in my lap. The nestling is important: human warmth is essential for real *maionese*. Then the stirring began, and I had to set a pace to be maintained until the end. Changing it or, God forbid, reversing the direction of your stirring, will result in a humiliating mess. Once the yolks are smooth, you add the oil. A drop or, if you are daring, two. You stir and let the yolks absorb the oil at their will: you cannot control or speed up this first alchemy. Each yolk has its own time, willingness, and temper in this delicate matter of amalgamation. I suspect the same holds true for the oil, but I can't prove it.

When the yolks, or the oil, have decided to combine, the mixture turns slightly paler and thicker. You must keep on stirring and add another drop of oil. Or two, but that might be pushing your luck. Stir, amalgamate, drop of oil, stir. Now I had reached the crucial point. Let not the palpitations of the heart change the stirring pace: this is the moment of truth! For this is when, for arcane reasons nobody will ever explain, the *maionese* can *impazzire*. That is, it might go crazy. You can interpret the terrifying phenomenon euphemistically as "curdling" but the literal translation, "going crazy," is much closer to what the *maionese* actually does. The smooth, silky delight suddenly becomes diabolically transformed. Its color turns; the monstrous thing is now slimy, then raggedy and wet—it looks as if it wants to slither right up and out of the bowl. And it would, if I couldn't control the wild tremor in my knees. Don't panic, I had to tell myself. Don't attempt to beat the thing down with the spoon.

When this happened, I would close my eyes, put the bowl down on the table, and admit my shame to the world. I could have quit here, given up. But I couldn't. I was in Rome, remember, with Lia looking on, counting on me. Moreover, the black shadow of war was over us, and two egg yolks were two egg yolks, a treasure not to be given up without a fight.

The rescue operation had to be swift. Tumble down five blacked-out flights of stairs, guided only by memory and the dim light of a candle held, against blackout regulations, by the two gossiping old biddies on the second-floor landing. Then across the courtyard, across the street, and after a brief struggle with the blackout curtain and outcoming customers, into the dairy store to buy one egg.

Feel for the right egg in the wire basket. Can't afford a wrong one, another crazy egg. Feel for the warmth. A cold egg is suspicious. A cold egg has been refrigerated. A refrigerated egg is not fresh. Cold is bad and warm is good.

Toss a coin to Signor Mario, the dairy store man. He would be smirking. He knew I made a crazy *maionese*. The whole world knew. He took the coin, still smirking. He bounced the coin on the marble counter, taking his time, smirking. He bounced the coin again, listening for the telltale sound of a fake.

Was he trying to make me crazy too? I hate you, sour-milk dealer, son of a cow and a chicken, give me my change. Please. The change, finally, and fast across the street, the court-yard, up the dark stairs, past the two biddies. They yelled af-ter me *Coraggio!*—courage! Two more flights, three steps at a time, across the threshold, through the hall into the kitchen, to the rescue with one warm egg in my hand. It was almost all right now, I could breathe. But let not overconfidence de-stroy me. Calm down, now, Lia is there.

Transfer the crazy substance to a cup, clean the *maionese* bowl, and separate the rescuer egg ever so carefully. Plop the yolk into the bowl. Sit down, stir the yolk slowly and care-fully, add a spoonful of the crazy to it. Stir. It worked: it was amalgamating, it was beautiful. Stir, add, stir and add. A won-der had come to pass: the *maionese* was sane again.

Now I could sing, or I could just listen to Lia. In her sweet Veneto accent, she sang of the mountains she left behind, of the blond Alpine trooper who was scaling the highest alp to pick her a mountain flower, an edelweiss. The song went up and down, now a whisper, now a trill, like the Alpine valleys and peaks. When she reached the peaks, Lia stopped kneading the pasta dough she was making, her arms bearing down on it, her neck stretched and high. A moment's pause, and sliding into a valley, the kneading resumed, her body bending and swaying with the rhythm of the song and the kneading.

My pace now followed Lia's song. Half the oil was gone, time for a pinch of salt; stir, add a few drops of lemon juice, stir. But now it was all automatic, the adding, the stirring. I was safe home. With Lia singing and kneading, the *maionese* went by itself, the spoon was around and around, simply tak-ing my arm along.

There must be something atavistic in the male blood that makes it rush, relent, rush with the peaks and the valleys, the roundness of Lia's breasts valleying and peaking, the stretch of her neck, the swaying of her hips. What a wonder it is seeing flour and water turn into pasta! When Lia was doing it, it was a miracle. Did she know? Stir, stir, a little lemon; stir, a little oil. The song went on, the peaks and the valleys. How simple and rewarding was the making of *maionese*!

At dinner, Papa will ask what we did all day. My sister will have danced as never before, my brother will have swum his fastest mile. And what have I done? Not much; nothing, really. Mamma will bring to the table the poached fish, and Lia will follow with the chilled wine and the *maionese*. Mamma will serve the fish, and Papa will sip the wine and taste the *maionese*. A ritual: he will barely dip his fork and bring a golden drop to the tip of his tongue. He will savor it; a suggestion of doubt will cross his face. He will take another sip of wine and retaste the *maionese*. Then he will look at me, a secret wink and a smile, and just say *Buona*. Good.

7

A Fountain of Rome

I DOUBT THAT RESPIGHI WOULD EVER have been inspired by our little Roman fountain. It was nothing more than a four-foot cast-iron cylinder with pretentious floral decorations and a single spigot. In its best days, it had produced a constant, generous, clear, singing stream of delicious, cold water; now it gave only a few drops of rusty liquid, preceded and followed by a sickly gurgling and coughing, a lament for the whole of Rome's bombed-out pipery. But it was our fountain; we kept a tin can under its spigot to collect its few tears and to show that we still cared. On the sidewalk at the corner of two residential streets, it had been the meeting point of our gang since grade school.

Now our ranks had shrunk a little. Some of the older boys—the ones who often had helped us with our homework—were in the army fighting on some remote front. One had followed his family north; the two Levi brothers had left all of a sudden, but we knew, or hoped we knew, they were safe somewhere.

We all lived—were born, most of us—within the radius of a few city blocks. In all seasons, practically at all hours, we could go to the fountain and find company, and it was rare if, in the course of a day, all of us would not be together at the fountain, if only for a few minutes.

The war had put more constrictions on our parents than on us. The increasing rationing of goods forced them into new life routines, logistics, and strategies, including the limitation of travel. For one thing, ration coupons could be redeemed only at their place of issue; for another, travel, for business or pleasure, was difficult and dangerous. For us, all this meant mostly a reduction of our allowances and the curtailing of our long vacations out of Rome. We substituted for them with day trips to the nearby beaches of Ostia or Anzio.

In a way the new situation spurred our imaginations to devise our own entertainment. We made the huge, beautiful park of Villa Borghese our own turf. We played pickup games of soccer; we had fights with kids from other neighborhoods. But mostly we congregated around our fountain, our headquarters and touchstone. We felt safe there. A soccer game could be started there at any time, even if there were only two players, or turned into a full-teamed tournament—five players per team, that is, instead of eleven—that would drag on for days.

Or we played *nizza,* a game that Carlo, the philosopher-historian in residence, told us went back to ancient Roman times. The only—and very affordable—equipment consisted of one broomstick. A six-inch section was sawed off and its two ends sharpened into points, producing a fuselike *nizza.* Place it on the ground, hit one of its sharp ends with the remaining long part of the broomstick, and the *nizza* will jump waist-high into the air. Bat it hard, and the *nizza* will fly like a bullet. A member of the opposite team has to pick it up and throw it back at the batter . . . and on and on, following definite rules that we changed at whim. Sometimes the *nizza* would make violent contact with someone's forehead, player's or bystander's. That was bad enough and bloody, but it was much worse if the *nizza* hit a neighbor's window. Even if covered by wartime antishatter paper strips, the glass would break. There was no use running away. It was well known that the culprits were the *ragazzacci della fontanella,* the bad boys of the fountain. We were all forced to develop a sense of civic responsibility, and pitch in, replace, and repaper the pane while listening to the protracted lamentations of the whole neighborhood.

No matter how involved we were in our games, or tall-tale telling, or deep philosophical conversations, we would be dispersed instantly by the simple clarion call *"Pranzo!"* or *"Cena!"* of a maid or a mother. We did not even need to say good-bye. We knew that we would meet again, shortly, at our special place.

September 8, 1943. General Eisenhower, in a radio broadcast, announced the armistice between the Allied forces and the Italians. A short time later in Italy, Marshal Badoglio, the prime minister, confirmed the armistice but gave only vague guidance to the Italian armed forces. In a flurry of orders and counterorders, he abandoned the Italian army, navy, and air force to their own devices, with the veiled implication that now Germany was Italy's enemy. Before dawn on September 9, King Victor Emmanuel III of the House of Savoy, ex-emperor of Ethiopia and ex-king of Albania, together with the queen, the crown prince, and Badoglio, abandoned the capital and drove to the Adriatic coast, ending up in Brindisi, a navy base near the heel of the Italian boot. The city of Brindisi was still under the control of the Italian military. On September 29, Badoglio signed another treaty with the British and Americans that spelled out in detail the terms of Italy's unconditional surrender. And on October 13, 1943, the king declared war on Nazi Germany, which gave Italy the status of a co-belligerent.

A few army divisions, poorly fed and poorly armed, confronted the Germans and were quickly disposed of. Many less heroic troops were quick to destroy arms, ammunitions, and military impedimenta—or trade them for civilian clothing—and then vanish. Some enterprising soldiers walked miles to surrender to the U.S. Fifth Army and, as they hoped they would be, were promptly taken prisoner and shipped to prison camps in the United States. Others were not so quick or lucky and were captured by their former comrades-in-arms, loaded and sealed into cattle cars, and carted away to Germany and a horrible fate.

North of the Allied occupied zone, in the rest of Italy, including Rome, the monarchy had been replaced by the Repubblica Sociale Fascista Italiana, a puppet government established and controlled by the Nazis. The new Fascists abandoned Rome as the seat of government and chose for their headquarters the small town of Salò, on the shores of Lake Garda, not too far from the Austrian border. German paratroopers landed in gliders and freed Mussolini from his jail in Campo Imperatore, on top of the Gran Sasso, considered inaccessible, and carted him off to recover in Germany.

The Fascist Militia had retrenched and taken over the abandoned institutions. Il Duce, now a sick shadow of himself, was propped up and established as head of the *repubblica*.

At the first opportunity, the entrenched old master sergeants of the Regno d'Italia, the Kingdom of Italy, rubber stamps poised, collected the scattered records, resurrected files and documents, and were ready again to do business drafting soldiers for the government. A miracle, but a surprise to no one. It was known without a doubt that when the world came to an end and Gabriel finally tooted his golden horn, an Italian sergeant quartermaster would be at his side to call the roll and rubber-stamp the poor souls' documents.

Shortly the Rome Military District Command resurfaced from the ashes, a bureaucratic phoenix. We—the five or six bad boys of the *fontanella* who were left—were now close to military service age. Some of us had been called up by the Military Command, passed medical inspection, been given matriculation numbers, told to which barracks to report, and sent home in *in congedo provvisorio,* "temporarily released from duty," to wait for the call to arms. They also gave us a stern warning that if we did not answer the call when it came, the Fascist MP would come after us within a week and ferret us out, no matter how deep in hiding we might be. The warning came with the admonition that, when found, the deserters would be shot.

Not many young people were willing to fight at this stage, nor in light of recent events, were there many left whom the Germans would trust. The main purpose of the draft, more than to recruit soldiers, was a military census, to know who was where. The new Military Command assumed that any man who did not answer the draft—if not already listed as a POW, dead, or missing in action—was a potential underground fighter, a partisan.

The Fascists, nonetheless, kept exhorting young people to volunteer and join again with the Germans in the fight. This new Fascist Republican Army, they proclaimed, would restore the Honor of the Violated Motherland and show those materialistic Sons of Mammon from across *Mare Nostrum,* Our Sea, that "Italian youth still possess the atavistic valor of the victorious Roman legions."

Having been fed that kind of bombastic rhetoric since grade school and having experienced its results, we thought the whole exercise pretty sickening. It became downright morbid when they began to enroll adolescents in a Rome or Death Battalion, a special unit pledged to die in the defense of Rome. Many boys—and girl auxiliaries—joined for the doubtful attraction of wearing a lugubrious black uniform (an exalted version of the old Balilla one), silver insignia of skull and crossbones included, and armed to the teeth with pistols and daggers. Their childish egos swelled to bursting, and for a while they roamed the streets of Rome, bullying anybody in sight without fear of reprisal.

But there we were: numbered, tagged, and *in congedo provvisorio,* waiting. What we were waiting for was an end to the madness. The Allies were pressing hard on "Fortress Germany"; the Russians were pounding the Eastern Front; guerrilla fighters were popping up all over. The Germans were faring badly on all fronts. The war couldn't last, it just couldn't last much longer.

Besides our political objections, joining the Fascist Army now, or being forced to join, would be pure insanity. If worse came to worst and we were called, we all had plans to disappear into the *macchia,* the mountain underbrush, hide there like rabbits in holes, and sweat it out for the duration.

As for the Mazzettis, once our elementary school days were over, our roads had taken different directions: they went for the study of letters and the classics, I for technology and the sciences. We attended different schools and had made different friends; our association became less intensive and more superficial. Anna and Tina had more girlish reasons to keep in touch, and through them we had scattered news of each other. As practically next-door neighbors, we still did meet on occasion, and, for a few moments, felt close again. A few of these encounters happened at night in the air-raid shelter in the *palazzo*'s cellar; sometimes the alarm would last for hours, and it gave us time to get up-to-date, talk of our schools and aspirations. Sooner or later our political convictions took over and heated up the conversations, but our long childhood friendship prevented differences of opinion from developing into animosity. Nonetheless, we sneaked out of the shelter and into the silence of the garden to keep our debates away from curious ears, and also to get away from the stale air of the shelter-cellar, barely lit by two or three stinking and soot-spewing candles, and from the black-clad old biddies' monotonous reciting of the litanies. *"Ave Maria!"* one would invoke, *"Gratia plena,"* the others would answer in chorus. *"Mater Dei!"* the single voice would insist. *"Ora pro nobis!"* the cumulative chant would answer. And on and on for hours, until all the beads of the rosary had been fingered, or the all-clear siren wailed.

The air alarms would go off even if Rome was not the target.

Twenty thousand feet up, hundreds of planes—wave after

wave—would fly over, directed to other destinations. Anti-aircraft guns would go off, only scratching the beautiful Roman sky with tracing bullets. Some of these, unspent, came down and exploded in the city. Then the guns were silenced, saving the ammunition for when the planes were low enough to be reached. With time, these "white" air raids became commonplace, and people would just go back to bed. But sleeping was not easy, disrupted by the constant possibility of danger, and by the commotion of self-appointed air wardens, who took these occasions to walk the streets and yell *"Luce! Luce!"* at any light that seeped from a window's blackout curtain.

Never counted among the *ragazzacci,* Federico, Piero, and Tina Mazzetti answered the appeal of the new government and volunteered in the new Fascist Brigades. Tina, leggy and tall, had lied about her age and was enrolled in the Fascist Women's Auxiliary. All three went north, and in a few months they had finished officer school. They came back to Rome on furlough, wearing battle fatigues, each boy carrying a dagger, a pistol, a submachine gun, and two hand grenades hooked to his bandolier.

We met by chance in the courtyard of the *palazzo.* Federico was more discreet, almost embarrassed by his display of force. He explained that they had been ordered to strut their firepower to impress friends and foes. Piero was more proud to show off, and indeed, he looked dangerous. I told him I was impressed: it was quite a way from when we were shooting slingshots and homemade bows and arrows. I advised him to be careful not to trip or stumble, please, or he could blow up the whole courtyard. A sudden chill fell between us, and he called me "a joker, a fence sitter, while the world is burning." I too—he told me—should come to my senses, stop being a coward and wear the uniform. Perhaps, I told him, but it could not be the same one as his. With nothing more to add, we were going to part icily, perfunctorily wishing each other good luck and promising that, if we ever met on opposite sides of a battlefield, we would not shoot at each other. Or at least not shoot to kill.

Tina broke the ice, giving me a good-bye hug with a "For old times' sake." She mentioned that, while putting her things in order, she'd found a scrap of paper that had fallen out of an old schoolbook. From the handwriting, it looked as if it went back to second or third grade. A headline in tentative capital letters said THE BEST OF FRIENDS, and underneath were smeared bloody thumbprints with our signatures. I remembered when we had pricked our fingers, inspired by mafia indoctrination tales. I returned her hug and said that perhaps we should now sign our names on a new piece of paper titled THE BEST OF ENEMIES.

Just hold the blood.

With the roiling of events on all European war fronts, and clear signs of a violent final face-off in sight, the underground organizations in all German-occupied countries turned from hiding to active fighting. In France, Belgium, Holland, Hungary, Albania, Yugoslavia, Greece, Italy, people took up arms and, like hornets, came out of their nests for painful stings to the enemy, then rushed back into hiding. It was a very dangerous game: if found fighting or in possession of arms (these had a wide interpretation: a kitchen knife would do), people were no longer "patriots" but "partisans."

In Italy the Comitato di liberazione nazionale (Committee for National Liberation) was formed to coordinate and direct the activities of the small bands of partisans that were popping up all over the country. Apart from our schooling—which became more and more intermittent thanks to the frequent air raids and our constant need to search and barter for food—we, the *ragazzacci della fontanella,* got involved in a nonfighting yet dangerous activity. We did not dare to call ourselves partisans. Partisans were the armed bands that, more and more, were coming out of hiding to fight, shoot, bomb, and kill. If taken, partisans were shot on the spot by the Fascists or hanged by the Germans. Either way, they became heroes. Dead heroes. Very visibly so, because the carcasses were left out for everybody to see. Being a hero romantically appealed to us; being a dead one gave us pause. Moreover, real partisans had war names like Eagle, Wolf, Tiger. We did not. We ran errands for Eagle and Wolf and Tiger, but we never met them. They could have been our parents and we would not have known it. On the other hand, if our parents had known what we were up to, they would have had heart failure.

I had been drawn into the action so slowly that it took me quite a while to realize that, yes, I was a very small fish but swimming with the sharks. It had begun with my professor of history and philosophy asking me for a small favor. Would I run an errand for him? He had a package to be delivered— not too far from my house. . . .

I liked Professor Gesmundo; I liked his fiery black eyes, his ascetic figure, and his fairness and sense of humor. I tended to associate him with the El Greco portrait of St. Francis from

our art history textbooks. I was not one of Professor C
mundo's best students; frankly, I was among the worst, esp
cially if compared with one of his super-duper students, my
older brother, Marco. I thought that the rendered favor would
earn me one in return. I complied.

The package turned out to be a book, to be delivered to
a Signor Andreini. His address was on the Via XXI Aprile,
on the eighth floor of a huge complex of *case popolari,* a
beehive of apartments for middle-income and blue-collar
tenants. There was a shaky elevator, out of service. The address was about seven miles from the school but, fortunately,
halfway to my house. Via XXI Aprile branched out of Via
Nomentana, a beautiful four-lane boulevard, flanked by old
chestnut trees that formed a canopy of branches over it. The
road had an almost imperceptible downward incline: going for the delivery, I could bicycle freewheeling almost all
the way; but in coming back, the long slight upward incline
took a toll on my legs. That, plus the many stairs, turned to be
quite an exercise, and when I got home, my mother commented that she had never seen me so worn-out after a day
of school.

A few days later Professor Gesmundo asked me again. He
trusted me, he said, and he had books to be returned to the
same address, the same Signor Andreini. The books I had
been ferrying around, he confided, were banned books;
heavy, yes, but not too dangerous, mostly Russian classics.
Books one day—he hoped—I would like to read. That information gave me a sense of the illicit, and just being connected with anything Russian (communist perhaps?) imparted
a feeling of secrecy. On the third trip, Signor Andreini gave
me a package for Professor Gesmundo. To thank me, he gave

...nan brioche, an offering probably sug-
...ooks.

...ia went by the Villa Torlonia, the Mus-
... The whole area was crowded with Fascist
...and policemen, in uniform or disguised in civilian
...es. They were known to stop people, especially student-
...ooking guys, at random, ask them for ID, and generally harass
them. It was a small revenge of barely literate people to assert
their power over spoiled, sissy young men. All branches of the
military or Fascist police were recruited from the poor Italian
south, and their accents identified them. They asked for *"doc-
umenti!"* sounding like *"dogu-men-dah,"* and that's the nickname we gave to all of them.

I pedaled by them, trying to conceal my anxiety over the
secret parcel and act as indifferent as I could.

The next day, after the delivery, Professor Gesmundo whispered a thanks and then, loudly, so that the whole class could
hear, ordered me to stay after class. Nothing unusual. I had been
kept after class so many times that by now it was a ritual.

He got right to the point. Studies aside, he admired my
spirit of independence, and he wanted reassurance that I trusted
him as he trusted me. Now he had pamphlets that were of a
more delicate nature. I figured out, by the hush-hush and para-
phrasing, that they were anti-Fascist and he wanted me to
know it without his saying so, wanted to make sure I really understood. He did not speak of duty or of patriotism. He asked
me to think it over, be really sure I wanted to help him with
the errands. If no, fine. If yes, great. Only, yes or no, for everybody's sake, keep it to myself.

We could all be damaged. Seriously damaged.

Would I and could I? Then, with a twinkle in his eye, he

added that I should not expect my grades to improve; if anything, I should expect to be treated more severely. He wanted everybody to see how much he disapproved of me, and probably he would belittle me in front of the class. It was possible that he would recommend to my parents that I get tutorial lessons.

In a short time, running around on my bike, I was delivering packages all over Rome. Sometimes they were simple brown packages, obviously containing papers; other times they were unwrapped books. These made me curious: why was I shuffling books, even if they were banned? Any reasonably stocked family library would have them. Did they contain secret messages? I remembered when in grade school I had played spies with Piero, trading books with words circled or underlined to form a phrase. I did stop, once or twice, to open the books and check for telltale signs, but I couldn't detect any. Either they were well-hidden or I wasn't smart enough to see them.

Then Professor Gesmundo asked me if I had friends I could trust. Really trust. Yes. Sergio and Tullio, the brothers. Mauro, Carlo, Fausto, Gianni, and the strapping six-foot-three Aldo the Long. Gesmundo told me that he was now busy with different matters, had no more time for these deliveries. Yet they were still important; as a matter of fact, the delivery addresses were multiplying by the day and I could not carry out all the deliveries by myself. I needed someone to help me.

Sergio and Tullio were enthusiastic. Carlo and Mauro were not. Fausto and Gianni were in, Aldo the Long only on a part-time basis: he was too visible.

In a short time my expanded delivery service was under way. We logged miles on foot and on increasingly rickety

bicycles. Jokingly, we called ourselves *fattorini,* message runners. Gesmundo faded out of the picture, and we picked up
from and delivered directly to Andreini. Then Andreini faded
away, and we reported to people he had sent us to, with names
like Gatto (Cat), Lepre (Hare), and Falco (Hawk). Only Sergio, Tullio, and I continued to operate as a group; the others
were doing errands for people we did not know. The addresses became movable meeting points, sometimes just
drops.

We knew that we were working for "the underground"
and that we had become links in a long chain, of which we
could not see either end. Very minor links, we knew, and that
knowledge gave us a sense of security. Who would chase after us when there were bigger fish to fry? With the Allies
pinned at Monte Cassino, things really began to heat up.
Monte Cassino, eighty miles south of Rome, was one of the
tallest mountains on the road between Naples and Rome.
On the very top of the mountain, the sixth-century Bene-
dictine abbey held one of the most valuable libraries of old
books and manuscripts in Europe. Unfortunately, it also dom-
inated the surrounding valleys and roads, making it a su-
perb strategic position in German hands. The Allies pounded
Monte Cassino's abbey mercilessly day and night, with artillery from the ground and bombardments from the air. The
Germans transformed the abbey rubble into a formidable
bunker, shooting from there at anything that moved in the valleys below, blocking the American Fifth Army's way to Rome
for the rainy, muddy winter months—the worst recorded in
many years. It became for both sides one of the most bloody
battles of the Italian campaign. The stone-by-stone destruction of the abbey was used by the Fascist propaganda as

proof of the Allies' criminal disrespect for Italian culture and art treasures. The battle of Monte Cassino had bought time for Germans and Fascists in preparing their defense of Rome, and when in the city, they became more violently arrogant with each passing hour.

We started ferrying things other than pamphlets. It began with a pocketful of nine-millimeter shells, then the barrel of a Beretta, parts of submachine guns. With the Americans landing at Anzio, we were moving dismantled but complete items, and we amazed ourselves at our newly acquired knowledge of firearms and how quickly we could assemble and disassemble them blindfolded, or in the utmost darkness of Sergio's cellar. It was not unusual for our school bags to hold, with our books, a hand grenade or two. Sometimes more.

Someone, zipping by on a bicycle, had lobbed a hand grenade into a truck loaded with Germans coming out of a movie theater, then zigzagged away into the traffic. In the next few days, another bicyclist tossed explosives at the Hotel Flora, on Via Veneto, the headquarters of the German Occupation High Command. Then again a grenade against the German guard of the Regina Coeli prison, and the bicyclist was never caught. Many were the victims in all the incidents, but their number was never divulged by the Germans. The attacks infuriated them. A poster was glued to all the Roman walls that said:

The German Command Declares: Pursuant to the attacks carried out by cyclists in broad daylight, from this moment on, without exception, the use of bicycles anywhere in the Open City of Rome is prohibited. Transgressors will be shot on the spot.

It took care of practically 80 percent of the Roman means of transportation.

That ordinance had its pros and cons for me. The good part was that I did not have to lug my bike up and down five flights of stairs every time I went on an errand. Besides the weight of the machine, I had to carry its heavy chain. Bicycles were so appealing to thieves that the chain I used to link my bike to the iron handrail of my landing was so heavy it could easily have been used to tie a cruiser to a dock. The bad part was that now the secret errands had to be done on foot. They took a lot more time out of my day and a lot of wear out of my cardboard-soled shoes.

Some legal smart-ass came up with the meaning of "bicycle:" a vehicle with *two* wheels. With the welding on of a third wheel—like a large training wheel—or a small, permanently affixed trailer—like a recycled perambulator—the machine would cease to be a *bicycle,* hence not subject to the order against its use. This idea was suggested to the Fascist police transportation authorities, with the plea that forbidding the use of bicycles would practically kill the town by starvation. It was speculated that the Italian police, and their extended families too, depended on bikes for survival.

For a while everybody in Rome was going around with these crazy contraptions. I complied by bolting to my bike a small wheel left over from a child's bike. But the idea of lugging the bicycle *and* its third wheel up the stairs gave me pause, so I ended up just going on foot.

By the middle of January 1944, given the deterioration of the Italian war front and the increased partisan bombings, the

Germans in Rome—with the collaboration of the Fascists—became virulent. Suspected people were arrested and taken to the infamous Gestapo headquarters and jail of Via Tasso, where they were interrogated, beaten, and tortured. The mere mention of Via Tasso, its reputation probably fostered by the jailers themselves, struck terror in people's hearts.

In school we had a *custode,* custodian-janitor, who took care of three or four classrooms on our floor. Signora Paolina, known just as Lina, was a middle-aged, round lady barely five feet tall, her black hair pulled back in a bun, with dark, perennially smiling eyes. She saw that the corridors were clean and clear of hazards, yelled at the students who ran down the stairs, cleaned the blackboards, and was the keeper of the chalk supply. She saved all the various objects left behind by the students and returned them—in exchange for a small tip at Christmas. She was well liked, a surrogate mother away from home. After school, once or twice a week, she also took care of Professor Gesmundo's apartment, keeping it neat and washing and ironing his laundry. Professor Gesmundo was a bachelor from Bari, near the heel of the Italian boot, as revealed by his accent, which, even if educated, had a marked open pronunciation of vowels. Signora Lina was very protective of her young professor, and from the allusions she made now and then, it was clear that she was trying to be a matchmaker.

On a Monday afternoon she went to Gesmundo's apartment. It had been marauded, all his books and papers strewn around. His only two pairs of shoes, including the ones he'd had at school in the morning, were abandoned on the floor.

Signora Lina went to the local police and reported what she had found. She was told to relax, he had been taken to Via Tasso, and why was it her business, anyway? She explained and was told that, since he had no direct family around, she could visit him on Thursdays, just for a few minutes, and bring him some clean clothes.

On Friday we saw Signora Lina in school, and her usually smiling eyes were wet and tearful. She confided, whispering, that she had seen Gesmundo. His face was a bloody pulp.

The news struck us with terror. And pity for the gentle professor. And fear for us messengers: had the marauders found our names among his papers?

After recovering from the first shock, I rushed off to see Signor Andreini for advice, but he had disappeared. Our last contact let us understand that if we were to quit now it was exactly what those Fascist bastards wanted: to scare off any resistance. The best thing to do was to lie low for a while, then resume our work when it was required.

Which we did.

I sometimes took my girlfriend along on my walks, stopping here and there to show her the beauty of Rome. Seen with her, the city assumed a new dimension. I repeated to her what I had learned from my father—or what I could remember, filling the gaps with pompous fabrications—describing the monuments and the works of art. Many of them now were covered by sandbags. Tall Roman columns were protected from shrapnel by spiraling piles of bags—a direct hit would fell column and bags; some statues had been removed to safe locations, leaving in their places plaques with their names and brief descriptions. I let my memory and my imagination re-create what was obscured by the sandbags, which, as the signs said, "were to protect these treasures from the Barbaric Ene-mies, who seek the destruction of our glorious past." As if my descriptions had not done damage enough.

Actually, the most precious work of art, the one I would have protected not with sandbags but with my life, was my girlfriend herself.

My taking her along was also the cause for cutting re-marks from my friends. They did not object to my carrying out my assigned duties in her company. They too took along their girls: a couple of young *innamorati* would raise less suspi-cion was the excuse. What they teased me about was my pla-tonic attachment to her, the preposterous fact that I did not even make an attempt on her virginity. They called me a monk. Because they frequently, with one mission accom-plished, tried for a second, less dangerous but more strenuous endeavor: a chance at breaking down the resistance of their girlfriends. Then the remote bushes of a park, the dark cor-ners of the forums, the most isolated seats of a movie house became their love nests. They all had their favorite safe spots for rushed, consensual sex.

We were all living in our parents' homes—and would do so until we got married—and even on the rare occasions when our parents were away, the ubiquitous, nosy neighbors and watchful housemaids forbade us the luxury of comfort-able, unhurried privacy. A school acquaintance of ours, son of an Italian diplomat who had lived a few years in prewar Amer-ica, had told us of the incredibly civilized freedom of Ameri-can youths. They could obtain their driving licenses at sixteen, and hence have access to their parents' huge American cars, with their king-size backseats. In our imaginations, with sour-grapes joking, we constructed these cars as fully accessorized bedrooms. How could we ever match that? Could you see us, we asked ourselves, attempting love on a bicycle seat?

But then, on the other hand, we had available to us what American youths perhaps did not have: the paid hospitality of the *case di tolleranza,* houses of tolerance, an elegant metaphor for cathouses, or bordellos. Or *case chiuse,* closed houses, so named not because of their inaccessibility—their doors being open sixteen hours a day—but because, by law, their windows' shutters had to be chained closed, so that the sins within could not seep outside.

There were several in Rome, known by their addresses. If you said to a friend "See you at Via Mario de' Fiori," there was no need, once the time was set, for further explanation. These houses were licensed and run under the medical supervision of the state and were of varying degrees of quality and cost. Going to a bordello was a boy's rite of passage; on his eighteenth birthday—the minimum age of admission, but frequently the admitting *maîtresse* closed one eye, or two— friends offered him a paid visit to a *casa chiusa.* It was there that men went to ogle parades of scantily clad ladies, of a range of age and pulchritude, and spend their hormonal ardor when it was banned by their girlfriends or spouses. In those days of confused sexual ethics, a trip to a bordello was considered an acceptable glandular safety valve, in order to preserve a wife to be's virginity. Because, especially in the Italian south, if the future groom obtained the favors of the bride to be before the wedding, she was automatically disqualified because she was a virgin no more.

But now most of the *case chiuse* were closed for real to all civilians, left open primarily for the Germans, and a few for the Italian military.

But I did not care, one way or the other.

I was a monk, and I had my girlfriend.

And I was in love.

8

Maresa

ALL THE MANY TIMES I HAD BEEN in love before were only crude rehearsals. This time, in the midst of the chaos, I felt as though my whole persona had been shelved, set aside, its existence devoted only to nurturing my love. Day and night—especially at night—my thoughts and my dreams were filled with my love. It was with me at school, with me when I walked, or swam, or studied; with me as I made pickups and deliveries, or in the darkness of an air-raid shelter. I spent hours making up preposterous scenarios, of which I was author, producer, and actor, but above all spectator: my love was always the protagonist, at center stage, inspiration and engine of the drama. My love had a life of its own; it skyrocketed me to dizzying heights of happiness and plunged me to the lowest levels of self-pity. With equal eagerness I nursed the happiness and fed the self-pity. When you can savor ecstasy and despair equally, I knew with the certainty of my seventeen years, that is love.

Shakespeare, Dante, Boccaccio, Virgil, Petrarca, Browning . . . anybody who had ever sung, written, or spoken about love should have consulted me. They did not know what they were talking about, they did not know what love is.

But then they did not know Maresa. Maria Teresa Boni.

In a way, she had always been part of the extended family of our brotherhood of the fountain. Like me, most of the boys had sisters, but two of the neighborhood families had only girls, and Maresa's was one of them. As we approached adolescence, the girls had their own autonomous circle, but sometimes, particularly when some special activity took place, the circles linked (our families dictated the nonsegregation of girls). Now a birthday, now a picnic, now an outing to the beach; even, sometimes, a dance.

So Maresa had always been one of us, but now, suddenly, I realized how different she was, besides not having a brother, from all the others.

She was a beauty, much more beautiful, and recognized as such, than anybody else. Her coal black hair framed a perfectly shaped face in which two dark, almond eyes sparkled. Her mouth was delicately shaped but readily stretched by a smile, her lips full and framed by dimples; the flash of her smile competed with and underlined the brilliance of her eyes. She was tall, and her stately posture emphasized the shape of her breasts; her walk was light and elegant, like that of a dancer. She was an A-student, an accomplished piano player, a diligent churchgoer. A paragon of excellence.

What surprised me was that such perfection was accompanied by a natural modesty, for Maresa was not the least bit conceited. And it surprised me even more that she did not have—by the time she was a mature sixteen—a full contingent of suitors. Perhaps her whole countenance suggested such a chaste, pure, unmatchable personality that most young men were put off, convinced of rejection even before trying. Perhaps an even greater deterrent to amorous approach was the fact that her family watched over her like the Pope over the Vatican treasures. Her mother and father had set up for her a strict curfew. If she was not home by the designated hour—to the minute—mother, or father, would come out of their house and wait for her on the sidewalk. Being as honorable as she was, Maresa would soon appear at the bend of the street, at which point she would be told to hurry up. If she was delayed for more than five minutes, a search party was on. Her older sister, her mother, or worst of all, her father would roam the neighborhood looking for her.

At that time Italy had pretty tight social rules, "laws of honor," especially for relations between the sexes, but that kind of behavior was extreme, a throwback, despite recent national attempts at more progressive thinking, to the times of the Crusades and of chastity belts. What's more, Maresa was rarely alone. She was practically inseparable from Velia, a next-door neighbor and a particularly disagreeable, know-it-all girl; she had taken it upon herself to act more as Maresa's perennial chaperone than as her companion. I began to think of them as M & V, interlocked like a monogram.

What prompted me to attempt an assault on that fortress is not too clear in my mind now. I know that, when it came to girls, my three years in long pants had not much improved my self-esteem. On a scale of zero to ten, it would have registered a three at best. It did not help that once, during a get-together with aunts and uncles, when the families' children's behavior and development were being evaluated, I had heard my mother say of me: "At school he is a mess, and he is not much to look at either." Then, after a long pause, in search of something alleviating, "But he has a nice body." I was swimming a lot then on the junior regional team, hoping to drown all my other shortcomings.

Perhaps it was on a dare. I think that it was Sergio—to whom I had confessed my admiration for Maresa's virtues and my curiosity about her maidenhood—who mumbled what a shame it would be if some outsider came and snatched Maresa away. One of us should propose to her, to save the integrity of the group. Perhaps, he said as a throwaway, I should be the one. What did I have to lose? Already too taken by Maresa to see the trap—Sergio as a laughing Nero, feeding a poor Christian to the Bonis' lions—I took the challenge.

An opening came a few days later. During a festive reunion of boys and girls at Velia's house, the conversation fell on school and anthropology and, by Maresa's admission, what a fascinating subject it was.

This was my chance to show off. The Lateran Museum, I mentioned casually, had the best anthropological collection in Rome—perhaps in all of Italy. If she wanted to see it, I knew it well enough to be her guide. I tried to be as nonchalant as I could—make this a take-it-or-leave-it kind of proposition—but I am sure that anybody in my vicinity heard the pounding of my heart.

And so it happened, incredibly enough, that we—Maresa, Velia, and I—saw the dugout canoes of Fiji, the straw skirts and ritual coconut masks of Pago Pago. The experience inspired me to save Maresa from the shark-infested waters of the South Pacific, nurse her on a deserted island on a diet of coconut milk and crab legs. (Somehow, in my dreams, I had let the sharks dispose of Velia.) Other cultural-intellectual outings followed, enough for Maresa's mother to check the dossier she had put together on me, to suspect my intentions. If she happened to answer my telephone calls, at first she denied Maresa's presence; then, on subsequent calls she asked me aggressively, "*Ma che vuoi? Ma che cerchi?* What do you want? What are you after?" Then finally she told me curtly to stop bothering Maresa. She was the one who invented the devil. My feelings were absolutely and purely platonic, even Maresa could see that. And when I told her of her mother policing my calls, Maresa was upset and offended. Her family should have trusted her judgment, she was not a baby anymore. So, in a way, Signora Boni became my accomplice; I believe that, more than for sincere interest in my company, Maresa accepted it to spite her mother.

Our trio's innocent excursions took on a clandestine tinge. For instance, when we went to the movies, a much forbidden and risky affair, we had to choose theaters at the other end of town. Unashamedly, to have an ally in my assault on the fort, I asked Velia, the excellent linguist, to tutor me in French. As subtly as one can in a poorly digested foreign language, I spoke of "*l'amour*" as different from "*l'amitié*" and finally managed "*Je suis tombe fou de Marese.*" Velia consoled me, somehow feeling romantically involved in my "*mal d'amour,*" and relented a bit in her watchdogging of Maresa. Wartime daily events slowed down my intentions, but finally, skipping the intermediary, I confessed my feelings to Maresa herself. We began to go out together alone, dodging Velia, and the covert nature of our meetings told me that Maresa liked me. We made appointments to meet in some far spot in the old part of Rome; I would be there way ahead of time, agonizingly waiting for her, finally feeling her coming even before she was in sight.

I held her hand; she let me. We walked all the ruins, and I was emperor and slave. We went to orchards at the outskirts of the city to purchase a few greens—with luck a few pieces of fruit—and food never tasted more like ambrosia. I confessed my love again, and I kissed her. She let me. I grew wings and floated above the earth. I wrote poems to her. To be honest, I plagiarized them from obscure, antique books I found around the house, shuffling verses. She accepted them. She brought me morsels pilfered from her larder. I kept them as sacred relics. I went to church just to catch sight of her from afar.

I secretly borrowed one of my family's assets. It was an expensive Rolleiflex camera, kept as a bartering treasure in case of need, and I took pictures of Maresa. Smiling portraits of her prone in a meadow, peeking from behind wildflowers. I taught myself to develop and print, and made enlargements of her portraits. She loved them. An uncle of hers, a professional photographer, judged them outstanding and told her so. I loved them too, but wanting to improve my newfound skill, I took many more. Looking back, I see that these were the first steps toward photography becoming my lifelong profession.

We walked in the blacked-out city, when in the abysmal dark of the streets, other people were only shadows with muffled voices, and the only real people were the two of us holding hands. For me, then, the sun was high and the world safe. And in daylight, when with her, I felt privileged and tall, my chest swollen with pride. I was a new person, of much worth, Maresa's elected. I felt the eyes of passersby drinking in her nonpareil beauty, and I was their envy. I asked her, and she cautiously told me that perhaps she loved me too. Perhaps. Just perhaps. The light went out of the sky and clouds boiled over my head. Perhaps? Well, even "perhaps" was enough, it was plenty for me. Or was it? No, I wanted more.

That turned out to be Maresa's weird makeup. She gave you a magic carpet, and once you were soaring to heaven, she yanked the rug out from under and watched you plummet. I began to feel like a living daisy, my heart being plucked bit by bit: she loves me, she loves me not . . .

She loves me. Then, in our embraces, we held each other a little harder, we kissed a bit longer. Posing for another photo, without my prompting, she unbuttoned a couple of buttons of her chaste white blouse. It was easy to see how fast she was becoming a woman, yet my love remained virtuous and pure. When our breathing got heavy, answering the stirring of the blood, I pulled myself away. Not even in my dreams did I allow myself to violate her purity, and if the devil seduced me to think of her flesh, I chastised myself as unworthy and profane.

She loves me not. Then I would soothe my despair by looking at her looking at me, smiling and pitiless, from her portraits all around my room. She told me that her feelings for me were unchanged, only she felt unsure that they could ever match the intensity of mine. She needed time. "Time will tell," she said, and I hated her. Time will tell, and I suspected that her need for time coincided with the appearance in the neighborhood of some tall, handsome idiot. She told me I was jealous, I called her a tease. She loves me, she loves me not. "You're a tease." "You're jealous." And when at practice I swam underwater, I held my breath till my lungs felt like they would burst, wanting to die.

I had indeed seen her, on the downtown Number 6 trolley that took us to school, chatting with such a fellow. He was tall, with almost Nordic features, his hair short, honey red, and curly. We knew him to be a university student, hence a few years older than us, supposedly the son of a retired army general. He was aloof, silent, and expressionless, like the fashion plates in magazines. We had named him Vladimir *il bello*—an extra in a Russian movie, playing a cute, fatuous noble—for his above-you-all pomposity. We disliked him immediately for, among other reasons, his overcoat, made of rich, perfectly styled camel hair. New. He wore it with its belt tight around his waist, its collar partially turned up—the man of the world. We resented his flaunting that supercoat in front of us, who to keep warm on chilly days had to put newspaper pages under our threadbare jackets. We thought he was too stupid to know that he was flirting with danger. People had been robbed and beaten for much less than a new camel-hair coat. And as if he were indeed an extra in a cast of thousands, we would see him periodically disappear and reappear waiting for the trolley, without knowing where he had gone or from where he had come.

Yes, we all saw Maresa chatting with Vladimir. More than once.

"What did you talk about?"

"With whom?"

"Vladimir."

"That's not his name. You're jealous."

"You're a tease. And a flirt."

She loves me not.

My friends, Sergio, Tullio, Fausto, and all the others worried about me. And about themselves. My changing moods, my moments of depression followed by foolish highs, and then again my wandering around in a noncaring stupor, scared them. We kept doing our "errands," and they were afraid that I had not been as careful as I once was and should be again.

"It's not a game. It was never a game," Tullio yelled at me. Tullio was four days older than me, but tall and powerfully built. My father had mentioned once that Tullio could have posed for a Greek-Roman statue of an athlete, and indeed he went on to win two Olympic medals. Tullio had a gentle, smiling disposition, but if provoked, he could be dangerous and you'd better listen to what he told you.

"One stupid move," he continued with irate concern, "and we're all in *un mare di merda*."

"And so are our families," added Fausto loudly, red in the face, his spittle reaching my face.

We would all be in a sea of shit. Their rebuke sobered me, at least for a time.

To understand, to be told what was happening to me, I went to have a talk with my longtime next-door friend, La Paloma. A couple of years older than me, hence supposedly wiser, she knew all there was to know about life and love, its ups and downs, about Sacred Love and Profane Love, and what a crock it all was. A generous girl of very generous proportions, she spent time talking to me, telling me I was not unique in my pain. Shakespeare, Dante, Boccaccio, Virgil, Petrarca, Browning, they all had been there, they would have told me so. And I was not worthless. I was worth, she said emphatically, ten Maresas and a hundred Vladimirs. And, after all, she said, I *was* something to look at and I had a nice body. I felt somewhat better, and she, not to waste the opportunity, led me into some Profane Love. In any situation of life, she considered that activity a comforting therapy. She was a thorough and dedicated nurse. I was easily sold on her medicine. And it was so much better than "take two aspirins."

We did not see Vladimir around for about three months; nobody knew what had happened to him or where he had gone. But then again, the old Number 6 trolley had been bombed, put out of commission with other trolleys in the general depot. No victims. Our trolley stop became deserted, and we all had to walk wherever we needed to go. Maresa had lost, together with old, rusty Number 6, her Vladimir.

Again, she and I walked together on the unsettled cobblestones of the streets.

She loves me?

9

Roma, Open City

ROME—IN DEFERENCE TO VATI-can City, the capital of world Catholicism, and for its universal artistic and historic value—was officially declared an open city, to be kept safe from the offenses of war, a protected haven for all inside its walls. It was in reality a city under siege. German and Fascist troops freely roamed the city—armed—with the official explanation that they were on rest and recreation leave. Since nobody had specified where "Eternal Rome" began or where it ended, military headquarters, barracks, and depots were left where they were or moved just outside the historic center of the city. By the same token, these same areas remained fair game to the Allied Air Force.

Food was so scarce that anything remotely edible was devoured or bartered. My mother had become, like all home cooks, a magician. While fresh shelled peas or fava beans made sumptuous entrées, their shells and stems—soaked, chopped, minced, mixed with potato peels—made incredible soups.

Added bulk and flavor was coaxed out of dandelion greens and other edible (what wasn't?) weeds plucked from gardens or empty lots. As a praise to her ingenuity, my father suggested that she should wear, instead of an apron, a long blue cape and carry a silver wand. It was thin humor, but humor is also sustaining.

Foods once fed to pets were now gourmet items. But then so were the precious beasts themselves. The grounds of the Forum and the Pantheon, for centuries the exclusive preserves of fat feral cats, were now deserted and meow-less. Whoever still had pets, out of either love or selfishness, kept them under lock and key. Rabbits and chickens, against all public health rules, became common urban livestock, kept in unclean, makeshift hutches around the house or on terraces and balconies. My sister, Anna, took it upon herself to tend to a couple of white hens; they did produce a few eggs, plus a lot of stink on the balcony just outside my bedroom and considerable misery to her—she had grown attached to them—when their moment of doom arrived.

With reservoirs, aqueducts, and water mains bombed out, water was rationed to a trickle on one certain or, more likely, uncertain day of the week, and only for a few hours. As a reserve against dire emergencies, when even that trickle would vanish, we filled all sorts of available containers, including washbasins and bathtubs. The daily need for water was partially met by filling demijohns and bottles at assigned public fountains. The waiting lines stretched for city blocks and, beginning at dawn, lasted for hours, and all that idle time was put to advantage in catching up on gossip or, more frequently, in picking fights right and left to vent people's mounting frustrations. Cooking gas had gone the way of the water, and whatever food was available was cooked on makeshift stoves fueled by scavenged wood. At night, the once beautiful Roman parks and gardens were alive with park bench demolishers and improvised lumberjacks destroying centuries-old chestnut trees.

Electricity was a metaphor for some sort of ectoplasm that seeped through the wires a few hours a week and tickled a lightbulb to anemic incandescence. It was used mostly to fire up the radio to listen to a lot of static interspersed by reports beamed from Radio London. They were our only news— besides the official propaganda—of the rest of the world. Light was supplied, in theory, by candles; but these were of such poor quality that, in their effort to fight darkness, they simply melted away in a flicker or two. More light was shed by portable acetylene lamps of the type used by miners, but the real items soon disappeared from the market. They were replaced by homemade contraptions constructed out of a couple of tin cans. The bottom can contained a few chunks of calcium carbide, the top one drip-dripped over it a few drops of water at a time, provoking a chemical reaction that produced acetylene gas. The gas hissed out of a tiny hole in the top of the apparatus and, when ignited, either produced the sought-after light or blew up the whole works, frequently maiming people. When operative, both candles and acetylene lamps produced a lot of sooty smoke. If we attempted to read at night, our nostrils became caked with smelly lampblack, and our eyes were soon irritated and red. That condition was our proof, when asking the leniency of a stern teacher the next day, that we had made a valiant effort to study.

As for clothing, tailors and mothers were achieving miracles of creativity in keeping modesty in and cold out. Clothes were passed on and on and turned inside out so many times that the real side of the fabric, let alone its color or texture, was long forgotten. When a shirt collar had exhausted its last thread, a common trick was to cut a rectangle of cloth from the shirt's back and with it reconstruct an original-looking collar; the missing piece in the back was then replaced with one stolen from a bedsheet. When this subterfuge became common, fashion took over: it became not only elegant but patriotic to sport a collar made of a totally different fabric, taken from another shirt too dead to be resurrected.

Italian ingenuity, brilliant in so many instances, ran amok in creating a synthetic fabric called Lanital (Italianwool), made from, of all things, milk casein. It was supposed to be a propaganda victory, a demonstration to the world that we could thumb our noses at English tweed and other imported fabrics. It was a real Pyrrhic victory; Lanital, besides having a ridiculously short life, when wet, released a nauseating stench of overfermented cheese and untended goat stables. When it rained hard, many people kept away from public transportation, preferring pneumonia to asphyxiation by cumulative Lanital exhalations. But walking was a sorry alternative, because in the rain the cardboard soles of our shoes would dissolve. Real leather went, in theory, for soldiers' boots; civilians had to use a leatherlike alternative made of compressed cardboard. The dedication of cobblers who had many times repapered our shoes could do nothing against the sudden torrential cloudbursts of Rome.

It took less than three years for our once comfortable, civilized lives to reach this point, and the end was not in sight. But it had been a slow and constant degradation, so we all got accustomed to (or should I say not surprised by?) any new hardship, and besides constantly griping, we made do and survived.

Actually, we did just that with a long list of "surrogates," improbable imitations of the once-imported real articles. Coffee, chocolate, butter, rubber, leather, wheat were only part of the long list of surrogates, strange concoctions that of the real articles had only the name.

Our daily lives were thus made up of trade-offs between dicey alternatives. Public transportation came to be known as "Roman roulette." Buses, the ones that had survived air raids, enjoyed a precarious longevity through ingenious transplants; they had been converted from diesel to *gassogeno,* a gas produced by wood burning. Welded onto the buses' backs were huge wood-burning, stovelike affairs that supplied the power. Somehow the vehicles wheezed along, with the conductors getting off every once in a while to restoke the fire. Frequently, when face-to-face with one of the many hills of Rome, a bus would just give up and faint away. Passengers were then asked to disembark and push. In warm weather, the request was seldom honored: it was quicker to walk to one's destination. But in cold weather, many passengers obliged and put shoulder to the stove. Civic action was rewarded by temporary warmth.

Electric trolley cars were even chancier. Nobody knew when electric power would come or go, and one could be stranded for hours. Sometimes forever. During power failures, gangs of pirates disguised as repairmen would steal lengths of the aerial copper wire and thus disable the whole works. On the black market, copper was worth its weight in gold—or enough, anyway, for the thieves to risk electrocution.

Apart from one's own feet, the most reliable means of transportation, and beast of burden, was the bicycle. Entire households were moved on it. But here too attrition by use had eliminated any bona fide tires, and the only ones available on the black market were made with surrogate rubber, some kind of fabric impregnated with tar and sand. The tires covered inner tubes so overpatched that they had, literally, patches on patches, and the combinations expired frequently, usually giving up their last breath with a bang. Whereupon a grown man would simply sit on the curb near the dead, useless vehicle and cry.

But subsistence depended on our bikes, so the next solution was to replace tire and tube with a length of garden hose filled with sawdust, wrapped around the wheel's rim and fed into itself. The ride was bumpy, as if one were going constantly over badly laid cobblestones, but it took you there. Only during daylight hours, however. Nobody would chance such a ride in the extreme darkness of the blackout. Blackouts had been enforced since the declaration of war. All homes, public offices, and shops had to make sure that from dusk to dawn no light could be seen from their windows or doors. Black curtains saw to it. Only one in three or four streetlights was left on, their regular bulbs replaced with blue bulbs of such low wattage that their light rarely reached the pavement. So there they were, suspended in the dark like interrupted lines of faint stars; travelers found their way following the glowing points, as in celestial navigation. Or by memory. Vehicles' headlights were painted black, leaving clear only a strip of one by three inches. That made them totally inadequate for driving at night, but sufficient to alert pedestrians that something was getting close and they'd better jump out of the way.

These expediencies and aggravations of daily life were overshadowed by something more debasing than all of them put together: fear. At any moment, day or night, the air-raid sirens reminded us, especially with the war getting closer, that we could go up in smoke or be buried under the rubble of our homes, or schools, or churches. We trained ourselves to go to bed dressed, or with our clothes perfectly lined up and ready to put on in the dark in seconds, so that we could be down in the nearest cellar or air-raid shelter even before the alarm sirens had stopped wailing. In 1944, on a January night, it was cold and damp in the cellar, but the constant rumble of the guns of Anzio's beachhead told us of the horror of the war, and how many people were worse off than we were. The "Liberators" were no more than thirty miles away. In Rome, the Germans and Fascists no longer attempted to carry on with the open city charade. They declared martial law. At any time, for any reason, they could stop any able-bodied people on the street and whisk them away. Even standing in line for water or outside a shop to fetch some rationed item could be dangerous, so waiting in line had become the duty of young children and disabled people.

Our daily ration of bread was down to fifty grams. Barely two ounces of a black, claylike substance that of wheat had only the chaff, and of bread only the name. If that was the answer to our prayer "Give us our daily bread," then a vengeful God was listening and punishing us for our sins. Once or, with luck, twice a week I was assigned the task of retrieving one or two small loaves of bread from Uncle Giorgio, my mother's brother. He was a jovial, rotund man who had worked his way up the bureaucratic ladder to become purchasing director for the Ministry of Internal Affairs, a position that made him a lot of friends among the suppliers of goods of all kinds. I liked him a lot: he was always full of practical jokes, and when I was little he always had special presents for me. My father liked him too—it was hard not to—but I heard him say that Uncle Giorgio had accumulated more wealth than a civil servant should have. But he did not judge him too harshly, my father told me. Giorgio was doing what anybody in his position would have done, what every-body in government was openly doing anyway; not only stealing but flaunting it too. My father must have felt a deep resentment on moral grounds. Once my mother remarked what a good provider her brother Giorgio was. For the first time—and the last—I heard my father yell at her. "So I'm not a good provider," he shouted, "but I'm not a thief either!" He then walked out in a fury, slamming the door.

True, Uncle Giorgio's household lacked for nothing, but he was a generous man; moreover, he had kept the food coupons of his son, my older cousin, who was fighting on the Russian front, and also the ones of my aunt's aged father, whose munching capabilities and old stomach were no match for our daily bread. Hence the good news of the alimentary surplus. The bad news was that his house was located smack in the center of town, some four miles from ours. But I did not mind the mission; I loved to walk, and my walk took me along the Borghese Gardens and through some of the most beautiful parts of the old city. The long walk gave me a chance to think, to indulge in my fantasies, to make up stories for myself, fight all my dragons, chase away all my demons. It was part catharsis, part elation.

The mood was different when we sat at the table. Even if dinner had become mostly a metaphor, my parents enforced the old ritual of the family being together for the evening meal. I will never forget the efforts of my mother, trying to be cheerful and making a big thing of her meager offerings. But even worse was the plight of my father. His pride was wounded by having to accept the alms of a piece of bread, and a not too honest one at that, and also by having to divide these few miserable crumbs equally among us. Indeed, bread has a sacred value in Italy, but when my father was dividing that bread, it was not the body of Christ he was breaking apart, it was his own. And it hurt him. I know because I saw the shining of tears in his eyes.

In the spring of 1942, for speaking up in defense of a Jewish colleague, my father had been expelled from the party and lost his job. Since then he had struggled, doing temporary jobs, or consulting, freelancing, and for a brief time, working with the Jewish architect, who had also lost his job, constructing exact models of famous landmarks, such as Michelangelo's Campidoglio. This, their first and last creation, took the space of a good-size room and was perfect to the last detail, equestrian statue of Marcus Aurelius included. They were hoping to exhibit it for a fee, but it was the wrong time. It was impossible to transport that masterpiece to other cities, and in Rome people could admire the real thing for free. Our family financial situation was severely curtailed.

Knowing that many other families were in the same boat was not a palliative for rumbling stomachs. Perhaps it was this humiliating feeling of inadequacy that made my father decide on our sortie, originally envisioned as a one-man breaking of the siege. He had a distant cousin, a retired army general turned farmer, in Avezzano, in the heart of Abruzzi. This area, once a swampy lake, had been reclaimed and turned into fertile farmland. My father's plan was daring but simple: get on a bike, go there, scrounge as much food as possible, and bring it home to feed the family. But his plan presented several hurdles: (1) there was no way to find out if the old cousin had anything to spare (was he still alive?). (2) Avezzano was about 65 miles east of Rome, on the other side of the Apennine mountains. (3) The condition of his bike was deplorable. (4) It was winter. And (5) the real Olympic-size hurdle: my mother.

No, she said. Never. A serious form of insanity had invaded him, she said. He would never make it, he would be killed.

But he remained adamant. It was, after all, a matter of reestablishing his self-esteem.

That evening they retired to their bedroom, and we could hear animated whisperings, muffled sniffling, pleadings, and mumblings for most of the night. In the morning, a decision had been reached. He would go. But accompanied by me, as a general assistant, mechanic, companion, and accomplice. Don Quixote and an emaciated Sancho Panza, tilting at windmills.

The preparations were swift. Check the bikes. There were two in the household besides mine, and we cannibalized one to make the others as mission-worthy as possible. Clothing: all the warmest we could wear, including newspapers to wrap inside our pants and under our jackets. And that was all. I suggested I carry a Beretta (I had put it together from several unserviceable ones) against bad encounters but then decided against it. If found unarmed, by whoever decided to stop us, we stood a chance of getting away with our skins; if armed, that chance was nonexistent.

We left just before dawn, sneaking out of town an hour before the lifting of the curfew. We pedaled in earnest, without much talk, setting a pace we hoped we could maintain. The going was smooth enough for the first fifteen miles, then we hit the uphill to Tivoli, in the Apennine foothills. We had been this way before, but in peacetime; we did not know, now, what we would find around the next corner. Inexplicably—since the fighting war had not yet passed by here—we saw farmhouses bombed out, a church with its bell tower in ruins. Once in a while, packed-earth paths replaced stretches of missing road.

When the grade became too steep, we walked our bikes, taking breaks once in a while, but brief ones: it was essential to get to Avezzano before nightfall. That goal, I began to realize, as the road kept climbing, had been set by wishful thinking. But my father was determined in his plan, and I admired him greatly. An old man of fifty-two, he was the one to prod me on. The changing vista of mountain peaks and deep ravines, gentle valleys and pastures, all mottled by the shadows of passing clouds, was incredibly beautiful, but we had neither the time nor the inclination to stop to admire it.

It was well into the afternoon, just when we were beginning to despair, that we reached the crest. From now on it was all downhill . . .

We made it to Avezzano late in the night, much, much later than we had hoped. But we had arrived, and safely. Father found his cousin alive and, considering the time of night, in reasonably good spirits. Ario was cordial, though he did not know quite what to make of our surprise visit. But essentials first: considering the condition we were in, what we needed was a bowl of hot soup, a generous glass of red wine, and sleep.

I woke up past noon the next day on a makeshift cot in a toolshed. By the empty cot near mine, I saw that my father was up; indeed, he and Ario had already exchanged all the family news, the good and the bad. Among the latter was the condition of Ario's farm, once a model farm, now in pitiful shape because of an almost complete lack of manpower. With the few helpers left either too old or too inexperienced to be of use, the farm's production had been embarrassingly poor. Moreover, its meager storehouses had been raided by both the Germans and roaming Italian "deserters." In Ario's old army mind, any soldier who chucked his uniform was a deserter; it did not matter to him that these men were still fighting, now as partisans against the Germans. He and his wife were left with barely enough to survive. This litany of woe was not promising. It was obviously leading to the impossibility of giving us help. His wife made us feel, perhaps without malice, that the dinner of unsalted boiled potatoes she offered us was quite an unplanned strain on her pantry. Ario suggested that a nearby farmer could provide us with something; he owed Ario a favor, and if there was something to be bought, and we introduced ourselves as Ario's relatives, we might not be charged black-market prices. We rested at Ario's farm the next day and fed on potatoes. Out of compassion, a scrawny boiled chicken was produced for dinner. That was a real feast.

Again we left before sunup. We stopped at the farm that Ario had suggested, and after some quibbling we left with two sacks of dried red kidney beans. If the farmer's scales were correct, he had sold us a hundred kilos of beans, but once I managed to strap a sack on the back of my bike, fifty kilos felt more like fifty tons. Wobbling wildly, we got on the road. By early evening, we had reached the crest again, mostly by walking and pushing uphill the creaking, overloaded machines. It being too late and too dangerous to continue, we cajoled a farmer into giving us asylum for the night—and a miraculous glass of goat's milk. He let us stay near the glowing embers of the hearth, but I know my father did not sleep much. He was either too tired or too worried. After all, two bicycles and two sacks of beans were a treasure to watch over.

When we got up the next morning, a thin dusting of snow had fallen. The farmer's wife said that they had expected much, much more than that at this time of year. She gave us another warm glass of goat's milk, and a Godspeed slice of bread and one of cheese, refusing any compensation. The world looked clean. The tops of the mountains were white against a crisp blue sky; the air was fresh and invigorating. Home was down there somewhere, at the end of a long but, blessedly, mostly downhill road. Only a partial blessing, this: often enough, faced with a particularly precipitous incline, we'd had to dismount and walk. With the weight of the load, the brake pads of our bikes—surrogate stuff, naturally—could not take it; they just heated up and melted away. My father commented that Mr. Isaac Newton should have eaten his apple and gotten on a bike. He would have found out soon enough about gravity: uphill or downhill, it is always against you. It had been many miles since my father had had a try at humor; things must have been good. He proclaimed also, *"Ah, qui ci facciamo una bella pisciatina!"* He was only suggesting that we, here and now, take a good piss. There was a celebratory tone in his voice, as if it behooved us to bless this land, leave our mark on this turf.

We propped our bikes one against the other and, to gain a better view, walked fifty or so paces onto the pristine white field. And the view was magnificent. But then, at the same time, we noticed affixed on a stick a crudely stenciled notice, like the keep-out signs made by farmers. This one said MINEN!

In any language, a land-mine field is scary enough, but in

163

German it had a peremptory, terrifying taste. We looked at each other without words, petrified, rooted to the spot. My mouth went dry, my mind both blank and crowded with a million horrible images. My every muscle became stiff and every joint locked. The simple act of turning my head became a painful effort. I was obeying my father's gesture, a silent, urgent order: Look back! See!

The dusting of snow, which had seemed merely beautiful at dawn, had saved us. Our feet trodding on our footprints, we tiptoed back to the road, and while we were retracing our steps, I wondered about the workings of the mind, my mind anyway. During those hesitant fifty paces, I thought how easy it was to make your body weightless, and of the old childish game of not stepping on a pavement's cracks. If you did, it meant bad luck. How deadly a game now: wrong step and . . . But, predominant above the gory vision was the question Who would get the beans?

We got the beans; they made it home by dark.

For dinner, Mother put a few cups of the treasured beans into a pot of water. Most of them floated to the surface, a most direct message that they were empty inside. Scooped out by worms and now their cozy dwellings. It took a mother's heroic—or desperate—optimism to rejoice.

"Dinner special!" she exclaimed. "Beans! And with extra protein!"

And they were good too. Excellent.

10

Otto

THE RECOUNTING TO MY FRIENDS of that bicycle run and related adventures gave me a hero's status. I was exposed also to a lot of teasing and ad hoc nicknames. They called me Bottecchia, after a bicycle racer of the twenties who, during the Tour de France, they told me, went up the Pyrenees with a hot-water bottle strapped on his head, overcoming the cold and winning the race. I told them to be careful and treat me with respect: my portion of wormy beans, I warned them, could do considerable harm, I could poison-gas them all.

Near our dried-out fountain, we kept exchanging childish quips and crude jokes, as if we had not grown any since grade school. But in the next moment we speculated like adult men about philosophy and politics.

With our ages ranging from seventeen to twenty, we filled the bill of *vitelloni*: too old to be calves, too immature to be bulls. Or we just followed the old human tendency: when faced by harsh, incomprehensible events, one retreats to child-hood. We did not want to admit this to each other, but we felt like straws with no control of where the wind would take us, wondering what was in store for us in the future, if there was a future to be had.

What took us out of that torpor, one day, was an unexpected apparition.

That was the time when, for unknown reasons, friends, acquaintances, or people vaguely known disappeared and were never seen again. Some were Jewish, some had to relocate because their houses had been bombed. Many had just packed up and left the tormented city, seeking safety—and possibly food—in some remote village.

People *left* Rome. Very few—if any—*came to* Rome.

But there he was, brand-new. He made an entrance among our group at the fountain as incongruous as his appearance: compact and blond, well clothed and, above all, well fed.

"I am Otto Bellini-Weber," he announced, taking one hand off the handlebar of his bike and giving a mixture of Roman-Fascist and Nazi salutes. In times past, people invited to approach our turf would get a welcoming sprinkling from the fountain or, if not invited, a serious soaking. Now, either way, our fountain was useless. Otto got only gaping stares.

We figured out that he had almost everything. He had a hyphenated name, which none of us had. He had a racing bicycle with gears and real rubber tires and handlebars bent like the wings of Stukas. He had boots of real leather, Wehrmacht issue, and a black leather jacket, pure Luftwaffe. He had a German father and an Italian mother, or vice versa. It was unclear, since the roles seemed to switch with his telling.

He had a gift for languages, enough to put to shame our

poorly learned smatterings of French or English. His Italian was good, but he spoke it with a foreign cadence, like a child brought up in a multilingual home. Sometimes his constructions became ponderous and officious, and he spoke at length of weighty subjects. Only later, discussing his pontifications among ourselves, did we realize that he had said nothing at all.

That healthy complexion, those clothes, those boots, that bike . . . He knew he had our attention and proceeded to tell us that he had just moved with his family into an apartment a few blocks away.

"I am enrolled in the junior year of your local lyceum. Is any of you, also?"

Some were, some not.

"Do you play soccer?"

Ask a stupid question. Our team was the best.

"On which field?"

Field? Did he say field? Here, in the street. He was standing on the goal line, between the fountain and the pile of our schoolbags under the mimosa tree.

"I am a good goalie," he boasted. "When do you play?"

Where was this guy coming from? The moon? These days we played when we had the inclination and the strength, and then only if someone could produce a bunch of rags that could be bundled, tied up, and turned into a surrogate ball.

He was in possession of a regulation, real leather *Fussball*.

Carlo and Mauro faked a few kicks at an imaginary ball. Otto abandoned the bicycle and took the goalie position, slapping his gloved hands on his knees. Black leather, lambskin-lined gloves. Luftwaffe, like the jacket.

"Shoot! Shoot! Watch this catch!" he yelled, catching the imaginary ball. Well, at least he had some sense of humor.

It was then that we first saw the scar. It was smooth and shiny, ascending diagonally from his left knee. We could see only the beginning of this magnificent scar, but, rolling up his lederhosen as far as they could go, he proudly showed us the rest. The scar went to the top of his thigh and there disappeared into thick blond hair, like a river into a forest. How he had acquired such a wonder never became clear, since he gave several explanations for it, all astounding. When he showed us its full magnificence, we were impressed. He assured us he had more, not as heroic, but scars just the same. Come summer, he would show us. We all had our share of accidents and mishaps (magnets for accidents, our parents called us) but had come through them scarless. Otto was scar-prone; he collected scars.

Where did he get the big one?

"Air raid, in France."

Believable enough. By his account, his father was a civil servant working at the German embassy—now a translator, because of his encyclopedic knowledge of languages, now a cryptographer, now an attaché—and for years had been moved from one German embassy to another. The family had followed him; besides France, Otto had lived in Poland, Hungary, Holland. As proof, he translated a few basic dirty words into several languages. Considering all the war-torn countries where he had been, his wounds were not that improbable.

But then he claimed that he was not the bombarded, as we thought, but the bombardier. His Messerschmitt had been shot down, knocked out of the sky, and he had parachuted.

We all had heard, even told ourselves, tall tales about fantastic adventures, but this one was so tall as to be stratospheric.

Most of us had problems in choosing our personas, wearing or shedding them with the moods, or the needs, of the day. The reassuring strength we drew from the group was that if any one of us slipped into playing a part for real, the others would bring him back to reality with whistles, boos, rude noises, and unmerciful teasing. But when we booed Otto, he was sincerely offended, almost to tears, at our incredulity. It did not take us long to realize that he believed his own stories. An Italo-German, or German-Italo, Walter Mitty. Could we have given him a wrong signal about our political feelings? And who was he, really?

"You must be from the moon," Sergio commented, then picked up his schoolbag and left the assembly. The bag contained five hand grenades, passed on to him to pass on to somebody else.

As the days went by, Otto became an assiduous presence at the fountain, popping up at the most unexpected times. And his presence made us uneasy. We had never welcomed him but, trying to be prudent, had never frozen him out either. Was he really dumb, or did he want us to believe that he was? He was smart enough to speak several languages, an A student (not many of us were), and yet he always had a story so naïvely fabricated that either he was really dumb or he thought we were all born yesterday.

He also had more, if not more accurate, news of the war. The Allied Anzio beachhead was expanding and shrinking daily, and Otto knew of the advances and retreats before we heard them from the official news. We were expecting to see the Allies break through and leap to Rome; soon the war would be over for us. But Otto said it would take a long time and finally the invaders would be thrown back into the sea; he knew that German reinforcements would be pouring in from the north. Another time he said that, win or lose, the Germans would fight to the last man, unlike us, the Italians. This was another odd thing about Otto, the way he would cast his lot now with the Germans, now with us, the Italians.

It was much easier for us when he declared himself for Germany. We could play our practical jokes on him with less remorse and more gusto. Our jokes were coarse and cruel, but he laughed at them even more than we did. Once, while we distracted him in conversation, Aldo the Long loosened his bicycle's brakes. Otto mounted the machine and, in his customary way, dove zigzagging downhill, roaring like an airplane, and met at the crossroads at the bottom of the hill with the side of a stalled bus. We raced to help him, straightening out his contorted bike and bandaging with our handkerchiefs his many scrapes. He was grateful, and thanked us.

We kept our arguments about fleeing and hiding out in the hills away from Otto's ears, of course, because Otto scared us. He kept saying that the Germans were only beginning to fight, that they were just successfully retrenching. Once the American, British, and Russian armies were lured into a compact space, Hitler would unleash the Final Secret Weapon, and *boom!* Good-bye, Allies!

The Wehrmacht, he said, faring badly? Had they not just paraded Anzio's American prisoners through the streets of Rome?

The bastard had a point there. We had seen strong, well-fed, impeccably uniformed SS units escort through the streets of Rome a line of bedraggled, disheveled Americans, hands on their heads, with the dirt and the stench of war still on their faces.

"Here!" the guards seemed to say with contempt. "Here are your liberators!"

Yes, Otto scared us.

What we wanted was for Otto to disappear and leave us alone. We could have told him off. But we didn't dare. The thought that he could be a spy, checking on us, had surfaced several times. What if his bizarre behavior was just an act to throw us off, what then? No, he was really too dumb to be an informer, and we were fish too small to deserve a spy of our own. And if he was not a spy, might it be an asset to have a German (even if half a one), the son of a quasi-important official, on our side?

How we could take advantage of it, we had not figured out.

While running one of my secret errands, I felt a presence bicycling at my side. Otto!

"*Heil,* comrade!" he yelled at me, slapping me on the back. "Going somewhere?"

"Just for a ride," I told him, startled and hoping he would not ask about the package.

"And you?"

"On patrol duty," he answered, in his usual no-nonsense tone. Ask a stupid question . . .

He tagged along without saying another word. The encounter was just a coincidence, I told myself. To be safe, I took him on a long detour around town before returning home, delivery canceled. The coincidence happened again the next day. And then again. Three times is not a coincidence anymore. If he was checking my comings and goings, he was not too subtle, but he had in effect put me out of business. Sergio and Tullio took over my rounds, more guardedly but unhindered. Otto had selected me as his target, but why? Perhaps he'd decided that I was the weakest link and, through me, he would catch all the others red-handed. Or was I paranoid?

I asked guidance from Carlo, the oldest of our group, who suggested that the only thing to do, at the moment, was play dumb, befriend the guy, and try to find out who he was, what he wanted.

Riding around for no good reason on the cobblestones of Rome on the makeshift tires of my bike (equipped with a flimsy, undetachable third wheel, by rule) was not a thing I considered too entertaining, but I did it as my duty. Once, as a friendly overture, I admired and complimented Otto's bike, equipped with a tiny trailer made with two baby carriage wheels. He insisted I try it, and for a spell we traded mounts. He became almost loquacious. He told me of all the foreign countries he had lived in, of all the friends he had made and lost. So many that he had given up trying to make new ones. I had stayed put in the house where I was born, I told him, and envied him all the places he had seen. If he wished, I would show him some of the sights of my beloved Rome.

If he had a hidden purpose, it did not surface during the next few afternoons. Once back home, I tried to recollect every word I had said to reassure myself that I had not let my guard down, had not given any grounds for suspicion. Once I let him lead our tour, and we ended at our little fountain. Aldo the Long and Fausto were there, but in a minute they excused themselves and were gone. Otto wanted to know about them, about the others. I told him the truth: we'd known each other since we could remember. We had gone to the same nursery school, and then elementary school, and then the same junior high, and now the lyceum. We all had older or younger brothers, some had sisters. Our friends' mothers yelled at us or advised us (sometime were even proud of us) and in general treated each of us as one of their own.

He wanted to know about me and my family. Was my mother also treating my friends that way? Well, she was known to have swatted Gianni a couple of times (if his mother were there, my mother had told him, she would have done the same). Otto then asked if the beautiful girl he had seen with me was somebody's sister—or was she my *"suitart"*? He meant "sweetheart" in English and then, to my puzzlement, translated it literally into Italian: *"dolcecuore."* It sounded funny, anatomical. Of all Maresa's parts, I told him with a chuckle, cupping my hands under imaginary breasts, her heart was not my foremost sweet objective. But yes, she was my girlfriend, I had high hopes of making out sometime. I tried my best imitation of a macho man, blushing a little.

Otto seemed surprised, somewhat disappointed by my answer. He saw clearly through my stupidly faked machismo. Did he have a *"suitart"*? I asked. He changed the subject, talking about school. He loved gym; I liked physics—except for the teacher being a bitch. And who did I have for history and philosophy? That bastard Professor Gesmundo, I told him, and I changed the subject. He did not press the issue, and we found a common interest: airplanes. He confided that his real aspiration was to become, one day, a test pilot. I wanted to become an aeronautical engineer. We both had designed and built model airplanes; we both had won flying competitions. We had heated discussions criticizing those who called our models "toy planes," and us too old to play with them. The idiots, we agreed, did not know that the design of a model was more complex than that of a real plane. A plane needed a pilot to tell it what to do, how to fly, and how to land. A model had to be designed so that automatically it could climb, fly, land, and correct by itself any situation that arose, take advantage of the wind and fly high with the hawks. We had found genuine common ground, and we promised to show each other our creations. Otto invited me to his house the next day, after school. Was his the spider's strategy? Was he spinning a web? The thought crossed my mind, but I accepted his invitation.

Though only three blocks away from our *palazzo,* and of the same vintage and architecture, Otto's building was a step up on the social scale. Ours had a *portiere,* a doorman-janitor; his had a *concierge.*

Otto himself opened the door and asked me to wait a moment in the foyer; he had to announce me to his mother. He returned in a few seconds and gestured to me to follow. He spoke in a low, subdued voice, quite a contrast to his usually assertive tone.

Otto's mother was reclining on the sofa, holding a large book on her lap. She wore a white silk robe with white fur trim, and white, fur-trimmed slippers. One of her legs, in sheer silk stockings, showed to just above her knee; she looked too young to be anybody's mother, blond and perfectly made up. I had seen such an apparition before, in the movies. Marlene

Dietrich. Perhaps Otto's mother had also. To reinforce the similitude, she was smoking a long, thin cigarette with a golden tip; on the coffee table beside her were a notepad and pencil. She looked at me without any particular expression, and I felt like something brought in by Otto the cat.

Then she looked at Otto, and he got the hint. He introduced me, pronouncing clearly my name, family name first, as in the army. I did what I had seen done in the movies. I slightly bowed my head and clicked my heels (as much as cardboard ones could click). She scanned me from toes to head. Otto, like a well-behaved butler, asked her, in Italian, if there was anything he could do for her; she answered with a few soft words in German. He replied in German and led me to his room, asking if I too would like some tea. I shook my head, and he left. Tea? In my house, that had disappeared with the dinosaurs. I tried to imagine my mother, or my friends' mothers, lounging in white silk in the middle of the afternoon, smoking, drinking tea, and reading books. I just couldn't.

The walls of Otto's room were covered with framed photos of his mother, the Blond Goddess, skiing, hiking, picking flowers in a field, wearing an Austrian costume. In some, she and Otto appeared looking adoringly at each other. There were two of her together with a middle-aged version of Otto, slightly shorter than she. Some were of that Otto, obviously his father, in and out of uniform. Where Otto and his father appeared together, they looked like twins except for the age difference. I was so lost in the photographs that I hardly heard him return.

I asked him, and he showed me the photos of his winning model airplanes; then he retrieved from the closet the one he was working on. The structure of the wing, meticulously crafted, was complete, and so was part of the fuselage. He had been working on it in spurts for some time, never finding a good reason or the enthusiasm to finish it. Perhaps now he would, perhaps we could work on it together. He suggested changing the model's name from Pelikan to Pinocchio. That was what only a few relatives called me. How did he know? Paranoia again? But then, given my long, pointy nose, it could have been a coincidence. Again? "Pin-ok-kioh," he proclaimed slowly, and then he held me by the shoulders and mock seriously kissed me stiffly on the cheeks, as a general would after pinning a medal on a soldier.

The whole scene—his sudden burst of friendship, Marlene Dietrich in the other room—made me uncomfortable. Otto smiled. Out of a drawer he produced a small box; inside, wrapped in a cloth, there was an engine for a model airplane—a miniature "internal combustion engine," as he called it—that he had bought in Switzerland. Since I had started building models, years ago, I had always wanted to own one, but I knew that I would never come closer than pictures in foreign flying models magazines. I told him so, and he let me touch and hold the engine. My admiration prompted him to show me more of his prized possessions; his tidy closet contained ski boots and tennis rackets and leather jackets and a military uniform. His father's? I asked, but he informed me that German civilians working abroad had been "militarized" so as to share a soldier's rights and duties, and command the same respect from "the natives." I thought it prudent to ask no more. When we parted, he shook my hand rigidly, the German way, but I thought he held it just a bit too long.

Once back home, I felt disoriented, as if I had intruded on a different world, my feelings for Otto and his family confused. I sat quietly in a corner of the living room, trying to figure things out.

My mother told me to quit staring at her, it was making her uncomfortable, and go do something.

During the next few days, Otto and I became inseparable. Actually, I could not shake him off. A few minutes after I left my house, no matter how surreptitiously I tried to sneak out, there was Otto. Going to school, coming from school, there he would be beside me, parade-ground steps and composure, barrel chest out, chin up, and that annoying habit of his, when walking, of twisting his whole torso to talk to me, as if his muscular neck was too massive to allow the turning of the head. I had to share with Otto my interceptions of Maresa on her evening outing to the dairy store for the family's daily ration. My hint "two is company, three is a crowd" did not register with Otto at all. I was paying a high price for keeping him away from the rest of the group. I had bought myself a new chaperone, a bodyguard, a shadow.

Almost two weeks went by, and I hardly saw any of my friends. When I happened on the fountain, Otto in tow, whoever was there found important things to do elsewhere and disappeared. Finally I was able to talk to Carlo, Sergio, and Tullio. Otto did not have a clue what we were up to, I told them. He was only a pathetic guy in search of friendship, making up stories, trying to be someone whom others would admire and accept, or simply like.

Their reaction was "so what else is new?" and I found them cold and distant. I was puzzled and hurt. Couldn't they see that I was doing what they had told me to do? Why the cold-shoulder treatment? I asked what was up, how things were going. The old, grandmotherly school janitor had told us that Professor Gesmundo had been taken to Via Tasso, all his books and address books confiscated. Did anybody hear if that had implicated us? Had anything abnormal or suspicious transpired? Piero Spagnolo and Peppino Sbrana, two recent volunteers, had vanished. Had they been taken away and jailed? What else had happened? Why was I not told?

Sergio, for an answer, congratulated me on my wrestling prowess and, pursing his lips in a kiss, said, "Darling, say hallo to Otto for us!"

The word had gotten around that a few days earlier, in gym class, Otto had chosen me as his wrestling opponent. Otto had accumulated brownie points with our gym teacher, a multidecorated Fascist Militia hero who had lost a hand on the Greek front; he had been put to pasture teaching phys ed and given the chance to vent his anger by bullying a bunch of schoolboys. I disliked him, and his arrogance, immensely. The dislike, unfortunately, was reciprocal. He liked to brandish his stump in my face and poke me with it, as if challenging me to fight back. The beast knew I could not and would not. Allowing Otto to wrestle me was a further way of humiliating me in front of the class. Otto could have cracked me like a dry twig. But once we were engaged on the carpet, I felt his solid, muscular body go suddenly limp, and he let me get out from under to entwine me again in *a corpo a corpo*. Otto emanated a heady, musky odor, and it took him a long time to pin my shoulders down; he almost made me win, and so obviously that the whole performance had been just as embarrassing as if he had trashed me in two moves.

Word of our "friendship" spread so fast that soon Maresa, chaperoned again by Velia, barely acknowledged my presence when I tried to approach her. Even Velia, our acquiescent accomplice for so long, shook her head at me disapprovingly.

I just had to get free from Otto.

I could see now why he couldn't keep any friends: he was a cannibal. I had faked, at least at the beginning, an acceptance of friendship, and he had swallowed me whole. And I had let him.

I felt some compassion for him, but enough was enough.

When he joined me on my way from school, I told him, in as cold a tone as I could muster, that today I wanted to see my *"suitart"* alone. And tomorrow. And the day after that too.

"If you had not wished for my company," he said stiffly, "you only had to say so." He made a perfect about-face and walked away. I watched him strut down the street, marching gait, chin high.

Somehow I felt really sorry for him.

It was cowardice that inspired me to explain things to Velia, the fear that in talking directly with Maresa I would choose the wrong words and make the situation not only worse but irreparable. I went to Velia's house and made her swear to secrecy, made her feel an accomplice again, this time in a matter of life or death. In my dejection, I said, I preferred to ignore the fact that even hinting at my, our, activities endangered all of us. I painted everything vaguely and in heroic tints. I'd known that rumors were abroad, I told her, that my masculinity had been doubted, but I'd had to take it stoically;

it was all an act to better deceive Otto, the informer. I begged Velia to intercede for me, to tell Maresa the truth. I was courting danger because just thinking of her, every second, gave me the strength . . .

Velia capitulated. She would try. Come Friday afternoon, she said, bring your books and we will have another French lesson. I did, and a miracle came to pass: not only was Maresa there but Velia left the room. "Going for milk," she said. "I'll be back in a while."

Words were hard to come by, and the few spoken were moist with Maresa's tears. We embraced, we kissed. Why did you not tell me? Kiss. Not to put you in danger. Embrace. It will take me time to forgive you. Kiss. Embrace. And the more we kissed the more I felt her body closing on mine, her breathing becoming harder. As if to make up for wasted time, for all the times we had not dared, I was asking and she was inviting me, openly offering her breasts, her body. I had to be an idiot not to see what was going on. She loves me! Oh, God, chaste, virginal Maresa, she loves me. At the realization of what was happening, my ardor, my brain, my whole body went limp. I had brought Maresa to the edge of the precipice— or had she brought me?—but at the last moment I was too wilted to jump.

Did I miss the test, was I really not man enough?

Velia returned to find us red in the face and short of breath, sitting on opposite sides of the room, somewhat disheveled, silently questioning each other.

That evening La Paloma, the Dove, saved me. Her real name was Magda, but we had always called her La Paloma (dove) for the romantic image the name evoked and for the implausibility of it when applied to her. The irony of that nickname, we felt, was the exotic Spanish element, inspired by a popular song about a white dove, whereas she did not have the bird's delicate, fluttering nature but only the tendency, when feeling more romantic than usual, to coo.

She was on the hefty side of fleshy, with long, jet-black hair, her pride and joy. This hairiness surfaced also on her limbs and upper lip, and she tried, with some success, to bleach it away. In summer, when fashion and weather permitted skimpy clothes, the long tufts of hair on her moist armpits were things of marvel and bewilderment for the rest of us. It had been so since adolescence, when we boys, every morning, inspected our bodies in search of another reluctantly sprouted hair. But then, she was a year or two older than we were and, I knew, more than that in experience. Set in a moonish face, her eyes were large, dark, and liquid, by design kept seductively half open, like her heart-shaped mouth. A most disconcerting trait of hers was, while looking with abandon into your eyes, to show the pink, pointed tip of her tongue and slowly moisten her lips. She thought of herself as very sexy and with such conviction that, at least for an innocent time, she convinced us too.

Since in the Roman book of macho etiquette, the Anglo-Saxon rule "gentlemen never tell" translated into "guys broadcast all, and then some," we all knew that Magda felt romantic a good deal of the time. A high school graduate in classics, she now tutored Latin and Greek; rumor had it that, in addition to these dead languages, she had instructed more than one young man in the lively complexities of male-female relations. Her teaching successes were matched proportionately by an

ebullient, contagious good humor expressed in her loud, inspired rendering of romantic songs and arias. She had a clear,
cultivated soprano voice, and the number of trills and flour-
ishes she used was a gauge of her bouts of *ars amatoria*. She
could really belt out a tune.

I wanted her to judge me, to tell me again who I was. I
told her what had happened; that for a brief second the
musky, inebriating smell of Maresa's body had made me think
of Otto's sweaty hold. La Paloma told me I had done the
honorable thing, had not taken advantage of a woman's moment of heat. There was nothing wrong with my machinery.
It happens, she said.

And to reassure me—and herself—of the correctness of
her evaluation, she proved to me that I was still man enough.
I passed the test, noisily, violently, and to exhaustion. She
asked me to open the window's shutters and give a Tarzan
yell into the black night, as loud as I could.

I did, and a great weight was lifted from my shoulders.

All around us, in Rome, things started to happen very fast.
Bombs exploded in bars and hotels occupied by German soldiers; four-pointed spikes were seeded on the streets to blow
up their tires; sand or sugar was slipped into the tanks of their
unattended cars and trucks to gum up the motors. It became
unsafe for Germans and Fascists to go around town alone, and
it became unsafe for civilians to be on the streets at all. It was
a time to lay low and not go out of the house, and even that
was not a guarantee of safety. The Germans began setting up
dragnets, sudden and swift operations in which trucks barricaded the streets around a city block and all able-bodied men

aged fifteen to seventy, with or without papers, were loaded onto the trucks and taken away. Then the houses on the block were raided, room by room. Anybody found with dangerous or suspicious materials was taken to jail; the others were sent to dig trenches at the front or to uproot orchards, vineyards, and railroad tracks.

A young woman had taken residence in the apartment just below that of Aldo-lungo. She was referred to as a *collaboratrice,* one of the many that for preference or profit consorted with German soldiers. They parked their Wehrmacht cars on the darkened street, near the apartment door, and left them unattended till dawn. One night, moved by patriotic ardor, Aldo and his friend Marcello decided to do something more active than just shuffling around bundles and papers. The car sitting there was asking for an act of real sabotage. They walked downstairs and managed to pour sugar into its gas tank, a really heroic gesture considering what it meant to lose a few spoons of the precious stuff. But the timing was wrong: a patrol of very young Fascist Militiamen, armed to the teeth, nabbed them and—for breaking the curfew—took them to the juvenile jail of San Lorenzo. It seems that the young Fascists, out to check the adherence to blackout rules, were too noisily busy to see the sugar action. Aldo-lungo and Marcello were not heard from for three days, when once again the train yards of San Lorenzo were subjected to another heavy Allied bombing. A stray bomb hit the juvenile jail and one moment Aldo and Marcello were prisoners, the next a wall of their cell was sheared off and they simply walked home. People who saw them come back described them as white as ghosts or, more colorfully, like fish dipped in flour before frying.

On March 23, 1944, a charge was set off in Via Rasella, in the center of Rome. It killed twenty-nine German soldiers.

On the night of March 24, 335 Italians, political prisoners, Jews, and petty criminals alike, were taken from local jails by their Fascist guardians and handed over to the Germans, who carried them in trucks to caves at the edge of the city, tied them together in bundles of three or four, and shot them. The caves were then blown up. Professor Gioacchino Gesmundo was among the victims.

On the morning of March 25, an edict was posted around town: "*Achtung!* Warning! Attention, All Citizens! As of today, the *Kommandantur,* as reprisal for attacks against German troops, will order the execution of ten Italians for every German struck. The order, in regard to the March 23 event, has been carried out." For good measure, an eager Fascist official had delivered a few more bodies than the *Kommandantur* had requested. Like a baker's dozen.

The Repubblica Fascista Sociale Italiana gave the general call to arms. Anybody of military age, whether conscripted or *in congedo provvisorio,* who did not report to barracks within a week would be considered a deserter and summarily treated as such. Notices with the names of the drafted were posted all over town.

My name appeared twice. As Private First Class Gian Franco and as Private First Class Giovanni Francesco. Same birth date, same father, same mother.

The sunset-to-dawn curfew was enforced with a vengeance.

In the middle of the night, two German Army trucks picked up the Bellini-Webers, loaded their luggage, and with other German civilians onboard, headed north.

By way of our *portiere,* I was given a small parcel. It

contained the model engine and a note: "Please accept this Swiss Internal Combustion Engine. Happy flights! Your friend, Otto."

The time had come to put into action our plans to "go to the *macchia*"—disappear in the underbrush.

We all dispersed, leaving our little Roman fountain unattended.

II

To Camp

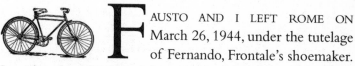

FAUSTO AND I LEFT ROME ON March 26, 1944, under the tutelage of Fernando, Frontale's shoemaker. It took only a few hours for us to decide to leave, and about the same amount of time to get ready: Fernando would not have waited for us much longer, and we had to grab that opportunity. As things were going, nobody knew when, or if, he would make another trip.

I barely had a chance to say good-bye to Maresa, and only by telephone. I took it as a good omen in itself that I could reach her; communicating by phone was an extremely iffy thing, the lines being down most of the time, or so overloaded that the home telephone had become mostly a decorative object. I crackled my eternal love for her; she crackled back, "I will think of you, please take care, please be careful," and then only the crackling was left on the line.

My parting from home was a mixture of sadness and excitement, almost as if I were leaving for summer camp. My brother had already found refuge in the parsonage of a country church, the parish priest conveniently being the uncle of his new fiancée. The safest place for me would be Frontale; Aunt Elena would see to my well-being and good behavior, away from the dangers of the open city.

My mother checked twice the contents of the knapsack to make sure I had not forgotten any important items, such as the protective Sunday missal, the one especially blessed by the Pope, and several changes of socks and underwear. She made sure that I had taken the best patched-over and mended pairs, so that her sister, Elena, would not think of her as a shoddy housekeeper. She also entrusted me with a short, sealed letter to Zia Elena; I did not read it, but knowing my mother, I am certain she was asking Elena not to spoil me, not to let me get away with any nonsense.

My father made sure that my bedroll was correctly and safely tied and loaned me his Swiss Army knife. It had been his inseparable companion since his youth, and I had to promise to take good care of it. It was honed like a razor; he had used it to sharpen thousands of drawing pencils. He was so fussy about it, that he made it sound as if the knife's safety was more important than mine. Like me, he could find no words to express what he felt. Then, with moist eyes, we said good-bye. We told each other that it was going to be a short separation: the worst would soon be over. The Americans of the Fifth Army were in Anzio, practically at Rome's doors, and nobody could stop them. Proof of their invincibility had reached the city only a few days before. U.S. Army rations had surfaced in Rome and were already available on the black market.

It was said that do-or-die scavengers had brought the packaged rations directly from the battlefront. As the American troops advanced, supplies followed; when they had to retreat, they buried them in the ground to dig up at their next advance—only by the next advance the supplies had disappeared and found their way to Rome. By the standards of the day, this story was believable. Unbelievable were the contents of the brick-shaped, carefully wax-papered cardboard boxes. To begin with, a tin can of soup, one of vegetables, one of meat, a small tin of butter, crackers, a chocolate bar, toothpicks, a pack of ten cigarettes, and waterproof matches. Around these goodies alone we could have built a Christmas feast, but the most outstanding items, and proof of the USA's unchallengeable superiority, were a well-wrapped *emergency* biscuit to be consumed *only* if one had been without food for more than twelve hours (the magic biscuit supplied enough nutrition and prevented hunger pains for the next twelve hours!) and a packet of *toilet paper*. How could anybody stand in the way of an army that considered as an emergency a condition that for us was everyday-normal and, moreover, supplied its soldiers not only with mouthwatering items such as meat, butter, and chocolate but even with the ultimate luxury? Toilet paper had been, for years, unobtainable on our markets; we imagined that only royalty and cardinals were privileged to its use.

It was a masterstroke of psychological warfare and, together with the scavengers' story, the brainchild of a propaganda genius. A few cartloads of those rations—however they were made to appear in Rome—did more to demolish whatever resistance remained against the Liberators than months of full-scale, lethal air raids.

. . .

We piled up on Fernando's motorcycle-cum-sidecar and left a little before dusk, so that by dark we would be in the countryside, away from Rome and out of the curfew area. Travel in the daylight was not recommended because of the danger of air attacks, but at night it was slow going. The motorcycle's headlight was painted the regulation black with a tiny clear slit to light the way. Fernando navigated by memory, mostly, and preferred not to use the light at all. It did not provide enough light to make any difference, he told us, and it could give us away to the bands of highway robbers—sometimes disguised as partisans—that were roaming all over. I wondered if this were true or if he said it just to make his mission sound more risky than it was. Instead of the light, it would have been more logical, really, to turn off the motor. Its racket, in the silence of the night, carried for miles and must have awakened the dead in the cemeteries we passed along the way. As a matter of fact, he did turn the motor off, now and then, to coast down a hill and save gasoline. Or when we had to disembark and push the machine down and up banks—where the road had been bombed out—to negotiate a piece of open, muddy field until the road was whole again.

Fausto and I welcomed these interruptions. They gave us a chance to move our limbs, sore from the jolts and our cramped positions. Fernando's machine was a decrepit old Gilera motorcycle, once a sporty, racy affair, now transformed into a beast of burden and kept alive by ingenious cannibalization of other machines. The homemade *seed-de-kar*—"side cart" would have been a more appropriate term—had been bolted onto its right side to carry produce and other goods from the country to the city. Human cargo had not been considered a possibility by the designer of the contraption, so any ride-smoothing

devices, such as springs, were not included. Whoever sat (eu-
phemism for a cross-legged, pretzel position) in it felt exposed
to immediate contact with all sorts of obstacles, real or imaginary, coming at him out of the dark, and the nervous system
suffered as much as the flesh and the bones. The other passen-
ger's place was behind Fernando. That space too had been
transformed in the service of commerce into a small platform
to which more cargo could be strapped. Fausto and I took
turns perching on that seat. The accommodation, physically,
was not that much better, but it gave the comfort of knowing
that any impact would be softened by Fernando's body.

Not that Fernando's driving could be called reckless, not
in the slowness of his night driving, anyway. But with the
light of day, it became enthusiastically frenetic. He would
launch the machine down the empty road and, without any
warning, take a ninety-degree turn into an open field, to hide
under a thicket of trees or behind a haystack. We would sit
there silently, the only noise the clunks and bangs of the engine's hot metal cooling off. Then, reassured that nothing was
moving as far as eye or ear could detect, Fernando would start
his contraption again and, with the three of us bouncing
wildly across the field, reach the road again. It was a rabbitlike
progression, rushing from hole to hole, then freezing to listen
for danger, then jumping out again. Between rabbit jumps,
happy to be alive, Fernando entertained us by belting out
raunchy parodies of operatic arias, possibly funny for someone in the right frame of mind.

Fernando was a born entertainer. Now in his late thirties,
since his apprenticeship he had been Frontale's shoemaker,
and a very talented one. In his one-room shop, always open to
the street, he custom-made beautiful boots and at the same

time entertained anybody willing to sit and be his audience. For us kids, not many years ago, it had been better than theater. Besides telling jokes and singing funny ditties and arias, Fernando could keep his eyes crossed for minutes at a time, or roll them every which way, one independent from the other. The performance we enjoyed most was the one of the cross-eyed cobbler. In repairing a shoe, he would pin two tacks on a sole and then, cross-eyed, after a suspenseful aiming of the hammer, right-handedly whack the nail on the left, flip the hammer in the air, catch it with his left and whack the nail on the right. As an encore, he would look cross-eyed at one kid and pull the nose of another; then, feigning annoyance with his handicap, he would whack the side of his head with a wooden last. It made a bloodcurdling crack, and his eyes became uncrossed. This part of the act required not only showmanship but perfect timing: while the audience concentrated its attention on his right hand and his crossed eyes, with the left he produced a perfectly synchronized sound effect by banging a wooden mallet on his stool.

He had put this special talent to good use. At the military draft examination, Fernando kept his eyes crossed for more than an hour and was rejected by the army doctor. With real, authentic documents attesting that he was "permanently discharged from military duty," he was free to pursue a most rewarding career in the black market. This allowed him to buy the motorcycle, a phony circulation permit for it, and grudgingly on the black market, the necessary gasoline coupons. Shortly, the spiraling profits afforded him a wife, a small farmhouse a few miles out of Frontale, and a mistress a few miles more down the road, at Le Madonnine. Presto, in good local tradition, both ladies became pregnant.

With rabbit jumps, stops for food and rest at various farmhouses, and slowdowns for road conditions, it took us twenty-seven hours to cover the 180 or so miles to Frontale. Or as close to it as Fernando would take us.

"If you are crazy enough not to believe what I told you about Frontale," he told us, "and still want to go there, that's your business. But you go without me."

The danger of being found by a German or a Fascist patrol carting two deserters was not part of the bargain. Being shot was definitely not part of it. Fernando left us at the fork of the provincial road, seven kilometers from Frontale but only two from Le Madonnine; generously, on his way home, he would swing by there and alert people that we were coming. It was a cold, dark, and drizzly night, but I knew the way well. By shortcuts through vineyards and orchards, we were at the Bertoldis', at Le Madonnine, in no time at all.

Only four years had passed since I had been at Le Madonnine, but it could just as well have been in a previous life. The Bertoldis' home was the same as always: only my perception of it was now different. The huge room where the whole family used to gather, the big fireplace, the great kitchen table, all seemed smaller and shabbier. The Bertoldis, the ones who were left home, were all there. They received me warmly, but not as a child coming back home, as in the past, rather as a guest due respectful hospitality. What made this clear to me was that Domenico, having fetched from a cupboard two of the "good glasses"—the ones reserved for guests or special occasions—offered us wine. A perfunctory gesture extended to visiting grown-ups.

Domenico, he of the perennial good humor and vitality, seemed spent and looked smaller and older than I remembered.

In answer to my "And how are you all?" he somberly brought me up-to-date. Anna, his wife, had died two years ago, and of the six daughters, only Erminia, now married, and Clara remained at home; the others were either taking care of their households or working as maids in faraway cities. Of the six sons, only three were around: Luigi, the oldest, exempted from military service because he was married with four children; Andrea, sent back home with one hand and one foot missing, lost to frostbite on the Greek front; and Baldo, the youngest, who had been allowed to remain home, thanks to Zia Elena's intercession with the authorities. Of the other three, two had been in the army in southern Italy at the time of the armistice and now were cut off from home, and the third was missing in action on the Russian front.

Fausto and I explained what brought us to Frontale. The mass shooting of hostages, the threat to all able-bodied Romans of deportation to Germany, the fear that our names had joined others' as accomplices of Professor Gesmundo, tortured by the Fascists and shot by the Germans; and being wanted by the military draft. It was not too far-fetched to presume that we had made the lists of the German police, the Fascist Militia, and the *carabinieri*. That was why, we told them, we chose the safety of Frontale and hoped to stay with Zia Elena until the Americans arrived, or the situation somehow changed for the better.

After a long pause, it was Andrea who gave us a brief but thorough presentation of the local situation. "As for staying with Elena," he said, "you better be prepared to share the hospitality with the SS. They have taken over Frontale. Not too far, in Apiro, there is a detachment of the antipartisan Fascist Black Brigade."

He paused, looking straight at us, to make sure we had absorbed what he was telling us.

"Here at Le Madonnine," he continued, "your grandfather's house was first taken over by a bunch of deserters in hiding, and when they fled, it was taken over by a family of refugees from Ancona, fanatical Fascists. Their twelve-year-old twin sonavabitches report to the militia anything that goes on around here. For candy.

"Patrols, German or Fascist, crisscross the countryside, night and day, ransacking farms and farmhouses, taking away all they want or anybody they suspect or dislike. A few weeks ago, they took Erminia's husband, Gigio, away, and her chickens and her only pig. Mount San Vicino is chock-full of disbanded soldiers, deserters, partisans, Jews, and political runaways. That is a load this whole area can take for only so long.

"If you are looking for safety, my friends," Andrea concluded, "you are better off back in Rome."

Andrea was a levelheaded man, and he had spoken calmly and deliberately to make us understand that what he was telling us was the bare, unadorned truth.

This was bad, much worse than what we had heard back in Rome and preferred not to believe. We tried to digest it in silence. Fausto was looking fixedly at me. If he was trying to make me feel guilty, he was succeeding. He had originally planned to stay with some rich relatives in a village on the Adriatic coast, forty miles southeast of Frontale. I had convinced him the war would pass by there at full force—it was the only retreat road open to the Germans on their way north, chased by the British Eighth Army; Frontale, by contrast, given its position and geography, would be totally out of the way, a safe haven . . .

Domenico broke our gloom. He stood up and said: *"La notte porta consiglio."* An old proverb and his advice to us: After a night's sleep, in the morning we would see things more clearly. We could make up our minds then.

Luigi suggested that, for safety, Fausto and I split up for the night. If anything untoward was to happen, at least one of us would have a chance to escape. With that kind of cheering up, I was assigned the Bertoldis' hayloft, Fausto the neighboring one, belonging to the Lanzonis, Gigio's family and Erminia's in-laws.

Erminia fetched a black oilcloth tarpaulin, big enough to cover the three of us, and together we accompanied Fausto to the Lanzonis' barn; it wasn't more than two hundred yards away, and we walked slowly in the cold drizzle. Under the dripping tarpaulin, swaying this way and that to avoid the mud puddles, we must have looked like a strange, shiny, six-legged beast, lost in the night and with nowhere to go.

Fausto's hayloft was dry and warm. Erminia made him promise not to move until she came to pick him up, at dawn. "What's the hurry?" was Fausto's disconsolate comment, and we parted.

On the way back, Erminia and I stopped at the Bertoldis' big chestnut tree. In years past, it had seen us climb its old branches like monkeys; it had heard our tall tales, told under its green, cool canopy in the heat of summer. Now its barren branches could not even protect us from the thin rain that drip-dripped on the oilcloth with the even measure of a clock.

Soon she would be—as would I—nineteen. She was wearing a dark sweater over dark clothes, and black woolen stockings. She was fuller and rounder than the last time I had seen her, and thick wooden clogs made her look taller. It felt strange to find myself with not a girl but a woman. It was not only her appearance but also her countenance, the way she spoke, that put her firmly in the ranks of the grown-ups, the mature.

She had a warm, soft voice, and the words came from deep within her.

Gigio Lanzoni, following the desire of his family, had asked her to marry him; she, following the desire of her family, had said yes. Don Girolamo had blessed the union, and they had gone to Venice for a one-day, happy honeymoon. Shortly afterward, Gigio had been drafted. He was sent to boot camp way up north and was just getting accustomed to wearing the stiff, scratchy green uniform when the September 8, 1943, *armistizio* happened and he was told to go home. He walked the three hundred miles, and popped up unannounced, just in time for the harvest. Then someone fingered him as a deserter, and the Fascists came and took him away, who knew where to. And to think that Erminia had been the one, back in 1941, to convince Gigio to quit the seminary and not become a priest. So, in something like two years, she had been married and unmarried and married and unmarried again.

But she had no time to cry. She was busy all day, and then some, running the house, the farm, the barn. She could have used some help and some more money. Baldo brought in some, but not enough, by making charcoal on San Vicino; he kept playing the half-wit and spent a lot of time running errands for the partisans on the mountain. Or perhaps he wasn't faking anything: to play that game, he really did have to be soft in the head. Sometimes, she said, she felt like wrapping all her possessions in a handkerchief and leaving, just disappearing . . .

Perhaps, I said, she should have traded places with Gigio, way back when he wanted to become a priest, and become a nun. I expected at least a small chuckle, but there was only silence.

Then she asked: What about you?

I was all right, I told her. At least I had not been married and unmarried and . . .

No, seriously!

Well, I could be all right . . . but once in a while I had this terrible emptiness inside. I told her about Maresa: how much in love I was, how she had told me that she loved me but at times I felt she was distant, as if a thin, icy veil were between us. I also realized that Maresa could not be the whole of my life, but I felt unable to get fired up about anything else. After so much phoniness, so many deceits—church, politics, flag waving—I didn't know what to believe, whom to trust.

"It seems only yesterday—you remember, don't you?— what I wanted most was to grow up. Now I would pay to go back."

"Oh, shut up!" she whispered. "You haven't grown up a bit. You are still talking crazy."

She linked her arm firmly around mine, and under the wet tarpaulin, feeling the warm closeness of our bodies, we walked home. The rain had become heavier, but it did not touch us at all. Actually, at that moment, nothing could have.

In the loft, the hay filled the moist air with a heady scent, like that of a field of wildflowers on a spring dawn, and it mixed with the seductive one of Erminia's bare skin. We held tight to each other, entwining our sorrows into a consoling warmth.

All night the rain drummed heavily on the clay tiles of the roof. But we did not hear it at all.

. . .

Next morning, as if to underline what Andrea had told us, partisans and Germans had a fight on the mountain road just outside Frontale. We had heard the church bell and, after a while, the gunfire exchanges, repeated and multiplied by the echoes bouncing from hill to hill. It lasted a long time, it seemed forever. Luigi and Andrea agreed that in the next few days, if not hours, Germans and Fascists would make life very difficult for everybody in the valley, and Fausto and I had better disappear, fast. If we were found out, it would be very painful for us and for all who had given refuge to us.

"Danger for danger," he told us, "the closest and safest place is San Vicino."

Baldo would lead us up.

12

Frontale

WHEN THE MORNING MIST lifts up from the valleys, it reveals rivers and green hills, well-ordered farms, orchards, and vineyards, in a landscape dotted with hilltop villages. It is like a curtain rising on a play: Le Marche.

Of all the regions of the country, Le Marche is one of the least known. The explanation for this anonymity is, in part, that it is a relatively small region: from north to south it is about one hundred miles long, and east to west about half that much. It is also one of the most mountainous and hilly: from the high peaks of the Central Apennines in the west, its hill-fringed valleys, like fingers reaching for the sea, descend to the Adriatic to the east, a configuration that has made the transportation of goods and ideas difficult and has always given the region a certain insularity.

Despite the tales of black marketeers and the occasional hints in Zia Elena's terse notes to us in Rome, Frontale seemed blessedly remote and isolated, like a forgotten Shangri-la.

Among the things we did not know about Le Marche was that its geographical anonymity and its remoteness had attracted many besides Fausto and me. Whole families, their homes bombed out, had found refuge with previously long-forgotten, distant relatives in Frontale. It was incredible, the Bertoldis told me, how many were the many-times-removed cousins who had materialized out of nowhere. In addition, after the armistice, many disbanded Italian soldiers who could not reach their homes in the north had sought safety on Frontale's mountain. San Vicino's difficult access and the cover and protection afforded by its deep forest and underbrush had also made it the base for groups of partisans. They operated at night, at times together, at times independently from one another, sabotaging and raiding the Fascist and German supply routes. They returned at dawn to their lairs on the mountain with the spoils of their actions and with enough scavenged goods to last till the next sortie. San Vicino had also acquired a strong strategic importance: it was within striking range of the Via Adriatica, the only large north-south thoroughfare at sea level along the Adriatic coast. Military convoys of troops and supplies kept it busy day and night, and the actions of the partisans provoked at times annoying delays and, at times, serious damage.

From Erminia, and later from my aunt herself, I learned that Zia Elena had not allowed these things to disrupt her life. She continued to tend the orchard and the vineyard, to cure, can, preserve, and store goodies in her cellar, and to go through the motions of running the post office. At six every morning—except Sundays—she opened the doors of the office, lined up all the rubber stamps, pencils, and registers, melted a bit of sealing wax so that the place had the smell of a working post office, and then opened the little window in the partition that separated the office proper from the theoretical public. She poked her head out, like a turtle's out of its shell, and when reassured that there was nobody in need of her services, put a call bell on the sill, just in case, and went about her business. The bell was pro forma: if anybody rang it, deaf as she was, she would not have heard it anyway.

Some said that what she did all day long was count her money. This is not true. What she did, to begin with, was keep her house, all twelve rooms of it, immaculately clean. In the fashion of the country, winter or summer, all windows would be flung open, and the rooms dusted and then the tiled floors wet-mopped and dried until they shone like mirrors. She was able to go through that exercise from room to room with alacrity, up and down the stairs, because she was in top shape— or perhaps she was in top shape because of it.

Another one of her daily activities was to meet the *corriera,* the mail coach. She put on her hobnailed mountain boots, took the mail pouch, the delivery register, and the red-green ordinance flag, hung the "At the *corriera* stop. Will be back soon" sign on the closed doors of the post office, and took off. Across the square she went, and past the church, past the schoolteacher's house, past the midwife's and another half dozen houses that clung to the sides of the precipitous road. Finally she reached bottom at Le Fontane, the covered public washhouse at the crossroads with the valley's provincial road. In fifteen minutes she had shed 425 feet of altitude. Then she positioned herself on the bridge over the brook and waited for the mail coach.

Even in the best of times, this was a rickety bus that made the rounds of the province's villages, carrying passengers, parcels, barnyard animals, and the mail. It belonged to the Italian National Postal Service, and took precedence over all other vehicles on the road. It announced itself with three bleating blasts of its horn, an unnecessary procedure since the grating noise of its gearbox could be heard miles away, reverberating in the valley. But the blasts were regulation blasts, as was Elena's, or Berto's before her, waving of the red side of the flag. Flag or no flag, the driver would have stopped to let people, things, and animals get in or out. There on the bridge the exchange took place. The driver delivered the incoming mail pouch, and Zia gave him the outgoing one; they checked the pouches' seals, signed each other's consignment registers, and exchanged the news of the day.

Then Zia waved the green side of the regulation flag, and the *corriera* was off with a great, agonizing lament of its engine. Zia climbed the steep road like a mountain goat and in half an hour was back again at her post office with barely a panting. She repeated this routine faithfully every day of the year, rain or shine. Except Sundays.

By the cold November of 1943, it had become an empty ceremony—nobody had seen or heard the *corriera* for months. But there was Elena every day, mail pouch and flag in hand, waiting at the bridge. She waited the regulation half hour and then went back up to Frontale. More than once, as she went by his church, Don Girolamo told her that age and celibacy had turned her daffy. Deaf and daffy, thought the rest of the village. Her answer, if she felt like dignifying anybody with one, was that soon she was due a government pension and she was not going to jeopardize it by not doing what she was paid to do. She was not the one who had declared the war; it was not her responsibility or concern.

But it would be, shortly. I translate directly from the accounts and diaries she left me. They are really no more than a series of dated notes written in post office style, sometimes in the heat of events, sometimes a bit later, simply relating the facts. Her most visible deviation from officialese is her liberal use of exclamation points.

November 10, 1943. I do not remember how, but that day the rumor spread around that the Germans were coming. Everybody nailed their houses shut and ran away. It looked like a ghost town! Thinking of my responsibility of the Office— even if the mails did not work anymore—I thought I should stay. I consulted with Don Girolamo, and he said that not even the devil himself would make him move. We concluded that going away was easy but coming back difficult, so we stayed. . . . A few other people remained, mostly old, with no place to go!

I was at the doorway thinking a thousand painful things, when a German soldier showed up, waving his machine gun at me!! Without ceremony he entered the house and started rummaging in and ransacking all the furniture in all twelve rooms, from first floor to last, writing on the door of each room with a piece of chalk who was going to use it.

By nighttime her house was full and the German headquarters for the zone installed. Respectful of her official position as postmistress, they left her a mattress and the use of the smallest room on the third floor. The kitchen was transformed right away into the officers' mess.

They cooked for twenty-six! What a mess it was!!!

They also left her free to run the post office, but with a warning. Operation of the telephone and telegraph was forbidden.

That night, perhaps in celebration of the new quarters,

they had a noisy good time with liquor, eggs, Marsala, and there was one who played the accordion. They sang and danced all night!! And I, poor me, prayed to Saint Anthony and the soul of my poor husband for help!

But at that moment she did not need much help. Her small, motherly figure, her smiling eyes, and her deafness gave her an air, cultivated, I am convinced, of helplessness that ingratiated her to the Germans, especially the older, simple soldiers in charge of the kitchen and of the daily running of the house. They called her Mama and gave her food out of their rations. She made herself invisible to the higher officers, except for offering—through intermediaries—to sew on a button or do some general mending, and they left her alone. She kept playing post office, shuffling papers, noisily rubber-stamping them, filling and sealing the mail pouch, and going to meet the nonexistent *corriera*. What she actually did was keep an ear to the ground, talking with Don Girolamo and the other souls left in Frontale and trading foodstuffs. Things went into the pouch, and things came out of the pouch, to and from the post office and down into her cellar.

December 12, 1943. The kitchen has become an arsenal! It is a continuous coming and going at all hours, and none too clean! The dining room is always occupied by officers who from there give orders and from the balcony review scrupulously the troops that march underneath in the square. My house, like many others, is getting fuller because some groups go away and some other groups come in.

The cleanup operations on Mount San Vicino did not go as expeditiously as the Germans and the Fascists had expected. The reason could have been that most of the German soldiers were veterans of the southern front, the North Africa front, or even the Russian front. Their hearts were not really in fighting anymore, certainly not in the cat-and-mouse game of mop-up operations. Trained in direct confrontation with an identifiable enemy, they were inefficient at fighting shadows. They were tired of feeling like targets—and that's what they were—being shot at or knifed or garroted when they least expected it, by anyone, young or old, man or woman, in civilian clothes. They tried a dragnet operation at the top of the mountain, but when the net was pulled closed, they found no fish inside. They blasted the base of the mountain with mortars and heavy machine guns for a full day, and when the troops moved in, they found a few dead cows and some hysterical sheep. Those who had more taste for that kind of war were the very young, untested recruits, the sixteen- or seventeen-year-old warriors put beside the seniors to learn and to help. But the old soldiers, who had seen the nasty face of war, were taken aback by the ferocity and brutality of the young ones, so this matchup did not work as expected.

Operations like these did not succeed in wiping out the partisans, but they definitely made their lives more difficult.

The partisans were kept constantly on the move and their supply lines ever thinner. Many were from the region's cities, towns, and villages; they used their civilian connections for support whenever they could. But now that these contacts were severely curtailed, they had to scrounge closer to their very temporary bases. At first they bought whatever they needed with money and, when that ran out, with "promissory victory notes." Their demands were difficult to ignore because, if refused, they would often take by force whatever they had asked for anyway.

It was a hard choice: people known to aid and abet the partisans were hanged on the spot by the Germans, shot by the Fascists, and left to rot in public view. And, for good measure, their homes and farms were sacked and burned down.

And, willing or not, people had only so much to give.

February 3, 1944. This little village, because of its very thick woods, among which there are a few farms and grottoes, has become known by all the disbanded stragglers coming from the south and the north.* An Assistance Committee has been established somewhere, and they are all sent to a precise address: San Vicino, the Mountain of the Cross. In this mountain are now living thousands and thousands of partisans and there is a Brigade Headquarters with a Colonel and other officers. In January Colonel Annibale was captured by the Germans and later died.

*Among the stragglers there is also a family of Milanese Jews coming from San Severino, where they were refugees because persecuted!! So Frontale is invaded by all sorts of people!!

During these months, different groups of Germans rotated in and out of Elena's house, but whoever came in took her and the post office for granted.

Toward the middle of February 1944, Zia Elena began meeting Baldo Bertoldi at the *corriera* stop. Baldo, with a little emphasis added to his natural gifts, looked and acted like the prototype of a village idiot, and as such the Germans left him free to come and go as he pleased. Most of his coming and going was from Le Madonnine, where Nonno Nicola's house remained under Elena's administration and cared for by the Bertoldis. It had been occupied, for a while, by seven disbanded Italian soldiers, who had, on the open market, the same value as outlaws or partisans. They had simply appeared one day and, nobody having had the heart to send them away, taken up residence in Nonno's house. Zia Elena's silence on the matter was taken as approval; with their supplies running low, she sent them, via Baldo, whatever food she could spare.

It has always remained unclear what made her do it, her position being at best a fluke of fate, a temporary blind spot in the Germans' military vision, a very dangerous playing with fire. Even more unclear is why, over time, she extended her supply efforts to other groups, the fighting groups. Nobody had threatened her into it, and as a matter of fact, considering her closeness to the German headquarters, it is difficult to understand why any outlaw would have trusted her with his life.

Obviously, Zia Elena refused to perceive her position as precarious. She even offered hospitality to three women refugees in her own house.

March 7, 1944. Last night toward midnight while we tried to sleep a few winks in the only room left to our use we heard

*the chairs move with which we had barricaded the door!! I
say "we" because with me there were three refugee women;
they all slept in a little bed and I on a mattress on the floor!
We were really scared when in the doorway appeared a captain of the SS who, smiling, was coming to approach us!!
Certainly his intentions could not be good, otherwise why
was he coming to us at that hour? But with all the unctuous
politeness we could muster we were able to send him away!!
Early this morning in good comprehensible Italian he told
one of the refugees that they were going to burn down my
house because I was harboring partisans! Fortunately orders
came for them to leave in the morning, and shortly afterward
another company arrived. It is true that I helped the partisans
who asked for food. I felt they all were sons of mothers, and
they got to call me "Mamma," and I never wanted to be paid
by anybody!! There was a Polish partisan, a certain Elio, who
particularly liked me and from whom I was always getting
news, who told me, smiling to soften the blow, that Fascists of
the Black Brigade were mounting a big raking operation and
to beware!!*

Elena passed the word to Baldo, and he and the seven
soldiers moved out of Le Madonnine and into the woods of
Mount San Vicino. Baldo still came down to the *corriera* stop
once or twice a week, behaving like a blabbering idiot. He
collected from Zia and from farms along the way whatever
he could.

German personnel kept rotating, remaining in Frontale an
average of one week. Perhaps they were using the village as a
rest and recreation post. But if "rest" might be justified when
comparing a frontline assignment with the relative quiet of

partisan containment, the "recreation" part was hard to figure. Perhaps being shot at occasionally—and not constantly—was recreation enough.

Zia Elena, being a sort of permanent guest in her own home, had slowly assumed the position of guide for the newcomers, showing them the ropes around the house and also where they could obtain minor services, such as laundry and mending, or even the cooking of ingredients supplied by the soldiers into something decent to eat, from some of the old people and refugees in and around the village. Increasingly, she acted as a liaison with Frontale's civilians, a sort of ombudsman but also responsible for their actions. In six months of occupation, none of the garrison's commanding officers had deemed it necessary, or perhaps they simply forgot, to collect the population's firearms. So it was up to Elena, now, to pass the word and be responsible for its execution. She saw to the collection of many rusted shooting irons, museum relics, and convinced some of the women to dig up a few real shotguns buried by the men who had disappeared. It was, she explained, a way to humor the Germans. When they caught Don Girolamo promenading around the square shouldering his trusty shotgun, Elena was able to convince them to let him go, gun and all, because, she explained, the old buzzard was born with that gun on his shoulder and had never harmed a sparrow in his life.

By the end of March, her post office activity had evidently increased. She had acquired an assistant.

March 28, 1944. I was intent at my office work when two big German cars stopped in front of the door. Three superior officers dismounted and entered the office with an open map

and demanded to know where was the house of a certain G.B.;
they were sure that from the post office they would get the right
directions! But I and my assistant knew that in the house of
G.B. there was a strong number of partisans all eighteen-,
twenty-, twenty-five-year-old youths. How to answer? After
pretending we did not understand, we showed them, with ges-
tures, the mountain road—the first house was way up in
Sandomenico! Once up there, they were told that G.B.'s
house was in Frontale! Imagine the anger of the officers, who
had told us before leaving: For false information we do "ka-
put." And so it would have been if, in the meantime, the par-
tisans had not run to ask for the help of men and arms and
reinforcements from the village of Casal Sampietro!!! It was
so that on their way back the German officers found the road
to Frontale blocked with machine guns, men, and muskets.
They attempted to escape, in vain!! With their drivers and es-
corts, they were made prisoners and brought to Commander
Falcon's group.

What Elena doesn't say is that, after giving the false directions, she made her assistant rush to the church to tell Don
Girolamo to say a fast service for the dead and toll the knell;
it warned the partisans that serious danger was on its way up
the mountain.

With prisoners on his hands, Commander Falcon pro-
posed an exchange to the German command. It was refused.
The six German prisoners were taken behind a barn and,
with the blessing of the partisans' priest, shot. In reprisal,
twelve partisans held by the Germans were hanged.

. . .

The Allies began their two-pronged push north, and the Germans, to stem their advance, moved the trained and tested, and perhaps now rested, troops south and unleashed their young soldiers and Fascist Militia, both mean and vengeful, on the partisans.

Fausto and I had been on the mountain less than a week.

13

Colonel Jim

COLONEL JIM COULD HAVE stepped out of one of the propaganda cartoons we were all familiar with. British officers were represented as tall, thin, and angular, nattily dressed, with handlebar mustaches over prominent, horsey teeth. When in color, the cartoons gave them ruddy complexions and rusty yellow hair; the portrait of the effeminate dandy was completed by a monocle and a thin bamboo stick, à la Charlie Chaplin. If you took away the monocle and the stick, you had Colonel Jim, or as he got to be known, for the way "Colonel" sounds when said out loud, the Kernel. In his midthirties, he was an intelligence officer attached to the British Eighth Army, dropped behind the enemy lines with a hundred and some pounds of radio equipment and a few contacts among the partisans. His main mission was to organize and manage the underground network that was collecting Allied soldiers on this side of the front and, with the help of accomplices, funnel them back to their proper side. These were usually escaped prisoners of war or shot-down fliers on the lam and once, I was told, an entire five-man Indian Sikh patrol that, turbans and all, had strayed behind the front line and got lost.

The Kernel's radio was the network's fixed base, or as fixed as it could be within the perimeter of Mount San Vicino. Another phantom radio roamed somewhere in the valley, never operating from the same spot, and in a code known only to the Kernel, informed him where and when someone was ready to be picked up; one or two of the Kernel's people would then be dispatched and the rescued, never more than two at a time, brought back to the camp on the mountain. From there a message was relayed to a radio behind the British line, which when I joined the group, was about ninety miles south of San Vicino. When the coast was expected to be clear, a relay point was chosen at the very last minute and the delivery was made at the appointed time. The network relied totally on the help—offered at great risk—of a few local farmers, who also, as best as they could, given the general scarcity of clothing, supplied the people to be rescued with civilian clothes.

Up to now the operation had run quite successfully and smoothly, even if sometimes things got sticky. Indian Sikhs, blacks, and six-foot-two Polish soldiers, if ever seen by someone too nosy (nobody was to be trusted), or even worse if stopped by a patrol, were quite hard to disguise as Italian peasants. One look was enough. It was essential then to make all movements, coming and going, in the darkest of night, and even more essential to know exactly the terrain so the distance could be covered between dusk and dawn. Moonlight was a mixed blessing; while it made us more visible, it also allowed for faster and more secure steps. With moonlight, the Kernel had taught us to blacken our hands and faces with burnt cork; at first we thought he was pulling our legs, but then we saw his wisdom. It was also hell afterward, with the dearth of soap, to get the black completely off, and our skin slowly acquired a permanent lined blackness.

A secondary but very important activity of the Kernel was to act as liaison—via radio—between the Allied Command and the partisan groups on San Vicino so that information could be exchanged and actions coordinated.

Kernel Jim's group consisted of five people, including me, with interchangeable duties: guide, sentry, cook, messenger, and generator. This last line of work was something that nobody lined up for and was assigned by drawing straws. The hand cranking of the radio's electric generator was not only tiring but also painfully boring. Autonomous and detached, the group was nevertheless under the protective wing of, and in constant contact with, Commander Falcon's Fifth Brigade of the National Liberation Army. Falcon, not his real name but appropriate to the kind of fighter he was, was in charge of the largest, strongest, and best-armed partisan group on the mountain; it was called a brigade because it was also in charge, more or less, of the other, ragtag groups that populated San Vicino and the surrounding countryside. Contact between the groups was maintained via messengers and runners, but discipline and unity among them was vague at best. Many of the people in hiding on the mountain were simply trying to avoid fighting and to keep away as much as possible from harm; some survived by petty thievery and minor banditry. Some were escaping religious persecution; many others were escaping civilian law or the military draft.

Some were like me; while searching for a sheltering haven, they had found themselves slapped with the label of partisan, fighting partisan at that, without much effort.

Baldo had brought Fausto and me up to the Kernel and vouched for us.

My acquaintance with Kernel Jim started on the right foot, so to speak. Baldo had introduced me as someone totally trustworthy, with an intimate knowledge of the area and its local farms, which was close to the truth, if a little inflated, and as an intellectual, master of many languages—which was many languages removed from reality. In Baldo's view, the fact that I had continued my schooling past the elementary grades entitled me to a seat in the Accademia Nazionale. It was true that my school curriculum had included many years of Latin, French, and English, but that did not take into account that the teaching of these languages was based not on actual conversation but on memorizing pages and pages of the classics—and even then I earned only bad marks. My melodramatic recitations to the bored classroom added nothing to correct pronunciation, or to my understanding of what I was talking about. French was relatively easy, involving mostly gargling the "r"s and pronouncing all the rest of the letters between pursed lips. But English was different. Our English teacher, who had never been closer to England than Rome, had spent valiant hours inculcating in us the mysteries of the English language. Yet the sound of "th" (rendered as "zee" by proper positioning of tongue and teeth, implemented by copious spittle spray) and of "h" (guttural aspiration of air, as in the last gasp of a drowning person) or even the vagaries of the simple "i" (as in "quickly!": "coo-eye-klee!") kept eluding her as much as they did us.

The Kernel's mastering of foreign languages must have followed the same kind of learning route, only via Oxford. He spoke Italian with an obvious reliance upon archaic words and structures. More than the languages themselves, what we had in common was a sense of humor about them. Or at least we thought so.

While shaking my hand, he recited Dante in a most natural conversational manner: *"Nel mezzo del cammin di nostra vita, mi ritrovai per una selva oscura . . ."*

I caught his jest and, as if answering a question, replied: "I shot an arrow into the air, it fell to earth, I knew not where."

Straight-faced, we continued for another couple of verses, as if involved in an exchange of deep thoughts, of questions and answers. My stature among the group was assured.

Baldo's introduction turned out to be essential. He had been the liaison, and source of supplies, between the group and the outside world for quite a while. He was trusted. Fausto and I had been seen as added ballast and two more mouths to care for. Our joining was, to say the least, not enthusiastically accepted. Fortunately, the situation was understood by both sides to be temporary. With that implied belief, they let us stay. For the next few days, we were trained in our duties in the various facets of the operation: how to man the generator, how to keep the site clean, how to clean and oil the generator, how to keep whatever was not in use packed up and ready to go, how to pack, unpack, and operate the generator in the dark, how to stand night guard crouched on a tree limb without falling asleep, or at least without falling off. And, for our rest and recreation, they gave up their turns so we could go and fetch water, and also cook for them.

This duty I took on with pleasure and, seemingly, to the pleasure of the rest of the group. Whatever I knew, I had learned, eagerly, at the side of our beautiful cook, Lia, or from the deliciously simple Bertoldis' kitchen, or on hunting-camping trips—right here on San Vicino!—with my zio Berto, or from that most frugal and fabulous cook Zia Elena. I had trusted Baldo to deliver my mother's note to Zia Elena, and on one of his contact trips he did so, but by that time she had already been informed of my presence on San Vicino. By way of Baldo, Elena excused herself for the impossibility of having me in her house, since it was already full of German guests, and along with the usual provisions for everybody, as a special message-gift to me, she sent an extra ham bone and a small jar of my favorite—she remembered!—cherry jam. I knew then that she was alive and well and that her heart was in the right place. The sack of general provisions contained some dried beans, some flour, and also a whole, small pro-sciutto. For her to deny herself a whole prosciutto (even if, in truth, an exceedingly small one) was a sign of the highest pa-triotism. In celebration of which, that evening, I prepared one of Uncle Berto's favorite soups: "thunder and lightning," the local interpretation of *pasta e fagioli,* a pasta and bean soup for which a ham bone is essential. Given the conditions, it was the best *tuoni e lampi* I ever made in my life, and the next day I received the greatest accolade from the Kernel.

"A medal! I will see that you get a medal for that soup," he said. "But, I say, don't you make it again while we're sup-posed to be in hiding."

The renown of the soup had spread around camp as fast as

its side effect: vigorous and sonorous flatulence. Which, considering our basic diet—rice, beans, potatoes, cabbage, all sorts of wild roots and root greens—was already a fact of camp life.

What we called camp was actually an abandoned house, a shepherd's shelter, square and low, and not in the best repair. Attached to its back, about twice as large as the house, was a covered shed, which had been used as a fold for the sheep when the flocks migrated from the valley's winter pastures to the higher spring and summer pastures. At its foot, San Vicino had patches of green mixed with underbrush, which turned, with the steep rising, into a thicker and thicker forest of chestnut and walnut trees. Two-thirds of the way up the mountain, the woods stopped abruptly to give space again to green and lush pastures; higher up these thinned out and, on the approach to the crest, turned into arid and stony soil. The steep inclines leading to the summit were, in places, almost vertical walls, perforated here and there by natural caves. Only thorny nettles, mountain weeds, wild sage, and rosemary grew there, making it ideal ground for goats.

Our camp was at the edge of the tree line, with the shelter proper partway into the woods and the sheepfold extending into the pasture. The fifteen- by twenty-foot room had thick walls built of fieldstones, with a door and two windows, by now gaping holes, patched closed by what, in some previous era, could have passed for blankets kept in place by twigs. The floor was bare earth; nonetheless, the whole affair—especially at that time of year and at that altitude—was a most welcome protection against the elements. Fausto and I nicknamed it "the San Vicino Plaza, a Four-Star Hotel." We gave it that rating because there was running water in every room (the space was divided into imaginary rooms, some actually separated from the rest by blankets hung on wires; when it rained, water leaked from cracks in the roof and tinkled into tin cans) and because, on clear nights, no fewer than four stars could be seen through these same cracks in the roof.

The sheepfold in the back did not rate as well. Its thatch roof was patched here and there with branches, and the sides of the shed, once totally open to the elements, had been closed in by walls of interwoven canes. The floor, compacted by years of trampling hooves and saturated with sheep manure and urine, had the heady smell of ammonia, which reminded us—with the misplaced nostalgia of urban types—of railroad station pissoirs. Its smell was, fortunately, somewhat cleansed away by the mountain breezes, which had easy access there. Our four-star hotel had a similar drawback: in past days the enterprising shepherds must have produced, for their benefit and our misery, great amounts of sheep's cheese. Unfortunately, all that remained of it now was its aroma: fermented by the heat of summer, preserved by the cold of winter, this smell was acrid, oily, and penetrating. After the briefest stay at the shelter, the clothes, the hair, the skin itself became absolutely impregnated by it, marked by it as if by a tattoo. None of the residents had found a way of washing it off, not even the prim colonel, who in honor of his favorite cheese, had given himself the battle name of Captain Stilton.

By assignment or by choice, each of us had his little corner to call home. Wooden planks raised a foot or so from the floor formed cots, over which lay a few blankets and our sleeping bags. The feet of the cots rested on upturned jar tops or saucers filled with kerosene: these were supposed to keep roaches and scorpions from climbing in bed with us. Near each cot, as a night table, was a cardboard box or orange crate to hold our personal properties. Mine included a toothbrush, a dull razor, a sliver of soap, a mess kit, a candle stub, a pocket-size version of one of my arty photographs of Maresa, and also one of my family, all together for Easter, three years ago.

Hotel San Vicino Plaza was not crowded, or at least it did not feel so. Fortunately, after a while, we found ourselves congenial; we took the scarcity of amenities in stride and even with a sense of humor. A good thing. Without it, as Captain Stilton would say, the situation would have tempted him to shoot all of us "spaghetti benders" in the middle of the night. He could take a lot, but snoring bothered him. Toto was the worst offender, but even asleep, his massive size prevented any retaliation from the rest of us.

The rest consisted, besides the Kernel, Fausto, and myself, of Luciano and Luca. Luciano was a hypertalkative, hyperactive Florentine, a fourth-year medical student who had been jailed for "subversive activities"—he'd been found signing prescriptions for a pharmacist friend dealing in black-market medicines. His father had bribed the police, paid a ransom really, for his escape. He could not stand still a moment, and paced around camp like a caged animal; he passed himself off as a ladies' man, an inexhaustible Latin lover, boasting continually and graphically, in his colorful Florentine dialect, of his *bischero*'s prowess. Of all, I liked him the least.

Luca was a gentle soul, pale and slim, at forty-one the eldest of the group; he was most reticent about his life story but did not make a mystery of having a loving wife and two children of school age. At one time he had been a teacher. He knew all the constellations in the sky and kept us entranced by pointing them out to us. He felt, and made us feel too, that a first-row seat in that big theater, looking at the stars' exquisite performance, was one of the pluses offered by a cold, crystal clear night on San Vicino. He also had an uncanny way of hunting and bringing to camp, with Toto's assistance, whatever scarce wild game—a hare, a pheasant, a stray chicken or turkey—was left on the mountain. Stealthily they would corner their prey, then pounce and quickly dispatch it with bare hands. This method of the hunt caused a great philosophical split between the Kernel and the rest of us. We thought that catching and promptly slaughtering the animals when they least expected it was a greatly humane act; he thought of it as "terribly uncivilized, not giving the buggers a sporting chance." These differences were set aside at dinner.

In a definite attempt to show off, I myself one day captured a stray fluffy white hen. Following Luca's example, I executed the prisoner, denuded it of its feathers, and split it in half. Then I pressed the two halves, flavored with mountain rosemary, between two red-hot bricks. The result, labeled *pollo al mattone*—even if only a small bite per customer—was highly appreciated. But the praises came with a strong reprimand and a biting tongue-lashing from Toto. I had left the white feathers to blow in the wind, and it looked as if half of San Vicino was covered in snow. I could just as well have put out a red flag to signal our presence.

During quiet days, I filled the long, dull hours writing interminable letters to Maresa, and poems. I would give them to her one day, I told myself, as a proof that she had been with me all the time. Often I read my honey-dripping poems to Fausto, not stopping for even a moment to think that my platonic pining could have been as boring as the sexual boasting of Luciano.

Sometimes, we came in possession of several bottles of wine—one of the very few commodities still plentiful in the area. Then we would all sit around in the dark and have a few glasses, telling each other of ourselves, mostly tall tales, trying to bask—in the middle of all the misery—in a little human warmth. But even so, the alternating of lull days with adrenaline-rush-filled ones was taking its toll on our collective nerves. One night—perhaps we had had more than a few—I was emboldened enough to recite to the captive audience one of my poems extolling Maresa's beauty and virtues. It was then that Luciano drunkenly broke in: *"O bischero!"* he said, "while you are masturbating in the mud, she is fucking the whole of Rome on feather beds!" He was still illustrating his speech with obscene pumping of his fist when I jumped at his throat and squeezed as hard as I could, my only desire to see his tongue and eyes pop out of his head. It took the combined efforts of Toto and Luca to wrench us apart.

"Fuck the both of you!" Toto yelled at us, kicking us into opposite corners. "You are drunk."

He was right. But I wanted to kill Luciano just the same.

It was the only unfriendly event within our group.

At the beginning of May, the Germans and Fascists mounted a full-force operation; in serious military fashion, they named it Operazione Vipera. A metaphor. Mount San Vicino was rich in vipers, and the proven way of disposing of them was by chopping their heads off.

From her privileged point of view in Frontale, Zia Elena could take the pulse of developments:

May 7, 1944. During the night a great number of Germans arrived with cannons and mortars and heavy guns for a big retata *operation. There were also many Fascists accompanied by two spies who had been with the partisans. They moved quick up the mountain toward Sandomenico, where several groups of partisans resided. But by the time the Germans arrived, the partisans had already run away into the forest.*

Infuriated by their lack of success, the Germans and Fascists blew up two farmhouses along the way and shot two couples—"heads of households, good people, in charge of large families"—on the spot and, it was said, threw their bodies into a lime pit. "But I sincerely hope that this is not true!!"

Zia Elena's hope remained just that.

On their return, the troops made a big display of artillery on Frontale's square. Whoever commanded the operation was furious. He imposed a total curfew, ordered a farm-to-farm and house-to-house search, and let the troops ransack and destroy. The state of siege lasted more than a week. A couple who came out of their house, breaking the curfew in search of food, were shot and killed on their doorstep. They were both eighty and were found entwined in a last embrace, one trying to protect the other.

Sharpshooters were posted at the railing on the square and ordered to shoot whatever moved in the valley, man or beast.

Zia Elena's diary doesn't say specifically what she did during this time. She did close the post office, and moved out of her room at headquarters to hole up in the church. There she and Don Girolamo and Gianna took care of a handful of refugees, women and children who had also sought the church's protection. Besides that, she lay low, like everybody else who managed to survive.

. . .

The Germans' detachment kept losing soldiers sent to stem the Allies' advance. The ones left became more virulent; the partisan activity increased. Falcon needed men and recruited Fausto away from us, luring him with the promise of a more direct contribution to the "liberation of our country." Luciano, who had promoted himself to doctor, also went to Falcon, to act as a medic. But his job was limited: both sides adopted the practice of shoot to kill, no prisoners taken. Prisoners meant more mouths to feed, and people needed to guard them—at this time, both unaffordable luxuries.

I kept hearing Tullio's voice: "It's not a game! It was never a game!" It was a reminder, if I ever needed one, that the final alternative was to be either safe or dead. The thought kept me alert every moment of the day.

I stuck with the Kernel. With the diminishing of our numbers, I had become more useful and my familiarity with the territory more essential. With Fascist and German patrols roaming the countryside, it came in handy to know all the nooks and crannies available for shelter. The Kernel taught me the basic tricks of a radio operator and let me have turns at it. One thing he did not reveal was the interpretation of incoming messages and the formulation of outgoing ones. Even the messages broadcast by Radio London to the partisans were in the form of popular sayings and bits of poems, or childish ditties, all with apparently inane meanings. "Maria is in love with Luigi. The rain is over, and the cow is jumping over the moon." The messages were spoken slowly and repeated over and over, as if meant for idiots who might have trouble understanding them the first time.

Colonel Jim would listen attentively, sometimes take notes, and then, at the set time and frequency, send the reply:

"Gather ye rosebuds while you may. Repeat: gather ye rosebuds . . ."

Since some of his messages were scraps of poetry we had exchanged in our bilingual mock conversations, I was convinced he was making the whole secret code up on the spot. A crazy way to puzzle and confuse the enemy, if they were listening.

"It's crazy," I told him, "as crazy as calling you Il Kernel." It reminded me, I said, of a grade school joke: a man who believed himself to be a kernel of corn was put in an asylum and, after a time, cured and released. But as soon as he was out the asylum's door, he began running and jumping from ditch to ditch, hiding. Brought back in, he was asked to explain his strange behavior. "I know I am not a kernel anymore," he said. "But has anybody informed the birds?"

The Kernel thought the story rational and the joke not very funny. But his next outgoing message was "The kernel is at peace: the birds have been told. Repeat: the kernel is at peace . . ."

Crazy. But crazy or not, twice already we had received this message: "When it rains, it pours. Maria better help Mario with the overshoes."

Both times, we were told to pack up and run within minutes. We escaped a major Fascist mop-up operation. The name for this kind of action was *retata,* dragnet, emulating what fishermen do: spread out the nets and see what fish get caught. The attackers advance slowly in a wide line, followed by another, more tight-knit one. The strategy is that the fish that escapes from the first net is mauled by the second. It was

a well-tested strategy, used in cities or on open fronts, but not
so easy to execute on the thickly wooded, steep slopes of San
Vicino. Rather than a net, the attacking troops put up a fire-
wall, firing at will. Mortars, machine guns, grenades, rifles,
nothing was spared. The partisans were quick to move from
spot to spot and burrow in shallow caves. Commander Falcon's strategy was to concentrate his counterattack in one
spot and punch a hole in the nets, pour as many fighters as
possible through it and then turn around and take the enemy
from behind.

There were not many victors, but a lot of bloodied and
dead bodies.

German or Fascist, whoever was in charge of these operations, considering the losses, decided to give it a rest. Perhaps San Vicino was not that important. Sooner or later the
mountain dwellers would need bullets, medicines, food, and
come out of the trees.

By now the air had the transparence and sweet softness of
spring, and the skies, even on the darkest nights, had the faint
luminescence of a billion stars. In a moment of contempla-
tion, just before he left, Fausto and I sat under a tree and
looked at the magnificence of the universe. It made us rejoice
that we were alive, but from that perspective, the worldwide
butchery seemed even more obscene and cruel. And senseless.
We willed ourselves good luck, promised to meet here again
once the world was saner, and parted saying only *"A presto,"*
see you soon.

With Fausto's departure I lost not only a friend but also an
audience for my rhapsodies about Maresa. He was the only
one of the group who knew her and could understand me. At
dusk, whenever I could, I took my loneliness to the lower

spring of the brook. From there I could see, down in the valley, the chimney smoke of Le Madonnine. In the tall, moist grass around the spring, protected as in a womb, I could enjoy my misery and think of Maresa, evanescent as a dream. I had to force myself to recall her every single feature and rebuild her whole. I tried to hear her soft, throaty voice in the gurgling of the brook, tried to evoke her fragrance. It was a hard task: the stench I had embedded in me made me feel unworthy of being close to her even in thought. And then the moment, the vicinity of Le Madonnine, the brook's earthy smell, so similar to that of Erminia's skin, the recent memories of her warmth, of the full roundness of her body, of her hurting embraces, brought back vividly Erminia's presence. And Maresa, with the help of my hormones, slowly dissolved into Erminia.

14

Bob

THE ELATION OF THE ADVENTURE, the exhilaration of learning new survival methods, the thrill of danger constantly present and challenging—it was all an alternating rush of adrenaline. When the rush subsided, I was empty, spent, insignificant. Alone. And with Fausto gone, even more so. I felt, illogically, like an abandoned child but fully realized that, at nineteen, I was not a child anymore.

I tried to take advantage of the camaraderie with the Kernel to get to know him better, but at that point he lowered a curtain. He obviously wanted to keep himself detached from me, from us. Where was he born? Was he married? Did he have a family? Brothers, sisters? He gave only vague answers, drawing a line between friendly interest and nosiness. Would he make new friends?

Suddenly I felt as if nobody needed me. But I missed everything: my friends, my family, my bed.

I was homesick.

I was in that frame of mind when I met Bob.

I was assigned, with Toto, to a retrieval mission. It was my third and his umpteenth. Toto had been with the group since the beginning; a quiet, withdrawn man, he was as big as an oak tree and as strong, and looked older than his midthirties. A disbanded soldier, he had a wife and children in the north, way up in Fascist-dominated Italy. It was most unsafe to return there now, but he made sure that one day he would by living every minute with the utmost care and caution. We teased him, saying that he moved as if walking on eggs; actually, he was making sure that he would not step on a mine. He had fought in Montenegro and in North Africa and seen things we had not. "I came with two," he would say, "and I'm going back with two." And by the scratching of his crotch, we knew he meant not just his feet. He was the one who gave full credence to the rumors that there were spies abroad on San Vicino and behaved accordingly. Nothing was too secure for him, and nobody was to be trusted.

We were to pick up an American pilot, we were told, at the Poppolis' farm—usually about a two-hour walk down into the valley, with cautious Toto, probably closer to three. We had to leave in the dark and come back in the dark, a night's work. If we could not make it in that time, then we had to hole up someplace and wait for the sun to go down again.

The night was moonless but clear and light; it was a safe trip with Toto leading the way. We avoided open fields and took detours to keep our distance from farmhouse watchdogs; in the quiet night, a traveler's movement would be given away by the progression of barking from farm to farm. I had learned a trick from Berto a long time ago: these haystack dogs (that's where they were supposed to be chained) were trained to guard chicken coops and sheepfolds from marauding foxes. If reassured that it was only a harmless wayfarer with no designs on the livestock going by, they would calm down. A couple of whistles would do the trick. I had tested the theory, and most of the time it worked. But cautious Toto did not allow that. If someone was bent on listening, it was better to let him think there was a fox going from farm to farm, and not a whistling idiot wandering in the night, he said. He had a point there. He was more worried, he added, when he did not hear barking. Patrol dogs were trained to sniff out their prey silently and take it by surprise, not scare it away. When you heard the vicious beasts' growls, it was too late: they were at your throat.

We stopped within sight of the Poppolis' farm and lay low on the dewy grass, listening for their dog to sound the alarm. This for Toto was the moment of truth. Give your signal, the one that proved it was you there in the dark and nobody else, and wait for the right signal to be given by the one person—and nobody else—who was supposed to give it. Even with all these precautions, one might easily fall into a trap or an ambush. It was, finally, a matter of gut feelings and trust. Or, mostly, trusting your gut feelings.

Aldo Poppoli came outside, released the dog from its wire run, took it inside, and closed the door. In a second he came out again with the dog on a short leash. In a stage whisper, Toto called out, "Hey, Dora!" The dog's name and Toto's unmistakable baritone cleared us.

Two candles, welded onto saucers by their melting wax, lit the kitchen table and barely defined the contours of the soot-darkened room. Aldo gestured to the loaf of coarse bread and the plate of cheese on the table and offered me a glass of wine. He knew Toto well and poured for him half a wineglass of rough, fiery grappa. Only someone of Toto's size could survive that pick-me-up. Although four years had passed since my uncle's funeral, Aldo recognized me as Berto's nephew; he acknowledged the sadness of having to meet again in a circumstance like this, not only without Berto's presence but having to whisper like thieves in the night. I agreed with him.

Toto made it understood this wasn't the time to socialize; it was a long way back, and we had to make it before dawn. Aldo took a candle from the table, opened a small door at the back of the room, and disappeared behind it. By the musty, wine-cask smell that reached us, I guessed he had gone to his wine cellar to get the American. Only after the war did I find out that many farmers had bricked off special hidden rooms somewhere on their farms, generally behind the cellars. There they hid the few precious things they wanted to keep secret from friends and foes alike. In his, Aldo also hid transient, outlawed guests.

My idea of an American pilot was someone in the mold of Clark Gable. I had seen him in an old movie, landing a biplane in a field at a blond girl's farm. Now, in wartime, I was imagining him tanned, broad-shouldered and square-faced, a devil-may-care, sarcastic smile on his lips, saluting a platinum Jean Harlow by touching with two fingers his flier's cap.

The person Aldo brought back from the cellar, Clark Gable he was not. This pilot was very tall and very thin, with an unkempt mop of straw yellow hair dominating a long, pale, beardless face. His light blue eyes peeked at us from behind Aldo, and his smile was definitely apologetic. He reeked of wine; he must have spent quite a few days cooped up in

Aldo's cellar, and his clothes had absorbed its odor like a sponge. The civilian jacket he wore was way too large for his thin frame and too short for his height, and so were his pants, which left a few inches of shin uncovered. My first thought was that, if he had a cork for a nose, his impersonation of a scarecrow would be perfect.

For a moment we all scrutinized each other in silence, and then his smile turned, like mine, into an expression of incredulity. Obviously what he saw did not fit his idea of real-life partisans. There we were: Toto, as aggressive as a gentle giant out of a storybook, holding an antiquated rifle as if it were a walking stick or a club (which, in fact, was pretty much all it was good for); and I, unarmed and as threatening as an unwashed kid up way past his bedtime.

Robert Moore was his name, and I was assigned to teach him the ropes around camp. I initiated him in the joys of the radio generator, and he took to it with real enthusiasm. Above all, he had to learn the escape routes and hiding places. Like a tour guide, I showed him the goat paths and the caves near the ravine. Hidden by the underbrush, some of the caves were holes in the rock, big enough for a shepherd to crawl in out of the weather; some were large enough to house a small flock. Others, opening onto the face of the cliff and harder to reach, burrowed into the mountain and formed a network of tunnels. It was easy to get lost, but the right tunnel resurfaced near the top of San Vicino. I explained to him and made him memorize the topography of the mountain and how it sat in the general scheme of our operations; I also informed him that, at the middle of the mountain's top, stood a thirty-foot-tall metal cross. It could be seen for miles and was the best orientation mark around.

We were on the northern side of the mountain. Ninety miles or so to the southeast, toward the sea, was the British Eighth Army. That was his destination, I believed, to be reached through underground stops just like ours; how many I did not know. Between here and there, the land was buzzing with Germans and Fascists, getting madder than bees disturbed in their honeycombs. Bob seemed more interested in the locations of the springs around us. His foremost desire was to wash himself; after the stay in Aldo's cellar, keeping clean and unsmelly had become his fetish. The past winter had been the longest, coldest, and wettest in local memory, and the springs were abundant and free-flowing. Bob loved to wash himself in the freezing water, as did I.

He was twenty-three, an engineer from Cincinnati, Ohio. Flying and engineering being the planned orientation of my future studies, I felt an immediate affinity with him. The fact was, he later explained to me, his title of engineer was for manning an engine in the railroad shunting yards of Cincinnati. This information confirmed for me the many traps of the English language, but it did not diminish my curiosity about him. He was only a few years older than I, but it would take me decades to catch up with the richness of his experiences, which he recounted in a matter-of-fact way, unemotionally.

His military career alone was enough to lift my sagging spirits. Volunteered for the army, was sent to the air corps to train as a pilot, ended up flying as a gunner in a reconnaissance plane. Shot down in North Africa, the plane landed just inside its own lines. Made sergeant, completed his training as pilot, went through the invasion of Sicily flying an artillery spotter plane and from there to southern Italy. While flying the one-seater Piper Cub, he was shot down again, by rifle fire, but landed safely on a tomato farm. This time he was captured and taken to a prison camp in Tuscany. Even though marked with red crosses (why? He did not know: there was no hospital or any sick prisoners around), the camp was bombed by the Allies (why? He did not know: perhaps they thought it was an ammunition dump). He was loaded onto a cattle train with other prisoners and had been moving north, destination Germany, when the train was blown up by partisans (why? He did not know: perhaps they thought it was a munitions train), at which point he found himself unharmed and free in the middle of the Italian countryside. Helped by farmers, rescued by partisans, he had been passed from place to place. And here he was, talking to me, alive and unscathed.

I asked him if he had developed any paranoia yet, or if by any chance he had some special amulet, some good-luck charm.

"Just myself!" he said, smiling. No, he wasn't Clark Gable. He piloted a Piper and not a Flying Fortress. Still, he was a pilot and an American. I told him how much shorter and less bumpy my road to San Vicino had been, how much closer to home I was, and I felt better.

Generally the stop at our station lasted two or three days, then people were moved along to the other relays. But now things were pretty hot, and Bob remained with us for close to two weeks. For a long spell we did not hear from the other radios, nor were our messages returned. We heard that two Polish soldiers had been taken by the Fascists before they could be signaled to us, and that the Poppolis' farm had been raided, but these pieces of bad news were unconfirmed. The antipartisan operations now became vicious: artillery and mortars pounded the mountainside and kept us and the other groups on the move and scattered. Falcon and his men had made quick sorties, had taken and shot prisoners. Many partisans had been shot, farms burned down. A few sabotage actions were ambushed, and there had been losses. All this confirmed the rumors that spies were about and informing the Germans. The Germans kept making artillery and mortar attacks, but not at random. Several shells came very close to Falcon's camp, and a couple of times they fell almost exactly where we ourselves had been only a few hours before.

Bob and I stuck together. Living close to Bob was safe, like living close to a lightning rod during a storm, I told him jokingly. I only hoped his good luck would rub off on me. But that was the extent of the humor we had left. We did not eat much, slept less; the days were long, spent in hiding, the nights busy moving from place to place, lugging our few items of survival and the heavy radio equipment. More than once I felt like dropping everything in a ravine, calling it quits, going off by myself, to face alone whatever was there to be faced. But Bob's detached curiosity and seraphic acceptance of events made me reconsider and go on for another day. His behavior, together with the teacupy sangfroid of Colonel Jim, was contagious to all of us.

To keep our minds off things and to while away whatever time was left, I taught dirty Italian words to Bob in exchange for his American Army English and the many meanings, depending on inflection, of "You kill me!" a declaration he used profusely. We spoke in whispers, and our conversations revolved about our families, airplanes, and girls, in mixed order. We agreed that we did not want to have a Jean Harlow as a girlfriend. I told him I knew someone with a mother like Marlene Dietrich, a fact that reinforced our determination

not to have any girlfriends or relatives looking like movie
stars. He said that his mother was a factory worker. The idea
of an American, factory-working mother was so foreign to
me that I could not imagine it. Frequently we halted our
talking, interrupted by the gunfire around the mountain or
in the valley, perking up our ears to detect how close the
shooting was.

We discovered we had in common a facility for repairing and creating things with our hands. For Falcon, we rebuilt
and put together, out of several damaged ones, a couple of rifles and a pistol. Bob always carried in his pocket a silver dollar he was working on; he had pinged away from a central
hole in the coin and obtained a perfectly shaped ring, which
he smoothed and polished with a soft pumice stone during
any free moment he had. I whittled at a hand-size model of a
P-41, with spinning propeller and detachable wings; I had
modified it several times following Bob's suggestions.

Slowly our conversations improved, each of us adding new
words to his dictionary. Our perennially insatiable appetites—
more a condition of constant starvation—brought us frequently
to the discussion of food. What did he eat at home? Beginning
with breakfast, Bob spoke of foods that came out of boxes, like
cornflakes (corn? *granturco?* That's animal feed!) and puffed
rice (c'mon, now: how do you *puff* rice?), all drowned in milk
that was more cream than milk (cream? *panna?* That's rich,
that's for pastries!); and eggs—at least two: fried, scrambled, or
poached—with a few fried strips of bacon (yes, pork belly, the
same stuff we use for cooking!). On more relaxed mornings
he had pancakes or waffles. With a lot of gesturing, by the ingredients list and the use of a hot surface for making them, we
reached the consensus that pancakes were *frittelle*—but not

fried (not fried *frittelle?*); as for waffles, they were left to the imagination—there was nothing, even remote, in my experience that could come close to what he was trying to describe. Pancakes and waffles were then slathered in butter and maple syrup (yuck! Drippings out of a tree? Like pine resin?).

Then, with breakfast over, Bob went on to the real nourishment of the day: where he was coming from, it turned out to be "meat 'n' potatoes." Seven days a week, twice a day. Now I really began to suspect his veracity; he was either teasing me or trying to show off and impress me. Meat? What kind of meat? Beef, mostly, and pork, and lamb—and all sorts of cold cuts. But after beef stew, steaks were his preference, juicy and burned on an open fire. Two-inch-thick steaks, a pound or more all for himself.

I knew then that he was teasing me. A steak is a thin piece of meat, pounded to make it tender and to look bigger than its three ounces—and, in good times, available once a week.

And me?

Breakfast: a cup of *caffè latte,* a bowl of warm milk with a touch of coffee, and a piece of bread with jam to dunk into it. Lunch? Start with a serving of *antipasto,* a slice of *prosciutto* or two, perhaps some slices of different salami (I was spreading it a bit thick myself now), or some *vitello tonnato*—thin slices of roast veal in a tuna sauce, and a *giardiniera* of pickled vegetables. But not much, just enough to whet the appetite, to prepare you for what follows. Pasta. A big dish of just drained, steaming hot pasta. With meat sauce, or white sauce, or pink sauce. With seafood sauce, or fish sauce, or clam sauce. Or a slice of *timballo,* baked pasta with a thousand goodies; or lasagna, yellow lasagna or green lasagna or yellow and green lasagna, with meat sauce or fish sauce or wild mushroom sauce. Then there would be sausages, grilled or stewed sausages with beans or lentils, and a big mixed green salad. In season, fresh, juicy ripe tomato salad, dressed in golden olive oil and fragrant vinegar; the whole meal accompanied by freshly baked, crusty bread. And then fresh fruit, lots of fresh fruit. Oh, I forgot the soups: *minestra, minestrina, minestrone . . .*

"Wow," he said, "I thought you Eye-talians only ate *spargetti* and meatballs!"

It was an exercise in masochism, excruciating our appetites, leaving us with watering mouths and rumbling stomachs. But we promised ourselves that when, and if, we got out of this mess, I would cook for him a real Italian meal to die for, a real "you kill me," and he would show me what a real American steak was.

Sometimes Luca would be present at our conversations, acting as a knowledgeable referee. He had relatives in the States, and he had heard about life there. Bob told us about his house—his parents' house—and its little garden; they even had a garage for their big Chevrolet. No, they were not rich: they were just a "blue-collar" family (that took me some time to figure out) like many others. I told him that I was born in a Roman apartment and had lived there all my life; for a garden, I'd had only the public ones or the parish play yard. He belonged to the Episcopal Church, one of the many Protestant denominations. Many? Protesting what? We had only one, the Roman Catholic. Well, two—if you counted the Jewish. When the conversation came to religion, Luca quietly absented himself.

The radio informed us that the Eighth was slowly moving closer and the Fifth was still holding at Anzio. The Kernel's activity now was mostly receiving and sending messages for the partisans. Bob and I tried to figure out the code of the messages; we divided the sentences into numbers of words and spaces, number of letters per word and numbers of vowels and consonants, and came up with nothing but a headache.

Once, with good-byes said and set to move him on to his next rendezvous, Bob and I were stopped at the very last minute. The radio had crackled alive and alerted us not to make the delivery. The relay was not secure, there was danger of a trap.

We tried to figure out the mystery of the spies. Our group's roster was small: the Kernel, Toto, Luca, Bob, and myself. No possibility of leakage there. We had frequent contacts with Falcon's groups, but they had more at stake than we did; there couldn't be leakage there.

Baldo had come up a few times, bringing ever more scarce food and no-news news. He was our only connection with the real world.

Baldo. The blood drained from my veins; a hundred suspicions swirled in my head, to be wiped away by excuses, only to resurface again. It could not be Baldo. But then . . .

We all got together and examined the facts. If he had wanted to betray us, we would have been wiped out by now; or perhaps whoever controlled him wanted the radio to keep operating to know what was going on on the mountain. Did they know the code? Was that the leak? And again: a few pickups and deliveries had gone awry shortly after Baldo's visits. But why, then, would the Germans interfere with our operation? Disposing of a few unimportant fugitives wasn't worth jeopardizing the interception of perhaps more valuable messages. And check this: for the last couple of weeks the food Baldo had brought up had been from German rations only. Was that a sign from Elena? Had she been telling us that

Baldo was in it with the Germans and we did not catch her message?

Baldo, crazy-smart; smart-crazy Baldo. He had always been the most loyal of friends. But also cunning. For money or favors, he would do anything. Dance on his hands, swallow cigarettes, eat chicken shit. Frequently, in the old days, he had taken the blame for something we had all done, and been proud to do it. But also, easily tricked by big words from the wrong person, he had betrayed us and laughed about it. But that was then, when we were children.

But, but, but. But what now? Now, I could not think.

The Kernel, Luca, and Toto could, and the more they thought, the worse it was for Baldo. In a short time there were no more doubts. He was too much of a risk.

It was put to a vote: the next time he showed up, Baldo was to be put against a tree and shot, as Falcon had done with another suspected spy. We would draw cards: whoever came up with the highest would shoot him. No, Toto suggested, not shot but strangled, to save a bullet. No, let's give him to Falcon and have Falcon do it.

Baldo's comings and goings had always been unscheduled. Let's hope he shows up today, said Toto, and we, or Falcon, will settle the matter.

Time would tell if he had been a spy or not.

I couldn't bear to stand there listening, let alone vote. Certainty and doubt were dueling in my brain, two worms tunneling in a rotten apple. I felt sick in the head, in the stomach, and walked away, my heart, my mind, and my body each going its own separate way.

. . .

It was Bob who came to fetch me the next morning, at the lower springs. I had taken him to this spot many times and told him stories of the village, of my childhood, and of my friends. It had been easy for him to guess where to find me, but he would never have guessed what I had been doing there. I had spent the night figuring out how to poison the brook. In the long run, the water would reach the Bertoldis down in the valley and poison them all, as Baldo had poisoned me.

"I got good news, kid," Bob said. I couldn't have cared less. I did not even acknowledge him.

"The Fifth has broken out of Anzio!" He beamed. "And they have taken Rome!"

Now I cared. I cared very much.

The news coming through the radio was confusing, even contradictory. Radio London was saying that, while the Fifth was consolidating its position in Rome, the Eighth Army, finally free from the Abruzzi muck, was chasing the Germans up the east coast; the American Liberation Forces' Radio said that the Fifth was after the Germans past Rome, having joined with the Eighth somewhere in the center of the peninsula. Whatever the strategies and movements of the two armies, it was clear that the Germans, if not in a rout, were now moving north in a rush, burning villages, uprooting orchards and vineyards, tearing up railroad rails, mining roads, and bridges. The front line was moving up the Italian boot as fast as a thermometer's mercury exposed to heat. It was hard to guess how long it would be before it reached us: perhaps only days, perhaps weeks. The main routes of escape from the south were the Via Adriatica on the east side of the country, the Aurelia and Cassia on the west, and the Via Flaminia, which coming from Rome slashed the country southwest to northeast to join with the Adriatica near Fano. Mount San Vicino was in that wedge of land between the latter two roads, just before they met. To show Bob what the troop movements were in relation to San Vicino, I drew on the ground a basic map of Italy.

The Germans were retreating north to their Gothic Line, which cut Italy in half, east to west, just north of Florence. It was a last stand to give their army time to disengage from Italy and move back into Germany, where it was needed most. To hinder this move, the Committee of National Liberation, following a directive from the Allies, gave the signal to the partisans all over Italy: attack whenever, wherever, and in whatever way possible. The Kernel had received and passed on to Falcon this message: *"Fratelli d'Italia! L'Italia s'è desta!"* Italian brothers! Italy is up and awake! There was no need of a code, this time, to understand the message.

I explained to Bob that the verses were from an old patriotic hymn and taught him a few bars.

"Fratelli d'Italia!" we sang as loudly as we could, throwing caution to the wind. He took his shirt off and waved it in the air like a flag, jumping around like a man possessed.

Sometimes, Bob could ree-ee-lly kill me.

15

Some People Are Lucky

ROME FELL ON JUNE 4, 1944. ON June 16, three groups of partisans, in a bold move, attacked the German headquarters in Frontale. The battle lasted six violent hours and was fought from house to house. There were many casualties on both sides, but no victors. At dusk the partisans collected their wounded and returned to the mountain; the Germans, recognizing the vulnerability of their fixed position, moved, farther down in the valley.

From Zia Elena's diary:

July 2, 1944. Even if totally cut off and with only the few bits of news from Radio London, we can feel the final rout is at hand. We can hear fighting going on day and night and also air bombings that make the earth shake! Great numbers of Fascists and Germans in retreat are taking horses, mules, carts, and taking away everything they can, even furniture and house-hold goods. ⋆ *They have brought in sappers with the order to blow up all they can, roads, bridges, and anything useful, even vineyards and olive trees.*

⋆ *Most of these things were found later along the provincial road, since they could not move fast enough with them!*

The partisans, 250 strong, came down from the mountain again to attack in force. Their goals were to obstruct the retreat and stop the mining of roads and bridges. Their first objective, because of its command of the valley, was Frontale. They fought their way in from the mountain road.

At this point things precipitate.

The German rear guard left in Frontale takes six women and six children from the church and lines them up at the square's railing, at the edge of the cliff. If the partisans do not desist and move back before sunset, when the shadow of the bell tower reaches the hostages, they will be machine-gunned. But also at this point, in the middle of hell, a miracle happens. Zia Elena, accompanied by Don Girolamo, asks the German captain in charge to let them trade places with the hostages.

The officer is a beardless youth who should be playing with the children! I tell him we are more important to the partisans than the children and I can ask them not to attack. The officer says yes, but he himself will shoot us with the machine gun if the partisans fire another shot!! So the partisans' commandant deems it opportune for now not to continue the battle.

The German retreat along the provincial road lasted four days. For four days Elena and Girolamo were kept in full view at the railing. They were given chairs to sit on and allowed to be brought food and water by Gianna twice a day; one at a time they were permitted to take care of personal needs, with Gianna remaining as a substitute. For four days they stared at a machine gun manned by a towheaded boy in a German soldier's uniform and waited for the bell tower's shadow to give them relief from the heat of the sun.

Then the Germans were gone.

Many old people, women, and children evacuated from their homes were reaching the San Vicino area like flotsam in front of a wave. Some on foot, some on makeshift carts, they carried their few belongings; some carried nothing. Not a few were German deserters, and they were most pitiful. Only a few days before they had arrogantly trampled on everything and everybody; now they were asking for clothes, for a crust of bread, for mercy. As a last humiliation, these were given to them, as alms to a beggar.

The presence of all these wandering people was hindering the quick and stinging partisan actions. Children, women, men, young, and old could be caught in the cross fire or, even worse, used by the retreating soldiers as hostages.

Other partisan groups, well-armed, had joined forces with Falcon, hoping to do as much harm as possible to the retreating Fascist and German troops. For many nights we heard the rumble of armor and trucks going north on the provincial road. We heard also, now and then, the crackle of rifle and machine-gun fire, and the whump of hand grenades and the thump of mortars hitting the mountain. Sometimes the mountain would echo back isolated yells and screams; they gave a terribly personalized, human texture to the fabric of battle, brutally rekindling my own doubts and fears.

I had set aside, for the moment, the problem of Baldo. I would deal with it when I came face-to-face with it. Or with him. One of the reasons I tried to keep it out of my mind was that, in my hurt, I had begun to identify Baldo with his twin, Erminia. Illogically, it was Baldo the traitor, Erminia the bitch: a two-headed monster. I had heard of twin identification, but that was between the twins themselves. That I should feel this way made no sense, and I knew it. Nonetheless I did, and it was painful.

The radio came up with a string of hurried, urgent messages. I ran to pass them on to Falcon's camp. The German rear guard, with several Fascist units, was approaching the southern slope of the mountain, destroying anything they had time to destroy in their path. *Operazione Terra Bruciata,* Operation Burnt Earth.

The Allied troops were at their heels.

The message I was given to bring back was that the bulk of Falcon's brigade was going to move north to continue the fight. Nonessential people could volunteer to follow or decide for themselves. As for our group, we'd better make plans while we had the time. But we should not count on Falcon's assistance. It was every man for himself.

Toto decided to go north; otherwise who knew when he would make it home. Colonel Jim would go, also. Having received no instructions to the contrary, he assumed his duty was to remain behind enemy lines. Bob would stay and wait for the Allies' arrival. Luca also was staying behind. For the first time he confided that he was a Jew and his home was only fifteen kilometers away. I would stay too. Rome would be on my side of the world again, and I could go home. It was all decided. Whoever was going had better get a move on. Those who were staying had better hide and duck and let the wave roll and foam over their heads.

The Kernel and I shook hands. Quoting from Dante, he said:

> *Sol si ritorni per la folle strada:*
> *Provi, se sa; chè tu qui rimarrai . . .*

Rummaging around in my memory (Milton, perhaps?), I came up with

> *Oh, how comely it is and how reviving*
> *To the spirits of just men long opprest!*
> *When God . . .*

And then the radio blew up. I saw the flash, the flame, and the smoke, but I did not hear any noise. I saw, clearly, splinters and pieces fly into the trees, and then another mortar shell fly in and then another, and flash and flame and smoke and dirt shaking loose branches and leaves.

I remember a great pain in my ears, and that when I tried to get up I could not. It took me a while to sit, legs spread out on the ground. And then I heard muffled voices and saw figures moving around. It all looked like an old silent movie, out of focus and cottony, discolored. I saw faces and lips moving, but I could not understand what they were doing or saying. Then I looked at my legs. They were naked and pitted. I was sure they had had pants on. . . . And then I saw that halfway between the top and the bottom of the right leg there was something red and clammy and pulpy. I couldn't understand what it was or who had put it there, and I almost didn't care. I was just very sleepy, and I would understand everything when I woke up.

I remember Luca wrapping something—was it my jacket?—around the leg and Toto carrying me and propping me seated in a niche in the rock, my feet barely inside it, and putting his rifle on my lap. "Just in case," I think he said; and Luca, "I will be back," then a waving of shrubs and branches, and muffled voices moving around and fading away. I remember feeling tired, and beginning to realize that something bad had happened to a leg, and that the leg was mine, because it was beginning to hurt. I remember, vaguely, that I felt surprised at not being mad at anybody, as I should have been, as my part required. It was like trying to bring back a dream, but instead a recurring, disconnected image kept coming up. It had to do with Greek theater, with actors having to wear masks and be true to the parts assigned to them at random: the god, the king, the soldier, the coward, the hero.

I think I slept and probably hallucinated. At one point I dreamt of hearing barking voices approaching and moving around and away, and dreamt the noise of branches being moved. I dreamt of lifting the gun and sighting to shoot, and I dreamt I saw at the end of my gun the muzzle of another gun, and behind it the pale, scared face of a young man wearing a too big German helmet and uniform. I dreamt, I think, that we looked at each other it seemed forever, not scared but puzzled mirror images, then the branches swished shut and I dreamt I was in darkness again.

. . .

The first thing I saw when I woke up was the jovial, round, black face of an American Army medic. He was changing the dressing on my knee, and it hurt.

"You're lucky, kid!" he said, smiling down at me. "Sawbones didn't like your scrawny leg, so he left it for you to keep."

They had turned the shed of Le Fontane into a first aid station. With me there were another dozen or so patched-up bodies.

"You are lucky," he repeated in a singsong lilt. "We like our heroes old around here. Kids we send back to school."

His good humor didn't do much for my pain; nonetheless it was encouraging. Some naughty metal, he explained to me, had gone through my knee, disassembled a few parts, and left them all hanging out. But things weren't terribly bad. So far, they had been able to stuff everything back in, but I had lost a lot of cheap Eye-talian blood. For two days now, they had been pumping into me some good secondhand stuff, made in the U.S. of A. And with that he stuck a needle in my thigh. "More good stuff," he said. "Only first-class here! Yessiree, no pain for you. You're lucky, kid . . ."

After Toto had hidden me away, the Germans had gone. Soon the Allies had arrived, and Luca, as promised, had come with a party to collect me, together with the other wounded on San Vicino. And many dead.

Luca came to visit again, but this time I was awake. He had brought from home a lunch pail of *tuoni e lampi* prepared by his wife, and I had a spoonful, just to please him.

He brought me up-to-date on the others. The Kernel and Toto, both full of scratches and sans radio, had made it north. Bob had caught a bad wound in his left arm and been sent to a field hospital far back inside the lines. As for himself, miraculously, Luca had found everybody alive and well at home and his house intact.

Luca had saved my possessions, and now he returned them to me. Wrapped in a dirty handkerchief were my father's Swiss Army knife, a fountain pen, my wristwatch with broken crystal, my ID papers folded around a couple of family photos and one of Maresa, and inside a crumpled piece of tissue paper, the ring made out of a silver dollar.

"Bob wanted me to give it to you, personally, if you came out of it alive," Luca said. "And he said to make sure I told you, 'From a hero to a hero.'"

For the first time I felt like smiling; I explained to Luca how this bit about the hero was something Bob and I had joked about; Bob had told me that in New York, with a loaf of bread, some cheese, some baloney, mustard, and mayonnaise, you could make a hero, but over here to make a hero— a real one—you had to bleed first. A joke. A lame joke.

"So," said Luca, "you qualify."

"Big hero! Ah! Really big!" And I told him of my encounter, perhaps imagined but probably real, with the German boy soldier.

"In all this fucking war, I didn't fire a single shot. Not even when I had my chance."

"If you had," said Luca, "that old piece of junk—I swear—would have blown up in your face. You are lucky."

So I was lucky.

I was going home, with a hole in a silver dollar and one in my knee.

As Bob used to say, some people are lucky.

16

"I Would Have Much Preferred . . ."

HISTORY BOOKS GIVE A DEFINITE date for the end of our war: April 25, 1945. But for some it was earlier than that, for others much later. For a few it never ended, and they still carry it within themselves.

On the morning of their fifth day as hostages, July 10, 1944, Zia Elena and Don Girolamo found themselves alone in Frontale's square. The Germans had gone; the war was over for Frontale. The front had moved farther north.

Some of the partisans followed the front. A few, feeling their sacrifices going unacknowledged and unrewarded, and finding themselves fully armed and trained, became bandits and highwaymen. But most of the local people returned to their homes and, together with other survivors, began to patch up and rebuild what was left of their houses and farms. Baldo survived physically unscathed, but somehow the workings of remorse or a bad conscience unhinged him. He totally lost his mind and became the persona that he had feigned for so long, the village idiot, entertaining the villagers with his simple-minded tricks. He earned a few pennies by collecting metal junk left by the passing armies, or helping farmers clear their fields. Erminia took care of him, feeding and clothing him as best as she could. Erminia, the smart and strong-willed one—and now a young widow—took charge of what was left of the Bertoldis' farm. Germans and Fascists on their hasty retreat had found time to burn and destroy most of Le Madonnine.

In 1945 Elena sold her half-destroyed house, disposed of all her goods, and moved to Rome. It took some doing to obtain her government pension because, she was told, it appeared that she had abandoned her government job, her post office, without written permission.

But eventually, the postwar government was generous with her. On June 4, 1947, the anniversary of the Liberation of Italy, by official decree, she was awarded the diploma of Patriot. A silver medal was pinned on her breast by a general of the National Liberation Front, in partisan garb.

"I would have much preferred," she declared, "that my poor, beloved Frontale had been spared the whole miserable catastrophe."

She lived many more years on her civil servant's pension and, having had her fill of politics, never got involved with any of the twelve political parties available to her in the New Italy.

For her old friend Don Girolamo, "that old fool," it was not the hardships of war but the blossoming of peace that made him unhinged.

When it had become apparent that the church bell was being used to alert the partisans, the Fascists had shot it down—and with it a good chunk of its tower. It was as if

Don Girò had lost a piece of his own flesh, but he understood that war is war, and he survived. After the Germans kept him hostage with his nose practically stuck to the muzzle of a machine gun for nearly a week, he had to be put in bed for a few days, but he kept his marbles and survived that ordeal too.

But when peace finally broke out, things began to happen of which he could not make any sense. For all his long adult life he had known what was wrong and what was right. Now there were so many grays that he was lost most of the time. He knew that if you were not a Fascist, you were a Communist and that was that. No argument there. Now that the Fascists were no more, what were you? You could be anything you wanted: Socialist, Liberal, Liberal-Socialist, Monarchist, National Unionist, Communist, Christian Democrat, Liberal-Demo-Christian—even a Neo-Fascist! It was, to say the least, confusing.

In his sermons now, he had to be careful to tiptoe around the issues. Soon enough, delegations of this or that kind of faithful had come to complain about one or two burning truths he had fired off from the pulpit.

With his behavior, and his age, he had become an embarrassment to the bishop's new bureaucrats, so they sent a young priest to assist him. This whippersnapper wore the cassock only inside the church; otherwise he sported a gray jacket and black beret—no biretta—just like a partisan, and raced around the parish on a noisy Vespa. When finally Don Girò let him preach, the young priest's sermons turned out to be political tirades: "Vote Demo-Christian! It will be your way of shoving the Cross up the nose of the godless Communists!"

They took another piece of Don Girò's flesh by retiring Gianna. Strong Gianna was let go after more than thirty years of selfless service to the church of San Paolo e Maria and absolute dedication of soul and (as rumors had it) body to Don Girolamo. It took two young nuns to replace her, and (crazy times) they had to build a separate bathroom for them in the parish house!

The straw that finally broke his old back came in 1948. The newly elected mayor of Frontale (a Communist), interpreting the will of the village, arranged to have a commemorative marble plaque affixed on a wall in the square. This memorial was inscribed with the names of all the people, of any army or civilians, who had died in Frontale and its surrounding woods and fields. The dedication was couched in official, mouth-filling words, but its meaning was "This plaque is not a thank-you note to these people for being dead. They did not wish to die or to be heroes. It is a memento, for whoever will stop and read this, of the madness of war."

They asked Zia Elena, as one of the local living heroes, to come back from Rome and unveil the plaque. She declined and suggested that Don Girolamo deserved that honor more than anybody else. And so it was. The dignitaries and most of the villagers stood at attention facing the wall, a trumpet was tooted, the mayor pulled a string, and the white sheet fell to the ground. Don Girolamo waved the aspersorium and sprinkled Holy Water at the plaque. And then he began to read it out loud. There were forty-six names on it, in alphabetical order, followed by sex, nationality, and age. Twenty-one men, Italian, eighteen to eighty-one years of age; four children, Italian, five to eleven years of age; seven women, Italian, nineteen to eighty; six men, German, sixteen to forty-eight; three men, Polish, twenty-three to forty-one; three (two men, one woman) American, twenty-one to thirty; two men, British, twenty-three and twenty-five.

Don Girolamo's voice cracked halfway through the list; then he could not continue. Words, as much as he tried, just came out as one painful, throaty lament. He was taken back to the parsonage, and the young priest continued the reading.

The next day at dawn they found Don Girò wandering in the vineyard, half-naked, blabbering and crying, repeating over and over what sounded like names. It appeared that he had spent the whole night there.

He was taken to the old priests' rest home, where he died two weeks later. Officially, he died of pneumonia, but Zia Elena's diagnosis was that the old goat had died of a broken heart.

He was, officially, ninety-three.

From the day we deserted our fountain, almost three years had passed before our group convened around it again. We were all there, having trickled back to Rome as fast as we could, once the madness was over.

Somehow we had seen the end of the war and none of us had died. Why not is a mystery, perhaps a miracle, because given the odds, most of us should have. We all carried scars, some deep inside. We came back to tell our stories, to show our wounds and hope that the telling would help mend them.

The long series of questions started without provocation, when we were too bored or too sad to talk about ourselves. Has anybody seen Pino? Is he back? And the son of the tailor, what's his name . . . Giorgio? Giggetto—would you believe it, that *finocchio*—walked all the way home from Messina! It must be 500 kilometers. No, more!

Which brought to mind Otto. Did anybody know what had happened to Otto?

Carlo knew. Carlo had seen action at Dongo, near the Swiss border, as part of the effort to stop the Fascists' and Germans' escape. He was close to where Mussolini and his mistress, Clara Petacci, dressed like German soldiers and hiding in a Wehrmacht truck, part of a convoy, were taken prisoner and shot. Their bodies were taken to Milan and hung upside down—like butchered beef—from the roof of a gas station in Piazzale Loreto. That same convoy also carried several Italian collaborators and many German civilian auxiliaries. They were all executed on the spot. Their carcasses were put on display, lined up on the pavement of the main square of Salò on Lake Garda.

It was among those bodies that Carlo saw Otto. He was sure: Otto was wearing only the ragged top part of a German officer's uniform, and Carlo recognized him from the old, familiar scar on his leg. The once magnificent body of Otto's mother lay near her son.

With unveiled sarcasm, people sang the Fascist hymn *"Giovinezza, giovinezza!"* and all over Italy they chiseled away from buildings and monuments all the symbols of the past dictatorship; Mussolini's statues were hammered into crumbs. Commander Puzi was the loudest at yelling *"Libertà! Libertà!"* and tore and burned his uniform in the middle of the courtyard, swearing that he had been a double agent working all along for the forces of freedom.

My father had his chance at him but said to Puzi's face that he would not waste his spittle on him.

Given the choice, instead of being locked up for a long time in a POW indoctrination camp, Federico and Piero Mazzetti elected to sweep minefields for a much briefer stint. A death wish, it was said, but I didn't want to believe it. They loved life too much. I much preferred to believe that they wanted to get over the past as quickly as possible, and get going again. Tina, on the other hand, not being allowed to dig up mines, became a serious drinker instead.

A surprise to all of us around the courtyard was the reappearance of Luigino Giggetto Tifini. Signora Tifini was a gentle widow who frequently discussed with my mother the difficulty of bringing up children, especially how to keep obnoxious males away from her beautiful daughter, Maria, just now finishing her university studies. And Luigino, the son, contemporary of my brother, Marco, was worrying her because he was a bit too effeminate. Coinciding with the Anzio landings, the family had made itself quite scarce for months, and their rare movements seemed furtive. Even their windows facing the courtyard had closed shutters. The widow and Maria made brief sorties only for the necessary available supplies. With the liberation of Rome, the shutters came open and the revelation flew out to stun us: for all that time the Tifinis had kept hidden three escaped American prisoners.

We speculated about the heroic logistics of the situation, and how they kept it secret, given the small parameters of our *palazzo*. We nasty boys commented on how Maria must have been happy with all those boys at hand, or vice versa. Then we found out that all three GIs were gay, and surely Giggetto had been the winner.

. . .

Signor Ulisse Mazzetti, after being released from a British prison camp in Ethiopia, chose exile and was allowed to remain in that country. In quite a short time he became an unofficial adviser to the Ethiopian government on matters of transportation and construction. His letters home grew less and less frequent, until they stopped completely. It became known, later, that he had acquired great wealth and a new Ethiopian family.

His legal wife, Signora Teresa Mazzetti, swore off politics. She dedicated herself to charity and to help church organizations care for the war dispossessed and the parish poor.

Signorina Ada had not followed the new Fascists north. With the first fall of Mussolini, on July 25, 1943, just before Victor Emmanuel's flight south, she had, in effect, been widowed and lost, in turn, her faith in all the rest of humanity. If humanity could be so vindictive and blasphemous, and behave with such savagery and infamy, and pile up such indignities on her idol, she wanted no part of it. Later, when the Germans freed Mussolini from his mountaintop imprisonment and propped him like a puppet at the head of the new Fascist Republic, she believed that this new Mussolini was an impostor, an impersonator, and remained faithful to her old idea of him. To protect it against any possible air-raid injury, she took down from the wall the portrait of Benito on horseback and turned it into a secret little shrine in a corner of her room.

After the end of the war, Ada was *epurata,* cleansed. She was fired without a pension and, like many other prominent Fascists, lost her eligibility for another government job.

Besides the Mazzettis, the closest Fascists I knew were the Paolis. I really wanted to find out about my old friends, and hoped to see them even if for a minute. Perhaps we could meet in Cattolica and play again in the sand. Acquaintances from Piacenza, their town, told me that the Paolis had disappeared, leaving behind only rumors. Someone had told them that young Vincenzo had been wounded on the Greek front (or was it the Russian?) and that Luisella, too much of a beauty to pass up, had been raped and impregnated by the long-toothed Britons, sons of Albion (just like in the old Fascist posters), or by the anti-Fascist partisans (or was it by Moroccan soldiers?). In the end, it seemed that the whole family—being, all told, decent and well-liked people—escaped the vindictiveness that had decimated the old governing class. They were helped to emigrate to Argentina with passports supplied by (or bought from?) the local bishop.

My mother had lost the help of a maid, a luxury now. But she rolled up her sleeves and went to work with renewed energy. First things first. The rumble of war barely over, she had all the rooms repainted to take away the soot (and with it the memory) of the miserable years past. She removed the anti-shatter paper strips from all the windows, leaving them open day and night to let in the air. When I came back home, she held me tight, not knowing whether to cry or to laugh. Then, considering my crutches, she gave me a rap on the head (a loving one, supposedly). She could have guessed, she said, that if left alone I would do something stupid and get hurt.

"So, we have a hero in the family!" she said reluctantly. That's me, I thought, the reluctant hero.

My older brother, Marco, had taken advantage of his months in hiding to prepare for his university exams. In very short order, he married his nineteen-year-old fiancée (the niece of the parish priest who had sheltered him. "Too young," people said, "but, oh! what a beautiful couple!"), took his engineering degree summa cum laude, and was immediately hired by an American company that was reestablishing its war-interrupted operations in Italy, headquarters in Rome. My parents were very proud of him and I, reluctantly, too. My younger sister, Anna, had blossomed into an absolute beauty, given up on her ballet ambitions (too demanding), and taken up tennis. Her social circle expanded to include la crème de la crème, not only of the neighborhood but of Rome.

My father formed a cooperative with two other architects. With Italy in ruins, they had their rebuilding work assured for years to come. They needed an expert administrator; the job, following my father's recommendation, was offered to Ada.

But only on one condition: she could not hang in her office anybody's portrait, on or off a horse.

She accepted.

I had resumed my studies. The university had set up accelerated courses for all those students who had lost time at warring. My stint had been a relatively short one, seven months, compared with those who had been away for four or five years. But in that short time my world had changed greatly. It was as if I had boarded a train that, after going through a long, dark tunnel, had emerged at an unknown place. My side had won, but I did not feel like a victor. I had won by default; I just as easily could have been the vanquished. For a time, I merely let things happen, without fighting them too much. I could find no reason for what had happened in the world. Both sides had drawn their swords in defense of their politics, their country, their religion. Both had God on their side. I tried to analyze my feelings, tried to figure out how a handful of despots had sunk the world in a bloodbath, how the masses had applauded and followed orders without questioning, jumping off cliffs into the sea and drowning like lemmings. A few thinkers had begged people to open their eyes, to wake up, but they were called Cassandras and punished. And when finally people woke up, it was too late. These kinds of mullings ended up making me ache all over, and I looked for revenge. I ended up throwing the crutches at flies on the wall, as if they were responsible. In these moments I found my identity; that was what I was: a fly on the wall, looking and seeing and remembering—but taking no part.

In 1946, although the official Italian economy was in shambles, the submerged one was booming. All that had been missing for so long was back on the market with a vengeance, the black market, that is. Illegal fortunes were made overnight, and the new rich, to impress the honestly poor, flaunted it. Money fetched money, and those who had none were considered stupid and antiquated. Things were done *"all'americana,"* the American way: fast, with brio and glamour, enterprisingly, agreeing on contracts with a handshake. Not the slow and staid, old-style, bureaucratic way. America, the victor, was sending big money to heal the wounds of the vanquished, so that the vanquished could get well and buy from America. Prime the pump, that's the American way! The money was given government to government, but much of it submerged at night into the private, shady economy, to resurface next day, laundered and shiny: new houses, new cars, new-furred mistresses, new businesses. A chicken in every pot, a car in every garage. We had seen that youthful, unencumbered lifestyle in Hollywood movies. Since 1938, American films had been banned, but now they had come back to fill Italian movie houses to standing room only.

While the wounds of the flesh were healing, my soul's were another matter. Maresa, when I came back to Rome, had welcomed me. Almost immediately she told me how much she had missed my friendship, the long talks, the long walks. Now our talks were easy but walks or embraces—with me on crutches—much less so (was it just the crutches?).

I spoke of love, she spoke of friendship. Friendship: love's assassin.

I felt self-conscious about my crutches, bothered to be looked at as a cripple. But, when I was with Maresa, it was even more embarrassing to be stared at not for the crutches but for her. She had become a star, or at least she really looked like one. With the return to our screens of the once banned Hollywood movies, Italy had discovered Ingrid Bergman, and if a painter had made a portrait of her Nordic beauty using a Mediterranean brush, he would have come up with Maresa. Maresa in turn had cropped her hair to look more like Ingrid, and their resemblance was uncanny. With my sense of identity already shaky, I felt myself becoming a mere satellite of that shiny Ingrid/Maresa star, known only as her sometime companion, her sometime friend, her one-time boyfriend.

Many times I thought bitterly of when Bob and I had decided to stay away from anybody looking like a movie star.

I lost my moorings completely when the old Number 6 trolley car reappeared as a sleek trolley bus, and with it Vladimir (his real name turned out to be a common Dino).

His reappearance was quite an unpleasant event for me. What was scary was that among all the faces Hollywood had brought to us (and plastered the walls of the city with) was Vladimir's visage—or Joseph Cotten's. The similarity—coloring, build, expression—was more than uncanny.

The creep had opened some sort of import-export office and become a frequent presence on Number 6, like most of us, going in the morning, coming in the evening. So did Maresa. It did not take long for Dino to become more than Maresa's occasional travel companion. He shamelessly offered her employment: Maresa Bergman, Dino Cotten. It was true that in striving to be *all'americana* we were all living vicariously the Hollywood image, borrowing postures, attitudes, ways of dressing and speaking, aping in general what we had seen on the screen. But this Ingrid/Cotten was too much. She accepted his offer and became his office assistant. Dino then assisted her in ditching her chastity, and in return, trying to catch up for lost time, she assisted him by giving him CinemaScope, wide-screen-size, full Technicolor sex. Every working day, and overtime on Saturday.

An envious, venomous Velia reported to me what Maresa had proudly confided in her. She had revolted and broken her family's puritanical restrictions, and had discovered in herself the inextinguishable desire, need, and ability for fornication.

Or, as Velia put succinctly, "The two of them are going at it like deranged rabbits."

It took me more than some time to get over Maresa. I had constructed for her a high pedestal of chaste purity, and now, in a simple special-effects film technique, that pedestal had dissolved into a rabbit hutch. I could not erase from my mind, not even for a second, the horrible vision of a nakedly oversexed Maresa "going at it." And, to twist the knife in the wound, Ingrid/Maresa kept smiling at me from all the walls of Rome, teasing me for all my lost times, all the times I had fought with my desire, saved my honor and hers, only to preserve the whole shebang for Dino.

For a long while it became impossible for me to think of anything but my naïve stupidity. I could not concentrate, especially on my studies. I could not look at mirrors; the only thing I saw was the face of an incurable romantic buffoon who wrote love letters to a whore while bullets were zipping around his head. Shakespeare, Dante, Boccaccio, Virgil, Petrarca, Browning . . . Gad, what idiots!

I simply had to quit this nonsense.

Like the whole country, I had to find a way to put myself back together.

17

The Partnership

I STILL LOVED TO TAKE LONG WALKS and talk to myself. Driven by an internal compass, like a homing bird, I would find myself going through the gardens of the Villa Borghese, by the Parco dei Daini, and then past the villa itself. The fountain of the sea monsters, and the fountain of Venus, the fountain of Apollo—we had raced our toy boats there— were now silent, their huge bowls empty, but still dear to me like old friends. The Borghese garden, in the heart of Rome, had suffered mightily from the war. Its manicured lawns and formal flower beds, flowering shrubs and trees, the little ponds and lakes, were dying for lack of upkeep since the beginning of the war, and whole acres had been demolished by the occupying armies' youthful, uncaring soldiers. Tent camps, temporary barracks, and truck and tank depots had been settled in and around the gardens, miles of barbwire separating them from the world. Now the armies were gone, but the deep scars remained. It was sad, even painful to look at them, like looking at scars on your own body. And yet the madness had passed, the destruction was over. By touching the scars, you could feel the healing in progress. Nearly three years after the liberation of Rome, two after the end of the war in Europe, the slow work of restoration had begun. One could begin to hope again.

I had been back in Rome, back at home, for almost two and a half years, and at this point I was finding the University School of Engineering hard-going. A regimented, disciplined life behind a desk seemed stifling, and I felt it was time I earned my keep. The war had left my parents' finances, like most everybody else's, not in the best shape, and I was still depending on them for my studies, my books, and the few (very few) lire of spending money.

A let's-do-it fervor was sweeping the country. Rebuild what is rebuildable, start anew what isn't, but let's do it now. In the midst of this, I felt as if I were idling in neutral and waiting until, with luck, I could get in gear and get going. Yes, it was time I did something, anything that would earn me some money, make me feel productive.

After all, I was healthy enough: my knee had healed but for a sharp pain that came and went once in a while with the change of weather, with excitement, when I needed an excuse. The therapy—miles of swimming—had worked miracles; I was told not to stand on my leg too long, but if I really had to, to rely on my crutches. But I abandoned them when I realized that I was making of them the emblem of my recent past, an advertisement as morbid as the kill silhouettes painted on a fighter plane's fuselage.

It was 1947 and it was spring again. It was high time to get going.

. . .

It was Sunday again.

Instead of going to Mass—as I'd promised Mamma—I indulged in my walk, heading for the Villa Borghese, remembering this same walk with my father, his explanation of the landmarks I went by. I reached the Pincio Terrace almost at noon. The huge terrace looks over all of Rome from way up, the best opera seat to have for that indescribable performance soon to begin. The old cannon on the Gianicolo Hill will boom at the stroke of noon and the bells of the myriad churches break loose in a joyous chorus. The view and the sound fill the soul and lift it.

I recognized Federico Mazzetti from a distance by his walk, like that of a ballet dancer or a soccer player, fluid and rhythmical. As ever, he was lean and gangling, which made him appear taller than he actually was. Because of his way of moving, as if always listening to an internal music, and the way he combed his hair back, smooth and shiny from lots of brilliantine, Piero and I had nicknamed him Fred, as in Astaire. Before the war, I had admired his unworried attitude toward life; he did not have a mean bone in his body. Now, having done his six-month stint clearing minefields—a line of work that aged people very quickly—Federico had returned home seemingly unchanged.

I had seen him before, of course, and Tina. Like me, they had come back to the old *palazzo* to stay with their family. Piero had not, opting instead to remain up north, working with a construction company. I had not spoken to the Mazzettis yet, and quite frankly I had not hurried an encounter, being unsure of how we would react to each other or how to behave. It was accepted etiquette to treat returning Fascist and German collaborators with the utmost scorn and contempt, rewarding their past arrogance by ignoring them. Some whose past offenses had been particularly unpopular had gotten public beatings as "cleansings." But the Mazzettis, as far as I was concerned, were different. We had known each other all of our lives, and to me, their going north with the Fascists was inevitable. They had no choice but to follow their beliefs.

Once Fred came close and recognized me—there in no-man's-land, as it were—the encounter played itself out naturally. After a moment's hesitation we embraced, patting each other's backs, then smiled as two friends who had not seen each other in a long time. The histories of our last few years were told fast, just summaries of major events, the listing of the chapters of a book in which we were the protagonists. We could fill in the details later, with time.

It was past noon. Sunday lunch would be served at one, and after a long stretch of make-do meals of pseudofood, a real meal made with real ingredients, cooked on a real stove and served on a real, properly appointed table, was something not to be delayed. My mother's way to express her gratitude for having her family all back together was to set up Sunday feasts. So was Signora Mazzetti's. If we walked quickly, we could make it with a little time to spare and, as a bonus, once we reached the courtyard, catch all the aromas wafting from the *palazzo*'s kitchens.

After that, Fred and I talked many times, trying to come to grips with our lives, with the war. I felt free to talk to him; we had been on opposite sides, how different from mine were his feelings? Now what? Our parents had called theirs the Great War so as not to confuse it with other, lesser ones. Perhaps, then, we should call our war the Huge War, the Monstrous War. Magazines and newspapers were, issue by issue, revising upward by the millions the global tally of losses for Russia, the U.S.A., Italy, France, Germany, Japan, and on and on. The figures were so big, the horrors so many, the events so terrible, that it was impossible to visualize them. Confronted by all this, we felt our own experiences inconsequential, ourselves so worthless as to be uncountable. At the ends of great figures followed by at least six zeros, one number more, one less, like a grain of sand in the Sahara desert—what difference did it make?

It was customary that, after a memorial celebration, the names of the missing would be called and the whole audience would stand up and yell in unison: *Presente!* Present! In spirit, that is.

One evening we came up with a new thought. Why not an accounting, a roll call of the people who survived? Then when your name was called, yelling *Presente!* that one more number, your number, made a big, a huge difference. It was a stupid thought, we agreed, but one that made our skins tingle with happiness and expectation. Walking in the street, we called our names and shouted in answer *Presente! Presente!* and a future was still there for us to have. We became giddy, and in rhythm with our steps, we sang our version of a popular song of the moment:

> *The only thing we own,* paisà,
> *Is the air in our lungs,* paisà!

So, let's use it to sing!
Let's forget the past, paisà:
Who has given, has given;
Who has taken, has taken;
Let's forget the past, and
Let's move on, paisà.

It had a good tempo for a brisk walk, and a simple philosophy, easy to understand. But, given human nature, not that easy to accept. The song did not make clear, for example, if the singer was the giver or the taker. For twenty years, some people had taken and taken, and for those who had given and given that wasn't so easy to forget.

Many of the big takers had escaped summary justice, and in order not to put the let's forget theory to the test, had fled, loot and all, to Portugal, Argentina, Brazil.

Others—the small takers and those who had been swept up by the Fascist cause—had remained to face the music. Their difficulty in reentering the fabric of civilian life (last choice for employment and banned from government jobs) was assuaged by belonging to a network of mutual assistance.

Fred had been helped by his network to find work in the darkrooms of Alinari, the oldest and largest photo library in Italy. At Alinari, photos of every single Italian panorama, cityscape, monument, painting, or sculpture, and details thereof, were on file. Studio Fratelli Alinari was also the official photographer of popes, kings, and all other personalities whose photos commanded a place on a wall. The reproductions (from postcard to mural size), if not already on the shelf, were custom-printed in the size and number desired. Fred hoped to step, one day, from the darkroom into the lights, behind a camera, an ambition spurred not only by his abilities but also by the incentive of switching from low apprentice pay to a professional salary.

How ironic, I told him. I had made a sort of reputation for myself by taking portraits of friends (especially of my ex-girlfriend), but I lacked a real darkroom, and I had to juggle my modest resources for film, chemicals, and papers. I had the use of a beautiful camera, a Rolleiflex, and I was using an enlarger I made myself. I had obtained some of its parts in exchange for making an enlargement of a dear departed, almost life size, giving it an oval shape with diffuse edges; the image in the middle, in soft focus, gave the whole thing an eerie, ectoplasmic appearance. It was very arty and so successful that I had been asked to make others for other people. I could almost turn the hobby into a small moneymaking activity, only I lacked capital and materials.

Fred confessed that, at work, he had saved a box of thrown-away scraps and leftover photographic paper for his use.

"I will bring you some," he said. "My contribution to a budding *artigiano*."

"*Artista,* please!" I corrected him.

For my ego, the difference between artisan and artist was similar to the one between a stonecutter and a Michelangelo.

The plan that emerged in our next few meetings was simple and followed the basic capitalistic canon. Detect, or promote, a "need in the marketplace" and fill it. To cover the somewhat morbid character of our enterprise, we decided that there were enough altruistic and charitable elements in it to make it honorable and creditable. How many people wouldn't be grateful to have clear, sizable pictures of their dear ones, in place of thumbed, yellowed, cracked, small snapshots?

We started by offering our services to our immediate circles of friends and acquaintances; we acquired experience, refined our technique, and put together a portfolio of samples. On delivery, we answered the final question of "How much?" by quoting a figure in line with a questioning lilt, then adjusting it, up or down, depending on the amount of happiness, or lack of it, expressed by the customer.

The actual laboratory work was done at night for several reasons. It did not interfere (not too much, yet) with my classes or Fred's job; it was easier to obtain a lightproof, darkroom environment, the supply of electricity being more stable at night (or not so prone to the ups and downs still common during the day) allowed for more constant exposures. And finally, since in our case "laboratory" was an exalted term for lavatory, we could lock ourselves in the little room and do our work with less chance of being disturbed. The choice had fallen on the bathroom of my house because the Mazzettis' household still included the superannuated grandfather, a slave to immediate, imperative needs that arose at any hour of the day or night.

Within two months we felt assured of our production capabilities and we had enough capital for a "market expansion." Advertising was out of the question. We were not equipped for mass production and, also, were very jealous of our little gold mine. Less dedicated or less honest operators could move in, take over, and turn our endeavor into a scam. These were so common at that time that most of the population at large had become very defensive and suspicious, so much so that they would not even trust their own image in a stranger's mirror.

And yet every day some gullible person fell again for old, well-publicized scams—like buying the ancient Roman gold coin just surfaced from the floor of the Colosseum—or new, incredibly imaginative ones. Remarkably good national health (probably due to years of a fat-free diet) prompted the discovery of previously unheard-of exotic and phony maladies, which naturally, would be cured by just as phony and expensive medicines; as one bogus sickness was cured, another one of epidemic proportions surfaced and again was cured by a miraculous snake oil.

As a counterpart to the physical world, an army of parapsychologists, mediums, hand readers, crystal-ball gazers, and tarot card interpreters had sprouted up overnight. They catered to all who searched for news of relatives lost in the great upheaval of the war and created for them elaborate scenarios. Once hooked, heartbroken people were milked dry by scoundrels who fed them little bits of sibylline news, week after week, always raising their hopes with the promise of more definitive good news the next time. The police bunko squad worked overtime, but the best thing it could do was to alert everybody to beware. Italy was suffering from a large inflation of wooden nickels.

These and other kinds of widespread cheating and swindling had soured the market for us, and the first and biggest hurdle to our expansion was to obtain the confidence of our prospective clients.

We obtained their addresses directly from city hall. Every day it displayed to the public the official notices of births, matrimonies, and deaths. Near these were unofficial bulletin boards full of queries asking for information on the whereabouts of missing people. Many of these notes were accompanied by photographs, mostly of soldiers, some of civilians, some of groups of people with one face circled. It was a heart-wrenching display of human misery, and we had to make quite an effort to reinforce our conviction that what we were doing was the right thing, that we were going to bring about, in all that Mount Everest of despair, a small hill of solace.

We took addresses from both bulletin boards, selecting them from the middle-class quarters of the city, houses of people with whom we could identify—and they with us.

At first we made our visits together, dressed as neatly as possible, dignified but not lugubrious. Fred insisted I use my crutches as props. Besides subliminally begging for a touch of pity, they reassured people that, whatever might develop, I was not capable of a fast escape. As briefly as possible, we explained the purpose of the visit, offered our condolences if appropriate (but without excessive gloom: the poor people had already seen enough of it), showed our portfolio with before and after samples, and gave right away a ballpark estimate of costs. When that point was reached, there wasn't much selling we could do: it was either yes or no. We just kept quiet and let them decide.

Once an order was in hand, we went to work and made the delivery as fast as possible. We returned the original and the new, restored print. "We will keep the negative on file," we assured our customers. "Any time you need other or larger prints, just let us know." And we left with them one or two of our calling cards:

F. & F. Artistic Photo Restoration
Any Size from Any Size
From Any Condition to Art Gallery Quality

There was some hype in that promise, but the cards were printed gray on gray, unboastfully.

By the end of winter, we were doing well; we did not depend anymore on Studio Alinari's scraps of material, and I could not only take my occasional girlfriends to the movies or dinner but even pay for it. Our success had its downside, though. The working nights got to be longer, and the constant transformation of laboratory back to lavatory and vice versa got to be a real chore.

Also, the patience of my family was growing thin; our supposedly temporary situation was getting to be as temporary as the Colosseum. Moreover, Fred had been found napping, more than once, in a corner of the Alinari darkroom, and I had been lulled, more than once, into gold-filled dreams during metallurgy class.

The situation was aggravated by another development. Made euphoric and bold by our success, we began promising to our customers things that we should not have, straying beyond restoration into artistic enlargements cum cosmetic surgery. A large number of the photos we were given to work on had certain features that bothered us. A large proportion of grandmothers sported fuzz on their upper lips (to be less diplomatic: definite mustaches) and, just as frequently, disapproving, scolding downturns of the mouth. In other photos, particularly of males, the magnesium flash had frozen them stiff with the wild, wide-open eyes of the possessed. Their photos had a gaze that followed you around the room, as the *malocchio* of the evil eye, searching and hexing you even in the dark. The darkroom safety light offered no safety at all.

These features, we thought, even allowing for a goodly amount of familial love, must also have bugged the photos' owners—and in some cases they told us so.

We promised, brazenly, to correct them.

A brainstorming session was due. In the evening we went to the local trattoria, ordered two expensive pizzas and a liter of good wine. We munched, sipped, talked, and thought. We went one more round. Then a third, but hold the pizza. When we left the place, it was night, a crisp and clear night. The sky was full of stars, we were full of wine and optimism, and we had a solution.

The name of our solution was La Paloma, the Dove. Our neighbor, my sporadic confidante, intermittent adviser, and (a few times) solace.

When I had been in need of her advice and counsel in matters of the heart, she had given generously of her knowledge, and I was grateful for her abundant friendship. But remuneration was not the reason I elected her to be our savior. She had several essential things to offer to the future of our operation. One, she had graduated from the Accademia delle Belle Arti and was a superlative illustrator, painter, and graphic artist. Two, at the moment she was unemployed in her field, keeping busy by tutoring in Latin and Greek. And, three, she lived in an apartment equipped with three bathrooms. Three.

A single child born when her parents were well past middle age, she lived with them in a huge apartment, its rooms arranged like an L, so as to form almost two apartments at right angles with each other. In the square-doughnut floor plan of our *palazzo,* her place was one floor below mine and adjacent, on the same floor, to Fred's. The *palazzo's* apartments were of different sizes, and hers was the largest, including what, with some hyperbole, was called the servants' quarter: a windowless room with its own bath-laundry-service room. The three-member family was servantless, and the "quarter" was used as a catchall space. It was there, just waiting for us.

We invited La Paloma (Magda) to the neutral grounds of our favorite trattoria. She was known as a *buona forchetta* (a good fork, a gourmand), and we thought that food and one or two glasses of wine would make her more responsive to our plans. She was already aware of our activities; still, we explained to her, casually but in detail, our present situation and our needs for the future. These really boiled down to two: finding a helping artistic, creative hand, and locating a fixed, somewhat more spacious laboratory than what we had now—and, ideally, everything close to home.

She put one and one together and came up with ten: How dumb were we, she asked, not to see that she had been there all along, under our very eyes, and with everything we needed? How could we not think of it?

We feigned amazement. How not, indeed! Was she serious?

She began to perspire with excitement. We said it was all so much of a surprise that we needed time to think about it. Then we offered her a partnership on the spot.

We walked home, arms linked. All the way she warbled La Tosca's *"Vissi d'arte, vissi d'amore."*

Indeed.

18

The Dead Are Dead

MAGDA'S PARENTS RARELY ventured out of the bottom leg of their apartment's L. Her mother, when not in church, spent most of the time in her workroom, embroidering church vestments and draperies. Her father was practically a recluse in his studio-library, immersed in his papers and books, cocooned in a thick cloud of cigar smoke. An eminent liberal lawyer and teacher of constitutional law, he had somehow allowed his name to be used to give credence to Fascist philosophies and then, fallen from grace, had been slowly elbowed out of the legal arena. Gentle, corpulent, and absentminded, he had taken refuge in the isolated sanctity of his studio. He made rare sorties for books, papers, and above all for his supply of cigars. Morning, noon, or night one of those fierce-smelling Toscani was propped in the corner of his mouth, emanating puffs of blue-white smoke that engulfed, stuck to, and permeated everything. We knew where he had been by the odoriferous trail he left behind, and like the warning bell at a railroad station, the smell of his cigar preceded him and heralded his arrival.

Magda had to promise her parents that her new activity would not interfere with their lives, a promise that we sealed with the gifts of a rainbow of spools of silk thread for her mother and a box of Toscani cigars for her father. The latter did not come in actual boxes but in bunches of ten, tied together like black kindling wood, which they closely resembled. I picked them out myself at the tobacconist's, choosing them carefully one by one. On the lap of my Nonno Nicola, an avid Toscani smoker, I had learned how to roll the abominable sticks between thumb and forefinger. The good ones had to be hard, knotty, and crackly, like a well-dried twig; only this would assure permanent embers and a continuous emission of foul smoke, a connoisseur's nirvana. I bought five bunches and put them in a decorated box; the three of us together made the presentation to him. Fred and I, to make sure he remembered who we were, reintroduced ourselves; the *Avvocato,* as he was known, said, "A pleasure!" and shook our hands, including Magda's.

The transfer of the operation went smoothly. In less than a week we were operating out of La Paloma's quarters. We made her an equal partner and felt the arrangement equitable. By the end of three weeks, the association had found its own pace. Fred delivered the finished work during his lunchtime break; in the afternoon, after university classes, I did a few rounds of prospecting; during the day, between tutoring lessons, La Paloma did some retouching; then, after dinner, we would all convene at her apartment. I did the rephotographing and enlarging, Fred did the processing and toning, and Magda the artistic work.

While Fred and I did our work in the darkness of the maid's quarter, Magda's was done in her spacious room, which had been set up as an artist's studio long before her enrollment at the Accademia delle Belle Arti, when she had shown an early talent for painting and drawing. Portraiture was her forte, and most of her works, until now, had been portraits of actors copied from movie magazines and, occasionally, studies of live models.

At home, La Paloma wore an ankle-length dressing gown of maroon velvet with white silk frills framing the cuffs and her ample cleavage. When ready to work, she put on a black velvet beret that officially declared she was in artist mode. At night she also turned on a brilliant swing-arm light clipped to her easel, which being focused only on the work area, left the rest of the room in a thousand-and-one-nights penumbra.

In a few days of work on the photographs, she gave proof of her talent for restoration and cosmetics; compared with her marvels, our previous work looked clumsy and patched up. Her needle-thin paintbrushes had the assurance and lightness of a plastic surgeon's scalpels, filling a crack here, erasing a wrinkle there.

Business was good. With the noticeable increase in its quality, we charged more for our work. Our income, even though now shared by three, grew substantially, so much so that we could reduce the workload. "Quality, not quantity" became our motto. Fred did not fall asleep on the job anymore, and his alertness was rewarded with a promotion to second assistant cameraman. I put in more time on my studies and began to catch up on fieldwork. La Paloma, now that she could practice her artistic skills in a professional way (being paid, that is), was happier than ever; she cut down on her tutoring and, following the "quality, not quantity" rule, kept only a few sturdy pupils. During the day, her musical repertory became truly eclectic, and her singing flew out of her windows like a silver ribbon of notes that brought joy to the neighborhood.

With our enhanced sense of well-being and the pooling of our talents, we became more creative. I copied the originals and made low-contrast enlargements. Fred developed them so that all the features were definite but barely visible, and from there La Paloma took over. What we gave her were merely the foundations, and on these she rebuilt, more than faces, entire personalities. Mustaches disappeared, lips' corners were turned up, a sparkle appeared in the eyes of grandmothers, and they became serene, looking from the wall with loving understanding. The staring, possessed eyes of other subjects were softened and the pupils made not to stare at you but to look a little to the side, as if to check that nothing untoward was happening behind your back. "Be reassured," all these images said, "I will be here when you need me."

All of this, we told ourselves, was priceless. La Paloma had an almost mystic feeling about her work. She felt that by making the images of these people more relaxed and serene, just possibly she was helping their souls too, wherever they might be, to experience some relief. It was heavy stuff, and when she fell into that mood we took her out and fed her pizza and wine.

Brushwork done, the images were artfully tinted and pinned to dry in a sort of gallery in Magda's room. I took them down from there and rephotographed them; then they were printed on a canvas-textured paper, processed by Fred to just the right softness. Once we had finished with them, we had a bit more than a *fotografia,* a little less than a *ritratto.*

We had a *fotratto,* a phortrait, an unabashed composite of photo(graphy) and (por)trait.

We said so in our revised calling cards:

★ ★ ★

F. M. F. FOTRATTI
Photo-Portraiture
From Your Originals, Old or New
Gallery Quality
★ ★ ★

Italy, having lost the war, was left with an immense amount of *residuati di guerra,* war leftovers. Many destroyed, half-destroyed, or just hors de combat war machines peppered the country-side. The Germans, in their final, hasty retreat, had left behind all sorts of materiel, and for their part, once the war was over, the Allies found it more economical to leave behind most of their own war apparatus than to ship it back home.

The Italian government solicited bids for collecting in huge depots all the "war residues," then bids for fixing, transforming, and making them in any way operative, and finally bids from wholesalers for merchandising and selling the resurrected, functioning goods. From Liberty ships to field kitchens, from Tiger tanks to Quonset huts, from airplanes to inflatable rafts, telephone systems to typewriters—everything was available on the open market.

Small and big industries leapt at the chance and transformed tanks into tractors, trucks into buses, parachutes into shirts, mountains of empty beer bottles into a flourishing, most fashionable glass industry. Never before had Italian creativity responded to a challenge with such ingenuity. For a long time afterward, it was practically impossible to have or to use something, anything that did not have a military past. And once the originals bit the dust, new products were inspired by them, then perfected and improved so successfully that they found their way around the world. Take a small compressor engine, snuggle it under a bike seat between two airplane tail wheels, and voilà, you have the Vespa scooter, the most long-lived, widely used means of transportation in the world.

The wheels of industry, of commerce, and of fashion were now spinning again, faster and faster, with the proud, aggressive joy of a reborn phoenix. Let others eat ashes!

To fulfill the need for faster transportation—for the benefit of the company—I decided to buy myself a motorcycle, one of the well-used swords turned into plowshares. After a long survey of machines, I was faced with a final, affordable choice: either a German BMW 500 or a British Triumph 350. Once enemies bent on destroying each other, now equally harmless leftovers of the Italian campaign. I went for the Triumph, not only out of a sense of loyalty but for the name. With a name like that, how could I miss?

La Paloma and Fred, after a few triumphal spins around town as passengers, decided the machine had a character of its own and deserved a less generic, more personalized name. Onomatopoeically, it was given a first and a family name: Paetaeppa Paetaeppe.

Life with Paetaeppa became a breeze. Pickups, deliveries, and all related errands took half the time or less.

It was hard not to remember, only a few years back—but it

seemed a century—when Professor Gesmundo stopped me just outside the classroom and told me he had seen me running around town on a bike. Did I have something more important to do than being in school? Did my parents know? I could not answer, but only lowered my head and blushed. A few days later he asked me for a favor: Could I deliver a small package for him? And that was the beginning of my bicycle running. I wonder why with all the miles of bicycling and bumping over the old Roman cobblestones my butt had not developed calluses; how not to remember how intensely I cursed the mystical, historical hills of Rome, having to push the miserable wreck of a bike up the steep inclines. But now, finally, I could rest on a cushioned seat and with a little twist of the wrist have the motor roar, and Paetaeppa would fly up any hill. There I was on a noisy magic carpet, barely feeling the old cobblestones, being—happily—a *fattorino*, a bike runner, again.

I used the time gained to my personal benefit—like carrying a conspicuously sexy girl (a fun loving countergirl from the photo-supply store) around town and even, in a most brazen and spiteful way, with the girl laughingly holding tight to my waist, running noisy circles under Maresa's windows.

I could also dedicate more time to my school assignments: among others, a paper on the theory of acoustics and its practice in sound engineering. For that purpose, I was doing work-study in a new film dubbing studio. I had made many friends among its staff, and they turned out to be as enthusiastic teachers as I was a pupil. Moreover, they had so much work that they welcomed a helping hand; the studio operated in shifts around the clock, and I could sign on whenever I had the time. The huge backlog of foreign films, barred by the war but now flooding the market, had to be dubbed, edited, and promoted for Italian audiences.

I told La Paloma of my fabulous experiences in the movie world (but not how peripheral they were), and how I had met the Italian voices of Gregory Peck and Gary Cooper (and, yes, Ingrid Bergman), and how much fun it was to see the movies in tiny snippets, played over and over again, till the dubber got it right and Gary and Gregory (and damn, yes, even Ingrid) were speaking Italian. In the long run it could become tedious work, but then at the end—it could take two or more weeks to dub a film—one was privileged to see a first-run movie before anybody else.

La Paloma enjoyed the anecdotes I brought to her like bouquets, and accepted them with childish pleasure; sometimes I had to throw in a few fabricated arabesques to fulfill her desire for details.

Then slowly her enthusiasm diminished, until even my more astonishing tales were received with indifference. She began singing sotto voce sad, tormented ballads, and in the morning, she did not bother to pull open the window drapes. Fred and I thought at first that she was going through one of those mysterious feminine phases, but when the mood persisted, actually got worse, we worried. And we were not alone. The baker, the dairy man, the tailor, the shoemaker—all the merchants and artisans who had shops on the street of our *palazzo*—worried about us. They felt there was a lesson somewhere in the fact that a liberal intellectual's daughter, an ex-Fascist Militiaman, and an ex-partisan had joined forces. They were aware that we had made a success of it; they had cheered us on and were

cheered in return by Magda's singing and our bouncy, contagious good humor. Now they asked us if things were all right,
if there was anything wrong. For a while they had not heard
Magda throw the windows open and welcome the morning
with one of her joyous victory trills. These had set the mood
of the neighborhood, reassured one and all that things were
okay with the world, but now . . . What was going on? They
spoke to us in whispers, as if there had been a death in the
house.

Magda's mood affected not only our morale but also our
business. It now took her a long time to return the work that
we passed on to her, and many times the portraits turned out
with scowls worse than the originals.

One night we found her easel light off, the studio in darkness, and Magda all bunched up on her sofa, a pillow among
the pillows, sobbing disconsolately.

She confessed. It had started with one: a grandmotherly
face kept staring at her, disapprovingly, from the wall. She had
to get up from a tangled, steamy embrace with a pupil to turn
the gazing photo toward the wall, but by then most of her
enthusiasm had vanished. Next time it was the piercing stare
of a mustachioed old man: she was convinced that she had
not tinted him yet, but when she went to turn him to face the
wall, he was a blushing pink. And so on. She confessed that
she had tried everything. She turned around all the photos,
even removed them, but no matter what she did, the images
of the dead were branded on her brain. They kept looking at
her, she sobbed, they just kept staring accusingly at her no
matter where she was, night or day. "It's like making love in a
cemetery," she wailed, tears flowing freely down her nose. "I
just can't! Oh, I'm sorry, I am so sorry!"

We tried to reassure her that, all told, she had no reason to apologize to us.

"The hell with you!" she fired back, sniffling loudly. "I am sorry for myself."

She said it as if we were the responsible ones.

We were the ones who had put her in that position of unfathomable, unhealthy unhappiness. It was no news to us that La Paloma equated sex with physical and mental health; her beliefs about that subject were decades ahead of the accepted norms. For a bride—and she intended to marry, once the white knight appeared—it was more valuable and much healthier, she affirmed, to bring to the wedding bed an enticing, varied, expert knowledge of sex rather than just cold virginity. "If my mother had known more and better," she used to say to prove her point, "she would have spurred my father into action and I wouldn't be an only child."

La Paloma's malaise caused us to reconsider the whole enterprise. Working on the photo portraits was only a part of it: with Fred pouring it on at the Alinari Studio (he had made it to first assistant cameraman) and me struggling to keep up with my accelerated studies and part-timing at the sound studio, we each spent an average of seventeen generally happy hours a day at work. We had been so busy, in fact, that summer had taken us by surprise.

Fred and I took a Sunday morning off and rode Paetaeppa a few miles out of Rome. We stopped on the bank of the Tiber and sat to bask in the sun and talk. We looked at the sky. We threw pebbles at the river. But neither sky nor river offered a solution. Perhaps, we agreed, our activity had run its course and should become a dear departed itself, once we had finished the work already commissioned.

The portrait work, we sheepishly agreed again, was making us uneasy too. We threw a few more pebbles into the river and watched the rings expand. Yes, it was time to move on to other things. It would be the best thing for Magda, for us. For the whole neighborhood, for that matter.

Together, Fred and I finished the backlog of portraits. Without Magda's touch, the images of the poor souls left our lab looking not much happier than when they had arrived. Not proud of our work, and to avoid confrontations, we slashed the prices. A big part of the profits went to take La Paloma to dinner, to the movies, anywhere we thought would lift her spirits. I took her up to the Roman Hills, with valiant Paetaeppa doing the equivalent of human sweating. On the steeper inclines, with Magda enthroned on the backseat, the front wheel frequently lifted off the ground, and the two of us, for a brief moment, must have looked as if we were riding a rearing steed. It gave me the willies, but thank God, it brought a faint giggle out of her. We had picnics, we had wine in the thick chestnut woods of the Castelli Romani; she made halfhearted attempts at seduction, I made pro forma capitulations; we achieved only wrinkled, grass-stained clothes. I saw it in her eyes: from somewhere the dead were watching her. I felt it myself.

The situation was hopeless.

The dubbing studio where I now spent many hours was part of a large film distribution company, which included a promotion-advertising section. Among the latter's duties was the translation of film titles (creation is more accurate: most of the Italian titles had no kinship with the films' original ones) and the design of their posters. This work was assigned to freelance artists who had to create images appealing to Italian tastes. I knew the head of that section, Giacomo Ala. He fancied himself, besides a great art lover and expert, an *"americano."* The studio had sent him to Hollywood for two weeks of indoctrination. The experience had transformed him. He made his new persona aping Hollywood movie actors, liked to be called Jack, and spoke an English that was, more or less, at the same low, slangy level as mine. He loved any chance to speak *"merikan,"* and I, who had had excellent tutors in Bob and U.S. Army field hospital personnel, was as good a foil as he could get. This link put us in a club of our own.

I had known Jack for a while when suddenly it became apparent to me that he was from the same mold as Magda. Only bigger. Tall, corpulent, he had a resonant voice and, in the presence of men, a John Wayne laconic, take-charge attitude. When in the presence of women, he became languid and seductive, full of Latin lover postures à la Rudolph Valentino. Struck by that realization, I found myself thinking that, perhaps, La Paloma's salvation was at hand.

"Hey, Jack!" I told him. "Ya gotta meet a swell babe I know, an artiste. She'll kill ya."

"Swell, kid. Ya're on."

Since La Paloma had sworn off all portraiture or any painting that involved the human face or body, it was difficult for me to develop a reasonable subterfuge. One evening, after receiving permission, I took her to visit the dubbing studio. She was fascinated by the techniques and even more by the artistry of the dubbing artists and how, one sequence at a time, they recited the Italian words perfectly synchronized with the screen actors' lip movements. Once a scene was recorded, another was projected and so on and so on. The studio was alive with creativity, each actor suggesting changes to translate correctly not only the dialogue but also the dramatic value of the dubbed scene. In that milieu, Magda seemed to perk up. On our way out, behaving as a proud host, I showed her the movie posters lining the lobby. A visit to an art gallery could not have been more compelling.

"This," I said pointing, "is *Casablanca*." Then, as a seasoned art critic, "The film is good. But the poster is flat."

She stepped back, looked at it bending her head this way and that, went closer, stepped back. "Too blue," she commented, "could use more red. More fire . . ."

On the way home, we elaborated on the artistry of movie posters, how a single image has to suggest the full, complex story and then some. By the time we reached her front door, she had agreed to come and meet Jack, sometime.

More than a meeting, it was a reunion of souls. Magda and Jack, having lost track of each other in a previous life, now found each other again in the ethereal, rarefied regions of Art. She promised to show him her portfolio. He promised to visit her studio.

They kept their promises. Magda suggested she try her hand at a poster, and Jack offered to see her trial sample.

Jack came to visit her studio frequently, to counsel her and check on the progress of her newfound artistry. Shortly the meeting of minds led to a clash of bodies, and theirs, like those of Titans, became a roaring, wall-shaking affair.

The silvery, trilled notes of *"Vissi d'arte, vissi d'amore"* poured again out of La Paloma's open window. The baker, the dairy man, the shoemaker, and the tailor looked up and smiled. Magda had donned again the black velvet beret and stabbed with long, large brushes at the work on her easel.

Not only were her posters accepted—and well paid for— but they became better and better. She developed a definite style of her own; compared with others, her posters jumped off the wall, full of sensuality and fire. Even the ones she did for quite chaste films suggested X-rated pleasures. Full- lipped, bosomy heroines and muscular, virile heroes led thou- sands of eager customers to movie box offices. The public loved the posters, and so did Jack.

La Paloma, our dove, soared high again, singing like a lark. The dead in her studio were dead. And buried.

19

Smile! Click!

ON A SEPTEMBER SUNDAY, Federico and I lean on the Pincio's marble balustrade and wait in silence. From here, in the Villa Borghese, all Rome is in front of us, its cupolas and towers and monuments all there to be counted; Saint Peter's Basilica dents the horizon with its presence and dominates it. The air is crisp, transparent, and everything has the clean lines and edges of an etching; colors are brilliant and come in a thousand hues, even the shadows glow with light. Exactly at noon, from the Gianicolo Hill across town, the old cannon will boom, and in a moment, as if at a starter's gun, all the church bells will let loose, calling and answering each other, making a joyful noise that, once heard, will not soon be forgotten. Thousands of birds give body to the sound, circling the air, rising and diving and rising again. The pealing is bounced back by the seven hills; here are the bells of Santa Maria Maggiore, and there of San Giovanni in Laterano, and then of San Paolo Fuori le Mura, of Sant' Andrea, of Aracoeli, and above them all *il Campanone,* the Big Bell. It is said that only a Roman, wherever and forever, will recognize the deep, sonorous, majestic voice of Saint Peter's bell: it makes the sky vibrate so that it will reach not only his ears but his heart.

September 1950. Halfway through the century. I've almost made it to twenty-five. One fourth of a century, and I've been thinking weighty thoughts, bouncing them off Fred, who is drinking in with me the crisp air, the magic of the moment.

Great advances have been made in the past half century, I pontificate, and Fred agrees. We fish a few achievements at random, trying to outdo each other. Einstein has told us that everything is relative; Freud has found that, way inside, our egos share room with our unconscious. With new chemistry, food is abundant; the surplus can be frozen, dehydrated, shrunk into pellets, and stored forever. But someone has counted that, out of 800 million children in the world, 480 million are starving.

"Once, a stone thrown by *un incazzato,*" says Fred, "by someone with his dander really up, could kill one man. Just one. Now the atom, that little bugger," he continues, "can kill hundreds of thousands in a flash."

"War," I add, "wasn't this last one supposed to end all wars? Two, three hundred years from now, perhaps less, historians will think of it as a popcorn fart."

As of now, the "Iron Curtain" has been closed shut. Us on one side, Them on the other. Here we are again, ready to go at it. Watch out for the rush, make way for the lemmings! Fred and I smile, as if to say, "So what's new?"

Compared with human history, our quarter of a century feels puny. But I am not complaining. I am still happy that the sun comes up again every morning. And if it doesn't, it cannot fool me. Fred agrees. We know it's there behind the clouds.

"I don't have in my genes"—I tell him—"the desire, like so many have, to change the world."

"I know," says Fred. "Curiosity. That's what you have. About this life's trek, about our traveling mates." He pauses a moment, then says, "Remember? Only a few years ago, Piero said you cannot sit on the fence forever. Sooner or later you got to get off, one side or the other."

I try to smile and tell him Piero was wrong. I was not "fence sitting." I was a fly on the wall, trying to find out who was right and who was wrong, curious to see what would happen.

"Flies get swatted," says Fred.

"So I was," I tell him. "But not too badly. I'm still here."

"Still with the fly act?"

"No. I've traded it for 'I'm a camera' syndrome. Almost the same: I try to put down on paper what the fly sees."

Which has developed into my profession, photography. People tell me I am pretty good at it, especially portraits (Fred snickers loudly: *pho*rtraits, you said?). I try to show a piece of the soul, more than just a face. Among the portraits on my studio walls, I still keep the one of smiling Maresa, not just because it sends a message of the sweetness of spring, a promise of happiness, but above all because it tells me of my luck. Lucky that things played out the way they did. Maresa turned out to be a very unhappy person; she would have destroyed me as she destroyed herself. Her infatuation with Dino ended badly, and now she is in self-imposed seclusion, isolated from family and friends.

So I am lucky, I tell Fred. Lucky to be ready to fall in love again. My girlfriend and I, we don't look like movie stars, we are just ourselves. Like me, but much worse, she has gone through the misery of war and survived it. We talk of perhaps marrying, one day. If and when. We will have to be sure of our steps. No more chances. We speculate for hours, almost a game. Where would we live, and how? My financial situation is still unsettled, and so is the national economy. Difficult, then, to make long-range plans. I met Erminia again when she came to Rome, at first as a guest of Zia Elena. She could not make a go of the farm at Le Madonnine, so she sold it for what she could get. Once that was divided among the surviving sisters and brothers, she took her little portion and came to Rome. Zia Elena found her a good job as the housekeeper of a very well-to-do family, and shortly she would move into her own servant quarters.

I went to see her as soon as Zia informed me of her presence in town. I took her out, I showed her the city, we went to dinner—I acting like a big-city jerk and she, to please me, like a green country girl, full of *ooo*s! and *aah*s! at everything. But the act did not last long; we knew each other too well. She could not take Frontale anymore, her soul was rotting there. The final blow came when Baldo, by accident or on purpose, had blown himself up by stepping on a land mine. So she remained alone, with the broken-down farm and her memories. The Frontale *paesani* would not let her forget that she had been raped—as had many in the area—and avoided her as if she had a contagious disease and not a war wound. The more we talked the better we understood each other, and our old friendship turned into what we wanted to believe to be love. And her laughter, the fact that I could make her laugh again, that we could laugh together, was like an invisible engagement ring. Parks and gardens saw us together, sitting on benches inventing imaginary plots for a future. We even imagined a pair of scrawny tots, one looking like her, one looking like me, cavorting in a chilly brook. It was fun, and much cheaper than going to the movies.

I have been exchanging news with Bob Moore, in Cincinnati. A few rare postcards at the beginning, Christmas affairs mostly, then lengthier and more frequent letters. I told him it was time for us to grow up, settle down, start families. He told me he had met again an old school friend of his, a cheerleader *then*. Gorgeous. They were planning to get engaged, and invited me to the wedding, if and when.

I have asked him, if and when, to come to my wedding. As a joke, I sent him the menu I would prepare for him—at least seven courses of *spar-getti* and meatballs, plus all the thick American steaks he could bring in a suitcase. I asked him to be my best man and carry the ring, the one he made out of a silver dollar. I still treasure it, safely guarded. Its value, on my money exchange, is much higher than gold and easily double that of platinum.

I accepted his invitation, if and when, to go to Cincinnati, if for no other reason than to meet a cheerleader *now*. Still gorgeous, I bet.

He has accepted mine; he could not pass up, he wrote, all those meatballs. He even suggested that I should say "Yes, I do" on top of old San Vicino. But, please, not in winter.

I cabled him back: "You kill me!"

Fred had just quit Alinari, too stifling. He needed a change of air, he needed to move. He was going north to coach a small soccer team, a job arranged by friends.

"It is the toy of a new-rich, washing-machine industrialist," Fred said to justify his move. "Up north every industry, big or small, has a team. A matter of pride," he continued. "They pay very well."

"A rich man!" I said. "You can get hitched, start a family."

He suddenly turned his face away from me. After a long pause, he turned back and, looking deeply into my eyes, said in a low voice he was going north with an old comrade from the Black Brigade.

"We have fought together. We almost died together," he added with great deliberation. "Now we're going to live to-gether."

It took me a minute to digest what he was saying. I remembered, way back, his exaggerated macho postures. Now I could explain them: they were a cover-up. He realized my dismay and, putting a soothing hand on my shoulder, said softly, "You are the only one to know."

He could have punched all my teeth out. But then, what are friends for?

So here I am, soon to be twenty-five. A milestone. With this birthday—I hope—there will be just one of me around. Three weeks ago the Military District of Rome summoned Giovanni Francesco and Gian Franco to report for duty. It turned out that I (we), like many people my age, had not fulfilled the obligatory military duty. No document existed to prove the contrary. To keep the record straight, the two of me were ordered to go to boot camp for military training, shortened from twenty-four to eighteen months. We'd better obey. Or else.

Following the Italian administrative tradition, I did my

best. I went to see the district's senior sergeant quartermaster. He gruffly admitted not knowing anything about my case; anyway there was nothing personal about it. He had seen this kind of thing before while serving under *Il Regno,* the Kingdom of Italy, under the Fascist Socialist Republic, and now with the new Repubblica Italiana. He was just doing his job, obeying orders, and frankly quite tired of it and hoping to retire soon. I thanked him for his equanimity, and—to wish him well for his coming retirement—I gave him an envelope, a gift. In it there was roughly two months of my earnings.

Out of gratitude, he met me a few days later at a local bar and gave me two beautifully decorated faux-parchments, one for each of me. On the top of the page, a central figure in Olympian garb—a crown on her head, a tall spear in one hand, a figurine of the winged victory in the other—represents Italy. On a panel at her right, factories with many tall, smoking chimneys: Industry. At her left, a man pushes down on a plow pulled by two oxen: Agriculture. Boughs of laurel leaves—Oh, Honor! Oh, Glory!—frame the page all around. In beautiful calligraphy the two similar documents declare that Private First Class Giovanni Francesco (and similarly, PFC Gian Franco) are given a *congedo permanente illimitato,* a permanent, unlimited discharge from military duty. The documents are completed by the flowery signatures of Major E. Rolitti, District Commander; Colonel O. Ricci, Commanding Officer; and Sergeant Major M. Simoni, recruiting clerk, all followed by stamps and seals. I keep both faux-parchments on the wall, in ornate faux-gold frames, as my official reassurance that I am done, twice and forever, with war.

. . .

Once I digest Fred's unexpected confession, I realize that nothing has changed between us. We are still the same as before. Perhaps closer.

It is easy, up here on the Pincio Terrace, to let your mind fly free, circle the air, reach for the sky. Everything seems possible, at hand. Fred and I lean on the balustrade and drink in the free spectacle. The bells' choir dies down, the pigeons settle, a child's balloon disappears into the sun.

"It's lunchtime," I say and wink at Fred.

"So it is. Let's go," he answers, smiling.

Then he lifts his hands in front of his eyes, his fingers forming the viewfinder of an imaginary camera. He frames me in a portrait.

"Smile!" he says. "Click!"

I make the same gesture, framing him.

"Smile!" I say. "Click!"

As in a snapshot, we freeze that moment in our minds. The shutter closes on a time of our lives.

Now the rest can begin.